WESTMAR COLLE W9-BQZ-185

The Fatherhood of God and
the Victorian Family

The Fatherhood of God and the Victorian Family

The Social Gospel in America

JANET FORSYTHE FISHBURN

FORTRESS PRESS PHILADELPHIA

BX
6495
.R3
F57

COPYRIGHT © 1981 BY FORTRESS PRESS

All rights reserved. No part of this publication may be reproduced, stored in a retrieval system, or transmitted in any form or by any means, electronic, mechanical, photocopying, recording, or otherwise, without the prior permission of the copyright owner.

Library of Congress Cataloging in Publication Data

Fishburn, Janet Forsythe, 1937–

    The fatherhood of God and the Victorian family.

    Bibliography: p.
    Includes index.
    1. Rauschenbusch, Walter, 1861–1918. 2. Social gospel—History. 3. United States—Church history—19th century. 4. United States—Church History—20th century. I. Title.
BX6495.R3F57 1982   261'.0973   81–43090
ISBN 0-8006-0671-X   AACR2

9025C81   Printed in the United States of America   1–671

101494

For Peter
Susan, Katherine, and Sally

Contents

Preface   ix

Part One

The Historical Context of the Social Gospel Movement: A Double Revolution

1. The Social Gospel Movement in Victorian Context   3

   The Social Gospel as a Movement   3
   Social Gospel Leaders: A Group Portrait   7
   Walter Rauschenbusch: A Study in Paradox   13

2. The Victorian Social Revolution   17

   Economic Structure and Labor Relations   18
   Family Structure and Personal Relations   22
   Church Structure and Social Relations   28

3. The Victorian Intellectual Revolution   35

   Social Change and Faculty Psychology   37
   Natural Evolution and Theology   46
   Social Darwinism and Evolutionary Theology   53

Contents

Part Two

The Social Gospel Movement:
An Ellipse with a Double Focus

4. Social Change and Applied Christianity (1865–1900)   67

    Liberal Social Darwinism and the Early Social Gospel   67
    Reconstruction: Nonwhite Americans and
        Civilized Progress   70
    Labor Conflicts: Social Darwinism and Social Gospel   75
    Urbanization: The City and Manifest Destiny   81

5. The Social Problem and the Kingdom of God
    (1890–1924)   95

    Social Darwinism and the Later Social Gospel   96
    Internationalism: War and Christian Manhood   102
    Socialism: Democracy and the Spirit of Jesus   111
    Feminism: The Family and the Kingdom of God   120

6. Theology for the Social Gospel (1900–1924)   129

    The Spiritual Intuition of "New Light" in Theology   131
    The Fatherhood of God: God the Absent Father   138
    The Brotherhood of Man: The Spirit of Jesus   144
    The Kingdom of God: Innocent Children of God   151

7. The Paradoxes of the Social Gospel Movement   159

    The Social Gospel Men and the Fatherhood of God   159
    Christian Manhood and Manifest Destiny   166
    Paired Paradox: Complementary or Contradictory   170

Notes   177

Bibliography   193

Index   201

Preface

This book is the story of a movement in the church (the Social Gospel) and of a man whose intellectual development (the theology of the social gospel) made a difference in the Protestant church in America. It is also the story of the difference between what people think they are doing and what they are actually doing. The theology of Walter Rauschenbusch, the central figure of this study, was influenced by a social philosophy that contradicted his intellectual and social objectives for the church.

The story is told as a chapter in the history of Christianity in Victorian America. In dealing with Rauschenbusch's life and thought, I have added a supporting cast to provide context, contrast, and local color. Rauschenbusch himself referred to other leaders of the Social Gospel movement as "pioneers." I have adopted his parlance to some extent in this regard, but I have also distinguished between social issues important to earlier leaders in the movement (Chapter 4) and those important to later leaders (Chapter 5).

In telling the Rauschenbusch story, I have tried to imagine what it was like to be a Christian in Victorian America. What were the major life experiences of the men of the Social Gospel? How did their experiences differ from those of their parents and grandparents? How did these men explain their experiences to themselves, and where did their life interpretations come from? How were the church and religion related to their lives?

My objective throughout has been to comprehend the meaning of the theology of the social gospel for the men who wrote it and for the Protestant church in Victorian America. In *Pattern and Meaning in*

Preface

History (London: Allen & Unwin, 1961) Wilhelm Dilthey portrayed the task of the historian as that of unearthing and re-creating the intentions of a people as these are expressed in written literature and social institutions. Dilthey suggested that history is understood by grasping the intentions and actions of people with reference to the social consequences of their acts. Following his suggestion, I have attended to the intentions stated in the literature of the Social Gospel and to the activities of movement leaders, as well as to the consequences for the church of their writing and activities.

In order to understand the stated intentions of Social Gospel leaders, I have used a method that biblical scholars use. I have attempted a critical interpretation of Rauschenbusch's *A Theology for the Social Gospel* by placing the book and the writer in cultural and social context. In order to exegete the vocabulary, philosophical assumptions, and mode of thought used by Rauschenbusch, it was necessary to survey a broad cross-section of literature written during the Victorian period. I have compared images central to his life and thought with patterns of meaning in the life and thought of five other movement leaders. In addition, in Chapter 7, I have compared his theology with that of "the Christian theological tradition," that is, theologies elaborated in dialogue with such major figures of that tradition as Augustine, Aquinas, Calvin, and Luther.

Bibliographically my approach was twofold. First, I read a broad selection of books that influenced and expressed what it was like to be a Victorian, including selected examples of social criticism, social philosophy, novels, religious thought and theology, religious novels, marriage and family literature, and autobiography. Within the religious literature, I studied, in addition to Social Gospel thought, the differences between books written by Calvinists, Unitarians, Transcendentalists, German philosophers and theologians, and the "new" evolutionary theologies. Second, I read selected interpretations of Victorian social and intellectual history written from the turn of the century to the present, attempting always to integrate observations from social history, church history, intellectual history, and family history in my re-creation of how the Social Gospel functioned in the world of Victorian America.

In the process, I have learned that the images people think in and live by—images such as the Fatherhood of God—emerge and crystallize over decades. During much of the Victorian period, people experienced continuing social change and a plurality of explanations about the world they lived in. Since the various images flow into one another and change with social circumstances, the time boundaries I have indicated in Part Two are suggestive, not arbitrary; they designate only the center of gravity in social issues and intellectual constructions during a given time period.

I have also learned that the thought categories eventually held in common by middle-class Victorians are with us even today. We still use some of their major distinctions, for example, between altruism and egotism. We struggle against their division of the world into masculine and feminine spheres. As a nation, we in the United States continue to be haunted by Victorian expectations of manifest destiny. Church members and clergy live in the shadow of the tradition we have inherited from our Victorian ancestors. For this reason the present study may help illuminate new dimensions in the relationship between religion and culture in America.

As much as possible I have let the Social Gospel figures speak for themselves. In drawing on the self-interpretations of a variety of people through autobiography, I have used their language. Consequently, most of the sexual references are in the generic forms, "man" and "woman."

Since completing my research I have become acquainted with several books that strengthen aspects of my conclusions about the Social Gospel movement. Corroborative evidence from Conrad Cherry in *Nature and Religious Imagination,* Ann Douglas in *The Feminization of American Culture,* and Dean Hoge in *Division in the Protestant House* has been integrated into the text of the book. That similar conclusions were reached by scholars working independently of one another substantiates the claim of Dilthey that there are recognizable patterns in history. I suspect that the patterns become visible only when the world-view under study is no longer viable.

PART ONE

THE HISTORICAL CONTEXT OF THE SOCIAL GOSPEL MOVEMENT: A DOUBLE REVOLUTION

The adjustment of the Christian message to the regeneration of the social order is plainly one of the most difficult tasks ever laid on the intellect of religious leaders. The pioneers of the social gospel have had a hard time trying to consolidate their old faith and their new aim. Some have lost their faith; others have come out of the struggle with crippled formulations of truth.

—Walter Rauschenbusch
A Theology for the Social Gospel

1

The Social Gospel Movement in Victorian Context

The Social Gospel movement of the Victorian era was and continues to be a lively impulse in American Protestant churches. The men who fathered the movement were formed intellectually and spiritually by the world of Victorian America. Walter Rauschenbusch, the most prominent Social Gospel advocate and writer, is only two generations removed from the civil rights and social concerns movements that flourished in churches during the 1960s. There is a clear line of continuity in the life experience, the social circumstances, and the intellectual assumptions of Rauschenbusch and other "new light" evangelical leaders of the movement. Their story is the story of the birth pangs of a middle class emerging in the midst of a social and intellectual revolution that transformed the nation.

The Social Gospel as a Movement

Walter Rauschenbusch, the lonely prophet of the social gospel, was reaching for the mature synthesis of Christian theology with the social gospel when he wrote *A Theology for the Social Gospel* in 1917.[1] He represents the culmination of a movement that developed a theology considered by some historians to be the only indigenous American theology.[2] The Social Gospel movement had its birth as such socially conscious evangelical ministers as Washington Gladden, Lyman Abbott, and Josiah Strong responded to the complex social issues emerging during reconstruction after the Civil War. Their ability to respond to those issues was complicated by the challenge of Darwinism to biblical interpretation and theology.

The Fatherhood of God and the Victorian Family

In his *Theology* Rauschenbusch hoped to convert both "the scientific mind" and the religious "conservative" by writing a theology "large enough" and "vital enough" to back the social gospel. He cited the Social Gospel movement and biblical historical method as the twin sources of the recovery of the social aspects of the gospel. The life experiences of movement leaders made them aware of "the social problem." Biblical scholars had rediscovered the long-overlooked emphasis on the kingdom of God in the gospel. For Rauschenbusch the doctrine of the "Kingdom of God" was the organizing center of the social gospel: "Without it, the idea of redeeming the social order will be but an annex to the orthodox conception of the scheme of Salvation."[3]

When Rauschenbusch used the term *social gospel* it meant either the Christian social message or the religious impulse that he believed was embodied and expressed in "the social movement" of the early twentieth century. The "pioneers of the social gospel" represented the ethical vitality of the Christian tradition needed to purify socialism of its potential excesses. Rauschenbusch expected that the synthesis of Christian ethics with the concern for class equality and social justice in "the social movement" would regenerate the social order. If the church did its part, Christian standards of morality would correct the idleness and greed inevitably produced by capitalism. The democratic ideals of freedom, justice, and equality could all be realized in the regenerated social order envisioned by Rauschenbusch.

Not all social gospel converts became movement leaders; some lost their faith. In the years between the Civil War and World War I, conflicts between religious faith and scientific "truth," outdated theology and the new social sciences, forced many of them out of the church. William Newton Clarke and Rauschenbusch found mutual support for the new social faith as members of the socially conscious Brotherhood of the Kingdom, which met annually between 1893 and 1913. By contrast, Robert Ingersoll, a contemporary of Clarke and son of a Congregational minister, earned national fame as "the great agnostic."

Membership in the Brotherhood of the Kingdom was a rare instance of contact between Social Gospel leaders. Gladden, Abbott, and Rauschenbusch knew one another through the Evangelical Alliance headed for many years by Josiah Strong. They were also aware of one another through preaching and publications. The men Rauschenbusch called "pioneers of the social gospel" were a movement in the sense of sharing a similar interpretation of personal experience and social circumstances, but they had no formal relationship with one another. Each man had experienced the struggle to adapt the faith of his youth to the life of a "modern" man. Each had suffered the loneliness of the prophet epitomized by Rauschenbusch.

Men like Gladden and Rauschenbusch were unique among the evangelicals Rauschenbusch called "conservative," because they applied humanitarian concern and evangelism to a pluralistic society suffering acute dislocation from industrialization and urbanization. They were also unique among theological liberals in retaining an evangelical concern for conversion, personal piety, and church renewal. Many socially conscious theological liberals eventually left the church. The men of the Social Gospel viewed the church as a source of social regeneration crucial to the social order.

Although the Rauschenbusch *Theology* represented the culmination of a series of liberalizing changes in the older evangelical theology, all Social Gospel leaders had adapted their religious thought to a Victorian world-view influenced by Social Darwinism. This was a source of the similarity in interpretation of life experience and social circumstance between leaders of the movement. Rauschenbusch noted that among the most influential convictions of modern life that modified religious thought were "belief in the universal reign of law, the doctrine of evolution, the control of nature by man, and the value of education and liberty as independent goods."[4] The modern convictions deemed new but not alien to theology by Rauschenbusch are found in some form in all Social Gospel thought. Most of the "new" liberal theology of the Rauschenbusch era was a synthesis of evolutionary concepts with Christian theology.

In the period between 1880 and World War I, many liberal theologians adapted theology to the new world-view embodied in Social Darwinism. Like the men of the Social Gospel, they had all inherited the unresolved theological issues of the first half of the nineteenth century. Major controversies concerning the sovereignty of God, the free will of man, the nature of sin, and church policy had led to an unprecedented pluralism in theological perspective. In addition to the differing views of Calvinist "old lights," evangelical "new lights," and Unitarian and

Transcendental perspectives, Social Darwinism was a new influence in theology after the Civil War. No one was untouched by the new scientific interpretation of man, nature, society, and history. As Social Darwinism gradually became the skeleton of a world-view affecting every area of American thought, church members and their pastors experienced an "ordeal of faith."[5] The distinctive mark of the Social Gospel theology was the integration of the "new" theology with earlier evangelical interest in moral renewal, humanitarian concern, and missionary zeal.

Movement leaders, as evangelists to both church and society, were consumed with a passion for the morality of individuals and the social order. The missionary zeal of Second Great Awakening conversionist preachers like Lyman Beecher and Charles Grandison Finney took on a social form of personal persuasion through pulpit, platform, and press in the Social Gospel. The monuments left behind by movement leaders were books, pamphlets, periodicals, and a few instances of political activity. Unlike Graham Taylor, a seminary professor with social gospel convictions, they founded no settlement houses and had little contact with the lower-class workers and unchurched poor, about whom they were concerned. They intended to regenerate the social order through the personal influence of church members and through their own influence on public opinion. Consequently they wrote two kinds of books: social commentary from a religious perspective meant for the general public, and theology for the church. In the process they were acknowledged as social critics by the general public and in church circles.[6]

Social Gospel evangelism was "an ellipse with two focuses": the individual and the social order. The preaching ministry of the movement had the double focus of inspirational sermons on Sunday morning and Sunday evening lectures in which community social problems were addressed. Evangelical interest in social issues was not new, but discussing such issues in church was an innovation. Many church members questioned the validity of clergy dealing with secular questions. Gladden's justification for this practice was his conviction that

> a great social problem was . . . forcing itself upon the thought of the world, a problem in the solution of which the Christian church must have a large concern. Primarily it must be a question of conduct, a question concerning

the relations of man to man, and it is the primary business of Christianity to define and regulate these relations. The application of Christian law to industrial society would, it seemed to me, solve this problem, and the church ought to know how to apply it.[7]

Social Gospel leaders viewed the Sunday evening sermon, which attracted business and professional men, as a two-way conduit between the church and society through which the "spirit" of Christianity could flow into the world. The church of the Social Gospel vision was potentially inclusive of all Americans. The conversion of the nation to Christianity would resolve social conflict, because Christian citizens would conduct themselves according to the spirit of cooperation, self-discipline, and self-sacrifice. In this way the secular order of society was gradually being transformed into the sacred order of the kingdom of God on earth. Josiah Strong anticipated the coincidence of Christianity and American society in the twentieth century:

> The ideal of Christianity is that of a society in which God's will is done as perfectly as it is in heaven: one in which absolute obedience is rendered to every law of our being, physical, moral, mental, spiritual, social: and this is nothing more nor less than the kingdom of God fully come to earth.[8]

The men of the Social Gospel responded to social, political, and economic events on the assumption that the secular order was evolving into a sacralized society.

Social Gospel Leaders: A Group Portrait

When Walter Rauschenbusch referred to the "social movement" in general, he meant that there was a common cultural concern with "the social problem." Since the Social Gospel movement was not an organization but a group of men who had life experiences, social circumstances, and a "new" theology in common, the movement was in a sense created by Rauschenbusch. It was he who noted that Gladden, Strong, and Abbott were movement "pioneers," and it was he who criticized the inadequacy of their theology.

Much of the coherence of the movement is related to the fact that the life experiences of the leaders were similar to each other and to those of the emerging middle class. As the unofficial historian of the movement, Rauschenbusch could name seventy to one-hundred clergy who were known as "social gospelers." All five of the men included in the group portrait were known to Rauschenbusch, either personally or through their work. Like Rauschenbusch, they had established reputations as public figures in some sense. All six men either wrote an autobiography or were the subject of a biography.[9] The Social Gospel movement of American church history exists in part because Walter Rauschenbusch, the professor of church history, was out front sketching the portrait.

If Social Gospel leaders like Lyman Abbott (1835–1922), Washington Gladden (1836–1918), Josiah Strong (1847–1916), William Newton Clarke (1841–1912), and Francis Greenwood Peabody (1847–1936) are typical of American clergy caught in the middle of a social and intellectual revolution, Walter Rauschenbusch is prototypical. As the youngest member of the group, with birth and death dates coincident with national war years, Rauschenbusch (1860–1918) was unusually sensitive to the evil of social conflict as it affected the lower classes, women, and children, who were the innocent victims of the industrial revolution and capitalism. While it is well known that Rauschenbusch was pastor of a German immigrant congregation in a New York City slum, it is less well known that Rauschenbusch lived out his early childhood years in a divided family.

As the child of German immigrants, Walter Rauschenbusch spent his early years in both Germany and America. In 1864 his mother took him and his two older sisters to live among her relatives in Westphalia for four years. During those years his father remained at Rochester Seminary, where he was a professor for German language students. In 1868, after a visit by the senior Rauschenbusch to his relatives in Germany, the family returned to the United States reunited. Although Walter Rauschenbusch eventually also became a Rochester Seminary professor, he did not want to be like his father in other ways. His childhood years had been marred by parental quarrels related to his father's drinking problem.

Walter Rauschenbusch yearned to be a respected man. Throughout his career he considered a private conversion experience to be "a source of right living." His account of his own first conversion at seventeen makes it clear that the experience represented his own personal commitment to sexual purity. He interpreted the experience as a conscious rejection of the possibility of being like the prodigal son of Scripture. By

8

his account, he prayed for help to his Father and got it. The juxtaposition of a father whom he did not admire as a model for Christian character with power received from God the Father is striking.

Rauschenbusch reported a second conversion experience that came in the midst of a vocational crisis. The first experience resulted in getting himself "under control" by prayer. The second related to channeling his sexual energy and desire by involving himself in meaningful work. He aspired to "participate in the dying of the Lord Jesus Christ, and in that way help to redeem humanity." The necessity of meaningful work for all men is important to the theology and social criticism of Rauschenbusch.[10]

The theology of Rauschenbusch was forged between Germany and America. Between 1879 and 1883 he studied and enjoyed the freedom of "Wanderjahre" in Germany. From 1883 to 1886 he studied at Rochester Seminary. He returned to Germany again in 1891 to study sociology and economics for a year. Although study in Germany was common for American seminary students at that time, the experience was different for Rauschenbusch as a bilingual German-American.

Throughout his career, Rauschenbusch suffered from the sense of isolation that he associated with the prophets of the Old Testament. Gladden, Abbott, and Strong had earlier thought of themselves as prophets crying in the wilderness. The double edge of the prophet as one who both identifies with and challenges the people of a nation was intensified in Rauschenbusch for several reasons. He was nearly deaf for most of his mature working years. His disability may have compounded the conflict normally experienced by first-generation Americans torn between a sense of rootlessness and a desire to be fully American.

His biographer relates that Rauschenbusch considered it his prophetic task to introduce "socialism" in the United States. He never sought fame, but when it came with the publication of *Christianity and the Social Crisis* in 1907 he enjoyed being a public figure. His optimism was high when he claimed in the book that the Brotherhood of the Kingdom had brought the social gospel into the mainstream of American Christianity. In 1914, buoyed by the rise in Protestant church membership, he thought the movement was at the height of its prominence.

His optimism was short-lived. In the years prior to American entrance into World War I in 1917, public opinion became overwhelmingly and irrationally anti-Germanic. When Rauschenbusch failed to publicly condemn the unprovoked German attack on Belgium, he found himself suddenly shunned by friends and colleagues. He died a lonely man in 1918, shortly after the publication of *A Theology for the Social Gospel.* It is one of the ironies of history that Rauschenbusch died a "lonely prophet," unwilling and unable to betray his dual loyalties symbolized by the doctrine of the Kingdom of God.

Although Rauschenbusch differs from the American Social Gospel leaders in his dual national loyalty and experience, in other respects their life patterns were remarkably similar. All except the Unitarian Peabody came from the evangelical conversionist tradition that grew out of the Second Great Awakening of the 1830s. All six men became ministers in a period in which requirements for ministry, the role of the minister in the church, worship forms, and the organization of the church changed.

Most of the Social Gospel men regarded the worship experiences of their childhood as rigid, cold, and restraining, broken only by the emotional excesses of midweek revival services and prayer meetings. Pressures on youth to experience a "change of heart" had become virtually a rite of passage after the Awakening. While the five men with evangelical backgrounds rejected the public conversion experience, they all continued to affirm the need for a clearly defined personal conversion in some form.[11] Most of them reported receiving "new light" while reading Scripture or praying for illumination. Only Peabody was not offended by the revival techniques of Dwight L. Moody. The private conversions of the Social Gospel men had the same objective as the public conversions of the Second Awakening tradition: personal morality and self-control.

The childhood years of five of the Social Gospel men were disrupted by either the death of a parent or a parental separation. Only William Newton Clarke was reared by his own parents. All except Clarke expressed negative reactions to their fathers and in some sense thought of themselves as fatherless sons. Of the six men, only Peabody was reared in the city. The other five made the difficult adjustment from the sense of personal relatedness they knew growing up in rural and small-town settings to the impersonal atmosphere of life in the city. As adults all six placed a high priority on the absolute necessity for a good family as the basis of individual morality and the health of society. All agreed that the city was not a suitable environment for a family.

During the student years of the Social Gospel men, curriculums in both colleges and seminaries were in transition. Abbott and Gladden were ordained to Congregational ministry without benefit of a seminary education. Clarke was ordained after a year of study at Hamilton Seminary after completing the four-year college curriculum of Hamilton College. Strong attended Lane Seminary, a seminary influenced by the evangelical fervor of Lyman Beecher, a former president there. Like Rauschenbusch, Peabody had the advantage of postgraduate study in Germany after completing college and seminary at Harvard, where he later became a faculty member. The curriculum during the college years of these men was the "old" classical course of Greek, Latin, history, and science. Their fourth-year courses in mental and moral science consisted of commonsense philosophy and natural theology.

The marriages of the Social Gospel men followed the conventional pattern of marrying a woman with a background similar to their own. The women went with them to their first pastorates as new brides. The first parish served by Abbott, Strong, Gladden, and Rauschenbusch was in each case a home mission assignment. Whereas Rauschenbusch went to the urban frontier, the others all served on the western frontier. These early experiences on the frontiers of mission left vivid and lasting impressions on the later advocates of the social gospel. Although Abbott, Strong, and Gladden spent their entire careers in the parish, they found time for writing, editing, and speaking, as well as denominational and ecumenical activities. Clarke and Rauschenbusch accepted seminary faculty appointments after beginning careers in the parish. Peabody's entire career was spent teaching social ethics at Harvard University.

The work world of Victorian men was one of suspension between the hope of success and the fear of failure and poverty. Recessions were frequent and alarming in an era in which job security and protection against unexpected expenses did not exist. Gladden and Abbott both apologized in their autobiographies for their lack of financial success. Yet both were able to provide the requisite live-in maid, considered a

11

necessity and mark of middle-class affluence. Both crossed the Atlantic several times, another sure sign of membership in the newly arrived middle class.

Victorian men worked compulsively, lest they be left with some unidentified void in their lives. Rauschenbusch hoped that he would never find himself with "nothing to do." Gladden confessed that he would not know what to do with leisure time. Vacation time meant visiting with family and friends. It was a time for fathers to swim and hike with their children, relieving mothers of their usual responsibility for household and children. Yet even when vacationing at summer cottages, Rauschenbusch wrote books and Abbott commuted to work in New York City during the week. Victorian patterns of work and play, filled as they were with friends and family, and constant vocational demands on men, were not conducive to silence or self-examination.

The work output of the Social Gospel men was prodigious. Gladden published thirty-one books, participated in denominational activities, regularly held a pastorate, edited several magazines, and traveled extensively to fill speaking engagements. Not all the Social Gospel men were as conspicuously productive as Gladden, but all worked steadily and continuously at similar projects.

The Social Gospel men thought of themselves as "men in the middle." Abbott considered his link with the progressive politics of his friend and colleague Theodore Roosevelt to be a middle way between reactionary and revolutionary politics. Gladden developed a reputation for having a mediating personality because of his activities as a labor arbitrator.[12] Josiah Strong attempted to mediate between the middle-class church member and the poor. Clarke and Rauschenbusch wanted to be mediating theologians. In each case, the characteristic of the Social Gospel figure is that of a mediator between conflicting forces, whether with respect to politics, labor problems, or fear of a social revolution.

A movement cannot exist unless it strikes chords of response in the public. The power of a prophetic figure is related to the ability of the prophet to verbalize a message which gives form to otherwise incoherent attitudes, reactions, and longings in the listener. A man like Gladden was a public figure because others could identify with his experience, and with his interpretation of their common experiences. The power of the Social Gospel movement is related less to its specific influence within ecclesiastical circles than to its general influence on an emerging American middle class. The Social Gospel men mediated the philosophy of Social Darwinism with the impulses of evangelical Christianity.

In Victorian America, the wide front porch symbolized a neutral zone where a family could be private in public. The social philosophy integral to the social gospel provided an outlook that made it possible to accept personal success and be aware of social problems at the same time, without incurring a debilitating sense of personal responsibility. It was a private, yet public, philosophy of life.

All the Social Gospel men can be described as men moving up. Even the educationally privileged Peabody shared the economic instability of the others as men-in-the-middle. Gladden and Rauschenbusch were the most charismatic figures in the group, because both were more sensitive to the personal alienation that accompanies moving up in America. In the movement known as the Social Gospel, the middle-class public found an expression of their own fear of falling back into poverty, combined with the loneliness that accompanies social acceleration. The men of the movement were expressing their fears, their longings, and their discomfort. In short, the Social Gospel movement facilitated the acceptance of a world-view adequate to the changed social circumstances of the middle class.

Walter Rauschenbusch: A Study in Paradox

There is some truth to the claim of Rauschenbusch that his theology was a culminating synthesis of the groundwork laid by the movement pioneers. He believed that his theology was important because he had worked out the implications of the doctrine of the Kingdom of God for other aspects of theology. Scholars, church leaders, social activists, and students have given more serious attention to *A Theology for the Social Gospel* than to any other single social gospel publication.[13] However, the *Theology* is the culmination of the story of the lives, the social events, the intellectual currents, and prior social gospel literature that comprise the Social Gospel movement.

From a historical perspective the movement was not a procession of pioneers preparing the way for a single prophet. Instead it is more like a two-stage process. The significant contributions of Gladden, Abbott, and Strong to the movement were in the form of response to social and intellectual issues between 1880 and 1900. Their orientation to the movement was that of social activists and theorists. The orientation of Clarke, Peabody, and Rauschenbusch to the movement was more intellectual. Although they were active in Social Gospel interests in the 1890s, their most significant contributions to the movement occurred primarily in the first two decades of the twentieth century.

For Gladden, Abbott, and Strong—all Congregational ministers— theology was secondary to issues affecting the church and society. Gladden and Abbott came to the Social Gospel through confrontations with post–Civil War social and intellectual dilemmas. Gladden's only attempt at constructive theology, *Present Day Theology* (1913), was written to refute criticism from conservative "old light" evangelicals that the Social Gospel had no theology. While Gladden was equally interested in the future of the church and the nation, his outspoken stance on social issues earned him a reputation as the "father" of the Social Gospel movement.

The more intellectual orientation of Clarke, Peabody, and Rauschenbusch to the movement resulted in a series of books written early in the twentieth century for purposes different from those of the earlier men. The later group possessed a self-consciousness unknown to the earlier men. The terms *Social Gospel* and *social movement* became common coinage in the 1890s, and the later men identified themselves with the religious aspects of the more general "social movement." The later group responded to a social situation in which it was increasingly clear that the "social question" was being raised more insistently by radical socialists. Rauschenbusch and Peabody came to be preoccupied with well-defined social questions concerning family, property, and the state.

The purpose of *A Theology for the Social Gospel* is typical of most social gospel theology and social criticism. It is meant to evaluate present social circumstances and to inspire the reader to respond in the present that in the near future the kingdom of God would come. The hope for a better future is substantiated by accumulating evidence of progress in the church and culture always pointing to fulfillment in the near future. Although the book was written during American armament preceding entrance into "the Great War," Rauschenbusch interpreted the war as God's way of awakening the world to a vision of international

14

cooperation. He believed that God used every event for the education and regeneration of the race.[14]

Rauschenbusch made no claim to systematic theology. He chose to discuss implications of the doctrine of the Kingdom of God for sin and salvation, atonement, eschatology, and the concept of God because he thought those particular doctrines in conservative theology locked believers into an otherworldly and selfish form of individual piety. He wanted to say that individual salvation is part of social salvation, but by itself is not Christian truth. He was convinced that the kingdom would come when Christians recognized that God, the Father of the race, was a democrat who wanted all men to demonstrate social solidarity with one another.[15]

The historical interpretation and themes of the *Theology* are common to all Social Gospel literature. The three pillars of Social Gospel thought were "the Fatherhood of God," "the Brotherhood of Man," and "the Kingdom of God." A shift in emphasis from the Fatherhood of God to the Brotherhood of Man occurred between the earlier and later phases of the movement. These three pillars of Social Gospel thought are common in Victorian literature, secular as well as religious. The Fatherhood of God was a part of a national vocabulary especially favored by labor leaders and politicians.

In Social Gospel parlance, the Fatherhood of God was more often related to social circumstances than to religious experience. Rauschenbusch used the terms *Kingdom of God* and *manifest destiny* interchangeably. The "Kingdom of God" was religious language connoting the destiny of the American democracy to demonstrate the brotherhood God intended for the world. In Social Gospel thought, the family represented the kingdom in microcosm and was considered a means of establishing the manifest destiny of America.

Social Gospel thought and historical interpretation revolve around a series of paired paradoxes. The pairs reflect the conflicts experienced by the men-in-the-middle, who resolved experienced tensions through a paradoxical interpretation of social circumstances. A paradox is a statement that appears to be contradictory but may actually be true. The basic paradox in Social Gospel thought is the claim that while church and society, theology and science, religion and culture may appear to be contradictory, they are in fact complementary. Armed with the hope of the coming kingdom, the men of the Social Gospel interpreted every social conflict up through the Great War as a temporary evil that would give way to God's greater good for America.

A paradox may also be defined as a statement that contradicts itself and therefore is false. There was one qualification in Social Gospel thought: "If only" the church were more vital, or theology large enough to inspire the church to fulfill its task of permeating society with "the Christian spirit," then the apparent contradictions would be resolved. Otherwise, the "spirit" would go elsewhere and the statements of hope would be false.

No theology can be understood without penetrating the content of the language, the thought structure, and the thought categories of the period in which it was written. This is especially true of the social gospel, which must be interpreted as part of the Victorian world that gave birth to the movement. Although the language of the Rauschenbusch *Theology* is less foreign than the obvious romanticism and idealism in the books of the earlier men, the philosophical assumptions in Rauschenbusch are those of the earlier period of the movement. In order to comprehend the full range of paradox in the Rauschenbusch book, the social and intellectual revolutions of mid-Victorian America must be comprehended. The roots of the reaction of Rauschenbusch to feminism, radical socialism, and internationalism had a history going back to pre–Civil War responses to change in the family, the economy, and the social order.

A century of history in which continuing social and intellectual change challenged the Protestant church is concealed behind the apparent synthesis and optimism of *A Theology for the Social Gospel.* In the doctrine of the Kingdom of God, Rauschenbusch gathered up the loose ends of once bitter religious controversies over biblical interpretation, evolutionary theory, Social Darwinism, and the new social sciences.

The Fatherhood of God and the Victorian Family is the history of a religious movement and a theology. It is the story of life in the century that preceded the 1917 publication of *A Theology for the Social Gospel.*

2

The Victorian Social
Revolution

The autobiographies of the Social Gospel men born between 1835 and 1847 relate experiences of a mid-Victorian social revolution that was over by the time Walter Rauschenbusch was born in 1860. The "pioneers" described how work patterns, education, and the church had changed compared to the work, schools, and churches they remembered from the small towns of their youth. Their recollections of altered daily living patterns give a personal dimension to the slow transformation of a once rural nation into an industrialized world power with a laissez-faire economic system.

The economic order and work patterns had been changing since the Revolution, but during the first half of the nineteenth century they were experienced as painfully disruptive of family structure and relationships. The Second Great Awakening and theological warfare of the 1830s dramatized other evidence that the Protestant church in America was to play a different role in society after the official separation of church and state. Protestant clergy became fearful of the "perils of Romanism" as Catholic immigrants attracted by economic opportunity poured into American cities. As the place of the Protestant church in the social order changed, so did the role and status of clergy in both church and society.

Contemporary use of the word *Victorian* as a synonym for "moralistic" captures only one element of the Victorian ethos. Early Victorian anxiety concerning the morality and self-discipline required to sustain individual freedom in the new democracy was intensified by economic and social change between 1800 and 1840.[1] The pioneers' formative years as clergy coincided with discernible shifts in economic theory, social theory, and the form of the novel that characterized mid-Victorian culture between 1840 and 1870. Henry Adams described the mid-Victorian period as a time when every man had to invent a "formula of his own for the universe" because the standard formulas had failed.[2] The Social Gospel pioneers responded to the social revolution by inventing a formula that offered the possibility of a moral populace, a moral nation, and a hopeful future.

Victorian, defined broadly, refers to a world-view—an interpretation of history, nature, the self, and society—that began to coalesce during the mid-Victorian years and gradually permeated middle-class culture during the late Victorian years between 1870 and 1900. These were years of Protestant cultural hegemony.[3] The Social Gospel pioneers played a significant role in that process by shaping an ethos of morality and optimism as they wedded the social impulse of early Victorian evangelical Christianity to the progressive interpretation of history of mid-Victorian Social Darwinism. Theirs was a theology of hope that invested the nation with the soul of a church.

Economic Structure and Labor Relations

In his *Recollections* (1909) Washington Gladden provides evidence of a general shift in the American economy that began in the Revolutionary era and preceded the full-scale industrial revolution experienced in mid-Victorian America. Gladden noted that his grandfather had owned his own farm, a circumstance less possible for the men of his father's generation but of vital importance to Gladden. Since the ancestral farm was only modestly successful, his grandfather was also a shoemaker who worked in his own home. This is a good example of the subsistence-farming and cottage-industry economy that gradually shifted to market-oriented production under merchant capitalists and prepared the way for manufacturing and the factory system.[4]

It was in Gladden's youth that men could no longer assume that they would inherit the family farm, or a portion of it. In part the frontier movement was motivated by a search for work. The fathers of both Gladden and Strong moved their brides and young families to the "western" frontier of Lewistown, Pennsylvania, and Hudson, Ohio, to improve their chances of economic opportunity.

The Victorian Social Revolution

When Gladden was six years old his father died. His mother sent him to the farm of his paternal grandfather for a time. Most of his boyhood and early school years were spent with his grandfather and an uncle in Owego, New York. Because of a lack of incentive and of a better alternative, Gladden lived with and worked as a printer's apprentice for five years when he finished public school at age sixteen. His boyhood and experience as a youth with economic instability and unsatisfying work partially account for his later sympathy for "the worker class." With his apprentice years behind him, he cherished his college years at Williams as "the shining days when all was new and all was bright as morning dew."[5] He later characterized this "new light" experience with education as his conversion. Education opened up a whole new life to him.

Early industrial conflicts between employees and employers, coming in the decades after the Civil War, were considered a form of war—industrial warfare. Gladden preached his first sermon on the issue while serving a congregation in industrial Springfield, Massachusetts, between 1875 and 1883. The men to whom he preached were affected by the depression of 1873 and general labor unrest. The Molly Maguires were hanged in 1877 for their part in a wildcat strike on the coalfields of Pennsylvania. Industrial problems affecting members of his congregation led Gladden to conclude that social problems could be solved by applying Christian love to the conflicts of an industrial society. Those early experiences led him to believe that saving souls meant saving the "manhood and character" of the workingman from the "immoral rules" of industry. This prompted his new insight and conviction that the church was not in the world to save the souls of a divinely elected group but to save the world itself: "The church is in the world to save the world; if it lacks the power to do this, and industrial society plunges into chaos . . . the church . . . will go to ruin with it."[6]

Gladden's career and his memory of the family farm economy of the early nineteenth century represent a knowledge of economic expansion that spans nearly a century. The Civil War briefly interrupted Northern industrial development that brought increasingly apparent prosperity to the middle class. But with the prosperity and new inventions that made daily living arrangements more comfortable for every new generation also came economic anxiety and fear of a sudden loss of work and income. Depression or a stock market panic occurred with monotonous regularity in every decade from 1860 to 1900. Labor strikes and riots raised the possibility of social "warfare." Just under the surface of historical optimism lay the uncertainties of the male work world. There was no assurance of economic security, short of establishing the great fortune of a captain of industry. Although many small gains were made in the cause of labor and unionization prior to 1900, it was not until the massive program of "progressive" legislation passed during the administration of Theodore Roosevelt that the middle- and lower-class employee could assume some protection from the whims of management.

Another facet of economic growth in the Victorian period was diversification and specialization in the division of labor. Division of labor changed the structure of family life as it became common for men in Gladden's era to work outside the home. Women became responsible for the domestic sphere of family and home as men became the sole source of family income. A division of parental labor replaced the family economy of the earlier rural pattern of family life. Men like Horace Bushnell longed for the simpler, earlier "age of homespun," when every member of the family contributed to the work and economy of the household. During the days of cottage industry the work of all family members had been necessary to the well-being of the family unit.[7]

The leaders of the Social Gospel movement responded to different aspects of the complex of social changes involved in the development of industrial capitalism. Early Social Gospel leaders responded to the plight of the worker by seeking to evangelize the worker class out of concern for social order and the future of the nation. Later figures, especially Peabody, observed the effects of capitalism on all classes of men. Peabody and Rauschenbusch developed a concern for national leadership related to their sense that middle-class men who lived off the capital provided by their father's work might be weak and effeminate. From the early 1870s on through the Great War, movement leaders considered work to be a necessary means of achieving manhood. The industrial revolution had its moral equivalent in the Victorian preoccupation with industry—or industriousness. Industry or work was not just a useful means to an end. In Victorian America, industry was a virtue and a primary moral quality.

The change from an agrarian to an industrial society removed men abruptly both from the realm of personal interaction with natural forces and from a domestic role in the family. Within the memory of the older Social Gospel men, the entire family unit had contributed to the provision of the necessities of life—a home, food, and clothing. As adults, none of these men was related to the land. They had no direct role in the provision of family food and clothing. Wives often handled family finances and became the family purchasing agent and home decorator. Although homemaking and work associated with the home had changed, women remained closer to nature in the new division of labor. Women kept kitchen gardens. They were responsible for flower gardens and flower arrangements. They were still aware of the rhythms of nature that affected housekeeping and child-rearing. A woman still needed a sunny day to dry the family laundry. Most important of all, a woman still experienced that most natural and exalted event, the giving of new life.

In the new family organization, the nonworking, domestically oriented middle-class woman lost an economic function as the male became the sole provider of family income. On the whole, the changes were less drastic for women than for men, because women continued to perform domestic duties similar to those of their mothers and grandmothers. Their womanhood depended on satisfactory achievement of duties within the limited arena of the domestic sphere.

The situation of the Victorian man was just the opposite. He had the whole world outside the home in which to prove his manhood. It was the meaning of manhood that had become problematic. Before the industrial revolution, manhood was a generic term used to connote virtue and righteousness before God. During the Victorian era, manhood came to stand for the worldly success of a man. Gladden and Abbott, apologizing for the modesty of their economic success, were measuring themselves by the male success ethos of Victorian culture. The American male had unfettered freedom in the new democratic society, but he had no assurance of successful manhood, especially if manhood meant economic success.

Gladden epitomized early Social Gospel response to the economic revolution when he said that he was interested in men, not commodities. Amid the plethora of labor-related issues addressed by the Social Gospel men over the years—violence, social disorder, just compensation, strikes, labor mediation, workers' rights, materialism, and social justice—it was finally the issue of moral manhood as the basis for peaceful social relations on which they all agreed. When Rauschenbusch, the only self-acknowledged socialist in the group, pleaded for social cooperation in the interest of a harmonious social order, the underlying philosophy was less socialist than it was an ethic for Christian manhood.

Family Structure and Personal Relations

By the end of the nineteenth century, American newspapers and magazines brimmed with speculation about the crisis of marriage and the family. Four developments gave rise to a steadily growing alarm: the rising divorce rate, the falling birthrate among "the better sort of people," the changing position of women, and the so-called revolution in morals.[8]

These were issues of grave concern to Walter Rauschenbusch and Francis G. Peabody. In the 1890s, feminists, socialists, and a handful of social scientists precipitated a heated public debate over love, sexuality, and marriage. The public, and social reformers, were uncomfortably aware that the divorce rate was rising and that middle-class family size was declining while lower-class family size appeared to be increasing. Meanwhile, prostitution had become big business. Radical proposals to alleviate the situation presupposed that people were marrying for economic reasons rather than for love, and that family life discouraged love, by which they meant sexual passion.[9] The reformers proposed solutions ranging from free love to simple divorce procedures, freeing women from domestic servitude, licensing prostitutes, giving women the vote, and a host of related reforms that drew the ire of evangelicals. The issues they found most provocative concerned sexuality and marriage.

The major issues to emerge were twofold. First, for most of the Victorian era it had been either assumed or implied that women had less "sex passion" than men. The high status of woman as the source of family affection lay in the assumption that women were naturally more pure than men because they had weaker erotic impulses. One of the reformers, psychologist Havelock Ellis, wrote that women did not lack "the sex passion." They were less erotic because they had not been taught to recognize their erotic impulses. To most evangelicals, this was a scandalous suggestion.

Novels began appearing in the 1890s suggesting that women could be seductive. In *The Damnation of Theron Ware,* Harold Frederic portrayed Celia Madden, a sensuous Catholic beauty, as deliberately appealing to the sensuality of Theron Ware, an innocent Methodist minister. Stopping short of an actual seduction scene, Frederic made the point that Celia had deliberately aroused the passions of the young clergyman. Evangelicals like Peabody protested the publication of such licentious literature.[10]

The second issue being debated was the nature of the marriage relationship. Was marriage a civil contract or a sacred covenant? Evangelicals found their assumption that marriage was an eternally binding covenant had to be spelled out in response to the radical proposal that, since marriage was only a civil contract, it could be dissolved by either party to the contract. Rauschenbusch and Peabody opposed all proposals to reform marriage or the family.

Large-scale industrialization occurred in the mid-Victorian period, 1830–70. Those early years of manufacturing and factories led to inevitable changes in family structure. Bride books, books about sexuality for young men and young women, and social commentary written by doctors and ministers concerning marriage, the family, and society addressed anxiety about sexuality and family relationships. The gradual development of a culturally shared family ethos that rationalized changes in family organization and the role of the sexes in marriage occurred between the Revolution and the Civil War. It was the same ethos assumed in early Social Gospel thought and defended by Rauschenbusch and Peabody early in the twentieth century.

According to the family ideal commonly assumed after the Civil War, the middle-class Victorian family was quite literally the "building block of society." The spirit of love and brotherhood learned in a stable, loving family was expected to flow naturally through the family into society. Eventually the spirit of brotherhood would permeate the world through the influence of a civilized America. Then the brotherhood of all men would literally mean "each for all, and all for each." In the future, the world would emulate the natural harmony and goodwill of the Victorian family.

Social Gospel men understood the family as the one stable social institution that guaranteed a hopeful future for the nation and the world. They accommodated to change in government, education, and church with equanimity, because change in those institutions meant they were becoming more Christianized. But they believed that the family, as the most nearly Christianized institution of the social order, set the pattern for personal and social relations that would characterize a fully realized democracy. Thus the health and stability of the family, and the continuation of the domestic role for women, were essential to their social philosophy. Rauschenbusch and Peabody opposed the possibility of change in the family or in the spheres of marital responsibility. A sign of progress to a social reformer like Ellis was a sign of potential social disintegration and decline to them.

When Josiah Strong in 1885 cited "the elevated status of woman" as evidence of nineteenth-century progress, he revealed an important clue to middle-class optimism: the family. With new forms of social relationships replacing those of the preindustrial period, the family acquired a disproportionate importance among social institutions as the essential and primary source of love and virtue. Victorians believed that only in the family was self-sacrificing behavior more natural than the self-interested competitive motives observed in society at large. A good woman was the only sure source of the inspiration necessary to ensure the good citizenship of men. Since a "good citizen" meant an individual capable of the self-sacrifice and self-control necessary to the level of voluntary social cooperation demanded in a democracy, mothers were indirectly the key to a Christianized America.

The difference in the family experience of the Social Gospel pioneers from that of their parents and grandparents is typical of how and why family structure was altered by loss of a family economy. As social patterns of an agrarian culture were replaced by those of an industrial culture, the large farm family was no longer necessary. Children were no longer needed to contribute to the work of the family; they became a luxury if not a liability. No Social Gospel figure was married more than once. As the death rate for women in childbirth decreased, the length of marriage increased. By the late Victorian period, marriage lasted into old age. Most of the parents of Social Gospel men had been separated by death in middle age, if not earlier, and had remarried.

The Social Gospel men and their wives all reared their children to adulthood; not one of them experienced the death of a child. Most of them had themselves been reared by aunts, uncles, and grandparents. In the two generations between them and their grandparents, the family had changed radically. It was smaller. The original unit of mother, father, and two to four children stayed together longer. Death intruded into the family circle less often. In the process, the family became a smaller, tighter circle isolated from the larger community. Its members were more dependent on one another, and less related to people outside the family.

The Victorian family gathered on a spacious front porch signified a major social change among the emerging middle class. The ambiance of family togetherness was publicly observable on the porch that served as an outdoor living room in warm weather. The durable wicker furniture, the family swing, the lush pots of hanging greenery and elaborate floral arrangements beckoned to the passerby. Yet, participation in the family gathering was by invitation only. Families living side by side were acquainted only if they chose to meet. Suburban living brought independence in many forms. The higher standard of living freed people from dependence on neighbors for the provision of life's necessities.

The price of economic independence was the loss of a natural social milieu in which men, women, and children intermingled as they worked, played, and worshiped together. The communal activities of shared labor in flax-scutching, harvesting, and the quilting bee quietly disappeared as machines and labor specialists performed those tasks more efficiently. Gone too was an informal sense of social responsibility to and for the well-being and moral health of the community. The white-steepled frame churches of the New England town square stood as a monument to preindustrial days, when the church naturally touched the lives of church members and the town population where they lived, worked, married, gave birth, and died.

Lyman Abbott was thinking of this kind of social relationship when he recalled that the pastoral prayer in such churches sounded like a newspaper report of community events during the week. The small circle of the rural community did breed gossip and undesirable forms of moralistic concern, but there was also the security of a web of social relationships in which social responsibility was a natural part of life.

The whole burden of socializing children and reinforcing morality fell to the family. The Victorian marriage ideal, built around the expectation that the couple would be "best earthly companions," replaced a web of social relationships involving both sexes. The combination of smaller families and increasing dependence of marriage partners on each other for companionship required a new rationale concerning sexuality. Lacking effective birth-control devices and social acceptance of birth control, the Victorian sexual ethos was, in effect, a natural form of birth control. In the process of adjusting sexual behavior to social circumstances, sexuality became a function of marriage, rather than an aspect of human nature. The sexual repression associated with the Victorian sexual ethos was a necessary adjustment to the social revolution behind the new family ethos.

The family ethos, the marriage ideal, and the sexual ethos are all implicit in Strong's phrase "the elevated status of woman." The Victorian lady was a woman on a pedestal because she was a model of moral purity. Just as male and female work was assigned to two spheres that were considered complementary, the sexual and marriage relationships were believed complementary in a way that was separate but equal. A marriage was a divinely ordained relationship in which the two people quite literally became one morally complete personality.

Man and woman needed each other for completion, because by nature the sexes possessed dissimilar but complementary characteristics. A man needed the more intuitive woman to inspire him and to evoke his potential. A woman needed the strength of a man she could admire to complement and evoke her maternal qualities. The complementarity of the married couple had three dimensions: mental, moral, and physical. Because the sexes were a mental foil for each other, acting as mutual stimulus and restraint, the average couple could reach a true view of any question by mutual consideration and correction. But man especially needed the correction of woman's way. The more aesthetic, intuitive woman needed the correction of a man's force and logic. "This male-female equilibrium is the law of growth and progress."[11]

The "correction" needed by the man was the love of a good woman who would inspire him to control his sexual desires. The complementarity of the sexes, a typical pattern of Victorian thought, was applied to all forms of social relationship. Gladden cited Ralph Waldo Emerson (1803–83) as his source of the idea that "an inevitable dualism bisects nature, so that each thing is a half, and suggests another thing to make it whole."[12] Virtually all Victorian literature reflected this differentiation of the sexes. Charles Darwin used the most common distinction in assigning sexual desire to the male and love and sympathy to the female.

The moral purity of woman and the self-control required of man in marriage led to the conclusion that the purpose of sexual intercourse was procreation. Consequently, a marriage without children was incomplete. A female was not a woman if she failed to become a mother. Ironically, the sexual act that potentially would complete her personhood was an invasion of her "purity" from which she was otherwise to be protected. The irony is reflected in ads, posters, and paintings of the late Victorian era. The lady pictured is delicate in a feminine yet motherly way. She was healthy, rosy-cheeked, slightly buxom, sometimes unbuttoned yet not seductive. Her dress was usually white or a light pastel, gauzy in an ethereal way, suggestive of the angelic realm. The Victorian marriage was built on an ideal of the complementarity of sexual self-sacrifice of both partners.

Chivalry was synonymous with male self-sacrifice in marriage. The early Victorians found young knights doing battle on behalf of women who were not their wives an inadequate model for the ideal man. Nevertheless, they admired the valor of the knight, energized by religious fervor, fighting to defend the honor of a lady.

Chivalry became a part of the language used by Victorians to describe marriage. Sexual self-sacrifice was understood in terms of the deference of the stronger to the weaker, or the self-sacrifice of the man to his fragile mate. Self-sacrifice on the part of the woman referred to her participation in procreation. The chivalric notion of deference of the stronger to the weaker was the controlling concept of all relationships, brother and sister as well as marriage.

The deference of the man to women and children symbolized by the knight of chivalry is a part of the Victorian concept of manhood. A woman was a complete person in the domestic sphere only if she became a mother. Her children were the product of her sphere and, as such, the symbol of her success as a person. The realm of successful manhood was the world of work. Financial prosperity and a high standard of living were the symbols of male success in the sphere of his "industry." The material products of his industry were the symbols of his success as a person.

The Victorians commonly cited the "perfect equality of the sexes" as evidence of the elevated status of woman. This meant perfect equality in separate spheres: man in the public sphere of his vocational world, woman in the private sphere of the domestic world. As the century wore on, the domestic sphere became "a refuge from the storm" for men. Increasingly, home was idealized as the safe harbor where all was harmony and cooperation. The outside world was the place of competition, distrust, and industrial warfare.

But home represented status as well as peace. While the male and female virtues were moral ideals, the Victorians did expect virtuous behavior to yield conspicuous evidence of success. If the husband cultivated the "manly virtues," his energy was going into his work. The standard of living a man provided for his family was evidence of his success. In this way sexual self-control was virtually equated with vocational success.

Middle-class men felt vocationally unsuccessful if they could not provide the expected symbols of success for their wives. Because immigration provided a large pool of cheap labor, it was common for middle-class families to employ a maid, until immigration laws reduced the availability of maids early in the twentieth century. Until almost 1890, Victorians expected to see material evidence of moral behavior. Status symbols were generally accepted as evidence of morality.

It is crucial to the social ethic of the social gospel to comprehend the Victorian understanding of the complementarity of the sexes and the chivalric ideal for men. The Victorian model for all social relations, including labor relations, comes from the marriage ideal of mutual self-sacrifice with emphasis on the manhood ethic of deference of the stronger to the weaker. Washington Gladden's idealistic expectations for labor mediation rested on his vision of the common table shared by labor and capital in familylike harmony and cooperation.[13] All the Social Gospel men drew their vision of the mutual self-sacrifice and cooperation in a well-ordered society from the Victorian family ideal.

Church Structure and Social Relations

Between 1820 and 1875, the Protestant Church in this country was gradually transformed from a traditional institution which claimed with certain real justification to be a guide and a leader to the American nation to an ad hoc organization which obtained its power by taking cues from the nonecclesiastical culture on which it was dependent.[14]

The Victorian Social Revolution

Like every other social institution, the church changed as the nation became industrial and urban during the Victorian era. It was not so much an "ad hoc organization" as it was a voluntary organization fated to compete for membership among denominations and sects when disestablishment made the church independent of any kind of government support. The sense of competition and the need for differentiation between religious groups surfaced in the theological controversies of the 1830s.

The "new light" evangelical identity of the Social Gospel men was a product of the "new measures" for conversion introduced into the moribund preaching tradition of "old light" Calvinist orthodoxy early in the nineteenth century by Charles G. Finney. One of Finney's most controversial measures, "the anxious bench," was a means of pressuring people who felt themselves to be under conviction of sin to experience the release of anxiety in a definable moment of conversion.

As a youth Washington Gladden suffered in the grips of an expectation of a conversion experience. He felt himself to be "an alien and outcast from the family of God" unless he could "regain the communion with God lost in the fall." He had been taught that a spiritual experience signified that the repentant sinner had gained the favor of God. He tried desperately, and unsuccessfully, to produce such an experience.[15] In the course of his ministry he developed a rationale for the continued need for conversion as the basis of morality and self-discipline. Influenced by his own misery, he determined to prevent others from engaging in that kind of unfruitful "discipline of soul-searching."

The "new light" evangelicals developed their self-image over against the "old light" Calvinism that they considered dull, dry, and unrelated to life. They wanted evidence that a converted heart really was a new heart. The evidence they came to expect was observable moral behavior and good works. The connection between conversion, morality, and social service in the social gospel is a socializing of the "new light" evangelical impulse. When Rauschenbusch pitted the social gospel against the otherworldly selfish piety of the "so-called evangelicals," he failed to mention the host of pre–Civil War reform movements and missionary zeal motivated by the "new light" evangelicals of the Second Awakening period.

The disestablishment of Congregationalism in Massachusetts in 1833 symbolized the new social situation of the Protestant churches. Until the beginning of the nineteenth century, when immigration added substantial numbers of Catholics to the population, the Protestant churches had been a guide to the nation, in part because they held a virtual monopoly on religion. In addition to the new competition between Protestant denominations, new sects like the Shakers, Mormons, and Christian Scientists offered a variety of religious alternatives to the once nearly established Congregational churches of New England.

It is no accident that the earliest Social Gospel leaders were all Congregational, or that they were obsessed with cooperative movements in the church and in society. Josiah Strong, the movement organization man, typifies a drive for social power through evangelism and consolidation in the church. Elected as secretary of the Evangelical Alliance in 1886, Strong was also a founder of the Federal Council of Churches, successor to the alliance in 1908. He was a founder of the Men and Religion Forward Movement, a source of hope so stimulating to Rauschenbusch that he called it one of the most promising events in Christianity since the Reformation.[16]

Strong expected the consolidation of religious power he sought through movements to morally invigorate the populace. In *Our Country* (1885), a book about American manifest destiny, he contrasted the national potential if led by social Christianity to the dangers to the nation posed by Mormonism, Catholicism, and alcoholism.

The Social Gospel movement was led by men who dreamed of a church strong enough to permeate the nation. In their lifetime both the church and the clergy had lost the social status and influence once taken for granted when the white-steepled church was the center of the community. Their yearning for a church with spiritual power came from childhood memories of small towns where life moved slowly, families worked and played together, and people were friendly and knew one another by name. They were aware that the movement of population out of small towns into urban environments meant the loss of a shared standard of morality and the social power of community sanction. They imagined the church becoming the soul and spiritual center of the nation, as the church on the square had once permeated the community atmosphere of the small towns of America.

The role of the pastor was changing as churches began to diversify in function and activities. William Newton Clarke contrasted the church organization of his youth to the suburban church he pastored in Newton Centre, Massachusetts. The total program of the small-town church of his childhood consisted of two Sunday services and a midweek prayer meeting. The church in Newton Centre was an organization consisting of multiple boards and countless other groups meeting for purposes ranging from education to mission to social events. Functionally, the church was replacing the small town as a gathering place for a social community.

If the church had become a social center and meeting place, the minister was becoming more like a community organizer than a man called by God to preach the gospel. No longer did clergy serve a single congregation for life. Nor did they spend long hours of preparation for preaching and teaching in studying the Bible and theology. The purpose of preaching—inspiration of the listener—no longer depended on biblical exegesis. Instead, this was the age of the minister as public figure and the "prince of the pulpit." The effectiveness rewarded with public attention and a call to a larger congregation depended more on personality than on scholarly aptitude or theological training. Henry Ward Beecher, friend and colleague of Lyman Abbott, had a well-established reputation as the "orator" of one of the largest congregations in the country, Plymouth Congregational Church in Brooklyn, New York. Beecher had the gift of communicating to a large congregation in a way that seemed personal to each individual. His gift was the ability to appear personal in a public situation.

The well-known orator-ministers and the Social Gospel men were exceptions as ministers who commanded attention in the public sphere, the work world of men. Church and religion during the Victorian era were more often associated with feminine and domestic pursuits than with the masculine work world. "The feminization of Protestantism in the early nineteenth century was conspicuous. Women flocked into churches and church-related organizations."[17]

By the end of the century William James, a Harvard colleague of Peabody, criticized the church for lacking the ability to inspire men to lives of ascetic discipline without robbing them of the kind of masculinity associated with athletics, military exploit, and national "enterprise and adventure." A church run by "oysters, ice-cream and fun" served only the feminine half of the population. The church, in his opinion, was serving the social needs of women but ignoring the masculine moral needs. The church had failed to set forth an ideal worthy of inspiring heroic manhood. "The contemporary ideals [for manhood] are quite as remarkable for the energy with which they make for heroic standards of life, as contemporary religion is remarkable for the way in which it neglects them."[18]

During the Victorian era there were two competing images for manhood: the Victorian gentleman and Christian manhood.[19] This dichotomy suggested that the moral Christian man was less successful—and therefore less manly—than the Victorian gentleman as a man of the world. James agonized over the dilemma in asking whether the saint or the strong man was the more ideal type. "The saint's type, and the knight's or gentleman's type, have always been rival claimants of this absolute ideality."[20] This was not a dilemma for the Social Gospel men. They wanted to be both moral men and men of the world by Victorian standards of manhood and success. They used the language of chivalry to clothe the Christian "saint."

The "knight" of the Social Gospel was both a moral man and a man of valor, fighting social evil on behalf of the woman he loved, God, and country. The self-sacrifice of male deference served the greater good of family and country. In the process, the "knight" envisioned by the Social Gospel would be playing an active and vital social role.

The Men and Religion Forward Movement impressed Rauschenbusch because it was concerned with the role of men in the church and of church men in society. In a culture where the power of a good woman might serve the nation through her influence in the domestic sphere, the "strenuous life" of the good man might serve the nation through his influence in the public sphere. Social Gospel proponents of an active role for men in the church and in religion were attempting to demonstrate that the church was not just the province of women and children.

The social gospel was a theology written by men for men. The Social Gospel movement countered the feminization of religion by directing male moral energy into cooperative movements that would reveal the social power of the church at the very center of society. In a day when some clergy suggested that the moral inspiration of pure women was the source of progress in civilization, the Social Gospel men pointed out that manifest destiny depended on the heroic morality of Christian gentlemen.

The pioneers of the Social Gospel movement lived through the years in which the nation was transformed from a rural, small-town culture into an industrial world power. A continuity with respect to religious belief and moral standards between the home, the church, and the community had existed when these men were growing up in small-town farms before the Civil War.

The nearly simultaneous developments of democratic freedom in the new republic and the social change that accompanied the industrial revolution produced an atmosphere of opportunity so open and unlimited that every individual was morally vulnerable. The sense of individual responsibility required by the new democracy was a risky experiment, even for a people with the deep religious roots of Puritan New England. But the accompanying alterations in social institutions intensified the awareness of vulnerability in a moral people. The real loss of common religious belief and an informal community enforcement of moral standards makes Victorian preoccupation with self-discipline seem less unreasonable.

As they carved out a new formula for explaining the universe, the pioneers were influenced in their choice of social philosophy and ethic by memories of the small-town church and its place in the community. As they interpreted the world in which they lived by 1880, they were attracted by social and religious thought that made it possible for men to be moral, hopeful, and successful. The form of Social Darwinism they adapted to religious thought was suitable to the need of the new middle class to be both prosperous and socially responsible. The formula of the Social Gospel pioneers involved a web of interdependent relationships between family, church, and nation that made the family and the church seem indispensable to the manifest destiny of the nation.

3

The Victorian Intellectual Revolution

Social Darwinism is usually associated with conservative right-wing politics. Such books as *What Social Classes Owe Each Other* by William Graham Sumner, originally published in 1883, are republished today in a series called "The Right-Wing Individualist Tradition in America." Then, as now, the central proposition of Sumner and his political heritage was that it is the duty of a good citizen to take care of himself.[1] This, Sumner claimed, was one of the implications of the scientific theory of the survival of the fittest.

Manifest destiny is a social form of the theory of the survival of the fittest advanced by Charles Darwin (1809–82) in connection with biological evolution. Although Darwin drew social implications from the theory, that was not his primary interest. Herbert Spencer (1820–1903), a contemporary of Darwin, was the major source of the social philosophy called Social Darwinism. Spencer applied Darwin's scientific empirical methods and the theory of evolution to history. His evidence of the manifest destiny of the Anglo-Saxon race was gratefully received and adopted by American social theorists.

The Social Darwinism of Herbert Spencer was a two-edged sword.[2] The Social Gospel men were one movement among many known at the end of the nineteenth century as political "progressives." Liberal Social Darwinists differed most in their political and social theory from conservatives like Sumner on the question of how manifest destiny was to be achieved. Was the competition of a laissez-faire economy a natural force dividing the fit from the unfit that required no intervention from government, as Sumner claimed? Or was the process one that could be ameliorated and possibly accelerated by means that would prevent a need for government social intervention? The liberals of the Social Gospel preferred amelioration but slowly and reluctantly came to the conclusion that very limited government intervention was acceptable, or even necessary.

The Social Darwinian philosophy that crystallized late in the nineteenth century was a system that gave specific content to intellectual currents and thought forms that began emerging after the Second Great Awakening. Social theorists contributing to a popular genre of literature concerning sexuality and the family in the pre–Civil War period held in common with Spencer a faculty psychology that was an underlying assumption in Spencer's system. Paradoxically, representatives of religion who saw evolutionary theory as an atheistic challenge to Christian belief contributed to the thought forms that opened the way to public acceptance of the evolutionary social theory that was the backbone of the Victorian world-view. The faculty psychology of the family ethos inherited by the Social Gospel men was an underlying assumption in their evolutionary theology.

The same family ethos based on the faculty psychology that appears in the thought of the early Social Gospel was present in the work and thought of Walter Rauschenbusch. Although the writing career of Rauschenbusch occurred much later than the early books of the "pioneers," his social philosophy, like theirs, was deeply influenced by the social thought of Henry George. He reported memorizing chapters from *Progress and Poverty* (1879), a book written by George during the period in which Social Darwinism became the source of the Victorian world-view.

Although the struggle to defend Christianity against the Darwinian challenge was not a part of the intellectual development of Rauschenbusch, his thought was significantly affected by the Social Darwinism of Henry George. Consequently, with reference to the intellectual foundations of the Social Gospel, the intellectual revolution touched off by the 1859 publication of Darwin's *Origin of Species* produced a social philosophy that appears intact in the three books written by Walter Rauschenbusch. By 1917, when Rauschenbusch wrote *A Theology for the Social Gospel,* the language of faculty psychology was no longer spoken. But the content of faculty psychology was carried into evolutionary theology through the influence of Social Darwinism.

Social Change and Faculty Psychology

At the time of the Second Great Awakening the legitimacy of the seemingly manipulative "new measures" of Finney was hotly debated. Men like Lyman Beecher (1775–1863), whose initial reaction to the pressures of "the anxious bench" was negative, eventually used Finney's technique because it worked. The use of new measures gave wide currency to a conversionist psychology that explained how and why Finney's conversions were legitimate.

> The conversionist psychology consisted of three parts: precepts, motives, and sanctions. The precepts were the legal directives, disclosures of what one must do in order to live up to God's system of moral government. The precepts were available in nature and conscience, but they were most clearly revealed in the commandments of the Bible. The motives were the spurs to decision and action, the mental impulses or the driving forces of human existence. The sanctions were the influences that made the motives effective and were of two types: the promise of reward and the threat of punishment. The key component for the revivalist was the sanction: it was his instrument for leading men to follow the right motives when choosing to follow God's precepts.[3]

The conversionist psychology of precepts, motives, and sanctions bears a resemblance to phrenology, a faculty psychology circulating among intellectuals in the same early years of the nineteenth century. Like the conversionist psychology, the faculty psychology of phrenology filled the vacuum left by the decline of the Calvinist view of human nature. Although phrenology was a popular craze, it attracted the attention of intellectuals concerned with health and morality as well as the laws of human consciousness. It was dignified by men like Henry Ward Beecher, a son of Lyman Beecher, who called it a "new science."

Physicians, educators, and clergy, all alarmed by the apparent loss of parental control over the vocation, courtship, and marriage of their children, eagerly appropriated the faculty psychology that moved the focus of parental responsibility to early childhood. In order to facilitate moral behavior in youth, the parental role in character formation consisted of permitting or encouraging the young child to choose the good as the best way of developing the moral faculties.[4] A phrenological chart was tacked to the wall at Fruitlands, Bronson Alcott's abortive experiment with a "consociate" family founded in 1843. Phrenology, a psychology of the faculties, provided the Transcendentalist educator with a blueprint for attempting to evoke the good in each family member.

The health, marriage, and child-rearing literature that proliferated during the first half of the nineteenth century was a major source of dissemination of faculty psychology. A genre of literature on health and personal hygiene complemented the books on sexuality and marriage of the period.[5] Many books combined advice about the need for "husbanding" of vital resources, fresh air, long walks, and proper diet with advice to the newlywed. For example, among the fifty books written by William Alcott (1798–1859), a prominent physician and educator, were separate treatises on self-control, vegetarianism, phrenology, and prudent regimen. Some of his books were for intellectuals; others, for the general public, were in the form of the popular gift book. *Physiology of Marriage* (1866), the last book published by the former editor of *The American Annals of Education,* was a synthesis of the various theories of his previous publications into a general social theory of morals.

Alcott's book, although primarily concerned with marriage, linked the success of the family to the well-being of the nation. His social theory, as well as the psychology he assumed, had been expressed earlier in a widely circulated book, *The Constitution of Man,* written by the English phrenologist George Combe (1788–1858). Phrenology was not a new science in 1828, when the first edition of Combe's book was published in England. When the official American edition of the book was published in 1850, its preface asserted that there were already 300,000 copies in circulation. For a segment of the literate public, phrenology provided a guide to child development as well as a social theory. Combe may have been the Dr. Spock of the nineteenth century.

Baby books published by Brentano in the 1890s contained a phrenology chart. In *The Baby's Biography* the writer repudiated "the popular misconception" that the faculties were manifested by "bumps on the head." Mothers were advised that readings revealing the child's disposition, religious and moral tendency, and vocational aptitudes involved measuring the "cranial contour and development as a whole." Readings could be taken as early as six years and constituted a virtual "mirror of the mind." Measuring the size of various head contours provided information by which the forty-two faculties could be graded. The sum of the gradings of various faculties predicted the child's potential vital power, motive power, and mental power in relation to the size of the brain.[6]

The synthesis of physiology with health, morality, and intelligence in faculty psychology was the basis of a moral philosophy that was also a social theory. When Victorians referred to the faculties, they meant three classes of human faculty like those described in Combe's phrenology: moral sentiment, the intellectual faculties, and the feelings or propensities that man held in common with animals. Animal propensities—feelings such as amativeness—were instinctive drives that had to be accompanied by moral sentiments if feelings or passions were to be properly controlled. Since moral sentiments, such as imitation, were also instinctive impulses capable of acting prior to an intellectual judgment, the formation of good moral habits early in life was imperative.

The higher nature of man included the moral sentiments and the various intellectual faculties. The five senses, as well as the reflecting faculty known as "moral sense" among evangelicals, were all faculties of the intellect.[7] Combe ascribed to moral sense the ability to judge, compare, and discriminate necessary to an intellect capable of directing the moral sentiments.

The lower nature of man, which included feelings of amativeness, philoprogenitiveness, adhesiveness, combativeness, secretiveness, acquisitiveness, and constructiveness, had remained constant as man advanced from an animal state to the present level of civilization. The animal propensities were always basically self-interested, but properly controlled they served a positive purpose: the preservation of the family, tribe, or nation. Therefore, amativeness, the "sex passion," was necessary for the preservation of the race because it stimulated the desire for a conjugal partner. Philoprogenitiveness, if properly channeled, was the source of parental love, the domestic affection "for young and tender beings." But any propensity could be used improperly if not accompanied by moral sentiment. Amativeness could lead to adultery. Philoprogenitiveness gone astray could lead to unmentionable forms of sexual deviancy. Since the power and function of animal propensities remained constant, the increase in the power of intellect and moral sentiment was the basis of the advances of the race and the progress of civilization. It was uniquely human to be able to seek the good of all men beyond the self-interested devotion to family, tribe, or nation of the animal propensities.[8]

A basic distinction between altruism and egotism, meaning self-sacrifice and self-interest, runs through Victorian social thought. The distinction refers to the human capacity to live according to the golden rule. Interpreted in Combe's terms, this meant that because of increased intellectual and moral powers, modern men were naturally capable of seeking the good of all men. The potential for altruistic behavior was developed in the individual by habitually choosing and doing the good. Choosing and doing the good meant using each of the forty-two faculties according to its God-given purpose. Morality and the proper use of the faculties operated according to the scientific laws of cause and effect. The positive use of each faculty would yield pleasure or reward; the negative use would yield pain or punishment. Faculties grew strong by habitual right use; they became weak or impaired if not used or if improperly used.[9]

Temperance, living according to the golden mean, was more than an evangelical crusade against alcohol. It was the Victorian way of life derived from a psychology that taught that each faculty must be kept in perfect equilibrium. Any faculty, in excess, could become insatiable and uncontrollable. Victorian prohibitions against masturbation were motivated by a fear of the erotic impulse run wild. The single life was considered unnatural because it gave no opportunity to develop the amative and philoprogenitive faculty. Overwork, the improper use of physical or mental faculties, was another Victorian anxiety related to the rule of keeping the golden mean. Combe wrote that daily work was necessary to physical well-being, but overindulgence could result in indigestion, sleeplessness, drinking, mental incapacity, or early death.[10]

Combe thought moral law was a predictable system of causes and effects operating like biological laws. Just as he ascribed the physical laws of the universe to God's natural order, he concluded that God had a similar design for the social order. Combe reasoned that just as God's natural order of creation was harmonious, the social order was also potentially harmonious if society would make it possible for all men to live by the good they already knew: the golden rule. "Civilization" would mean that every individual was able to use the faculties according to their natural organic law. If social circumstances were conducive, then each individual would voluntarily fulfill the moral law, and this would automatically contribute to the progress of civilization.[11]

Although Combe believed all men to be innately good and innocent of sin at birth, human happiness depended on each individual being in harmony with physical and moral law. Despite belief that a tendency toward vice could be physically inherited, he considered the intellectual enlightenment of the age so powerful a formative agent that even a tendency toward vice could be overcome. Combe concluded that the only reason for immoral behavior in a civilized nation was ignorance, but that could be remedied by education.

For the late Victorians, phrenology was a "science" that provided a method by which they could measure moral and mental development and predict the potential of their children. It was also the source of a child psychology that emphasized parental responsibility in early childhood, since good or bad habits developed before the age of moral accountability, when a child could reason about moral choices. The good habits acquired before the age of reason were the necessary foundation for the natural development of good moral judgment.

Combe used a principle of "natural law" as his unifying theory to explain man, society, and history. By "natural law" he meant the inner law of physical objects which could be determined by means of external observation. Moral law was known by observing the behavior of good men. For a child, moral law was learned by exercising the imitative faculty, thus positively activating a moral sentiment. It followed that moral judgment would then naturally know and choose the good as the intellectual faculties developed. Parents who were exemplary role models for morality were essential to the moral development of the child and to the future of civilization.

In Combe's system, if every part of the whole functioned properly, eventually the social order would be perfectly predictable. He was counting on the voluntary goodness of all men to fulfill their own potential and the destiny of history. Social disorder was a characteristic of barbarism and the barbaric past. Combe expected modern civilization to be a social order freed from war and violence.

Savage man, the barbarian in any era, was "ignorant, ferocious, sensual and superstitious," because his mental and moral faculties were underdeveloped. The savage lacked the mental faculty to perceive the relations of objects and was unable to project the future consequences of an act. The savage was sensuously active because he could not make the pragmatic judgments necessary to self-control capable of deferred gratification. He was unable to see the continuity in natural law.

This continuity was obvious to civilized man, who naturally knew himself to be the intelligent, responsible subject of an all-bountiful Creator. The civilized man studied all the works of the Creator, including the human cranium, to know God's laws and obey them. A civilized man knew that the world was organized to gratify the animal, intellectual, and moral power of man.[12] By studying the works of the Creator inductively, Combe assumed that man could understand the grand design of God's plan for humanity.

Late Victorian social theory revolved around a distinction between "civilized" and "barbarian" individuals and nations that served as a standard both of moral judgment and of historical interpretation. Combe's theory provides the content for the terms as they were used. "Barbarism" meant an immoral way of life led by barbarians who did not know any better because their intellectual and moral faculties were underdeveloped. "Civilization" referred to a self-controlled way of life led by men with properly developed faculties capable of appreciating the continuity in natural law.

Combe was typical in believing that he knew God's design for mankind. Alcott too claimed a healthy future for the nation if readers would only heed his advice about sexuality and marriage. His book, which assumed a faculty psychology, explains the rationale of the Victorian family ethos.[13] In *Physiology of Marriage,* Alcott worked out the implications for marriage of a social theory like that found in Combe's *Constitution of Man.*

Alcott claimed that sexual self-control in marriage was necessary to the good health of the partners, their progeny, the family, and the nation. According to him, "the family is the foundation of the social edifice and part of the order of creation."[14] Family members were to promote the "holiness, usefulness and happiness of each other." Christian love meant suffering for others, and the deference of the older and stronger to the younger and weaker. The social progress of the nation depended on the purity of the family.

Alcott described marriage as an extension of the brother-sister relationship. The sexes served each other as mutual correctives in that sisters taught a boy not to be too "coarse and sensual." Finding a marriage partner, from this point of view, was to find a "help-meet and educator."[15] Young men were advised to regard every woman as they would their mother or sister, because woman was naturally and constitutionally pure and it was man's duty to keep her so. He observed that the purpose of male desire was to keep men from being celibate in an age when women were "sickly, expensive and ambitious for the children." Marriage, both a duty and a necessity, was "the golden chain that binds society together." Alcott said that "amativeness" impelled men to marry in the interest of preserving the morality necessary to social order. The amative faculty was also the instinct necessary to the physical reproduction of the species which resulted from enjoying the exercise of the "sex desire."[16]

The amative faculty impelled a man to marry, but in a woman it was the force behind a desire for friendship. Victorian women were thought to be more naturally sociable than men. Alcott never said that exercising the sexual faculty was not pleasurable, only that it should not be over-indulged because of the "delicacy, sensibility and modesty" of the female. Nor did he say that a woman had no sexual desire, just that she did not "crave" sex the way the male did.

Self-restraint in marriage would reward the naturally coarse and sensual male with polish and purity. Alcott did not say that sex was a sin. But he did say that, like every other faculty, it had only one purpose: procreation. This implied that the amative faculty used for anything other than procreation was a vice. For the man who practiced self-restraint, Alcott promised the immediate rewards of health and vigor of a physical, mental, and moral nature. Like other Victorians, he believed that while seminal fluid did not sustain life and health, an unnatural loss of it might be an impairment. Finally, he drew out the social implications of purity in marriage. The sexual appetite, in proper balance, "will be the lever to raise up the world."[17] This was virtually a doctrine of progress by self-control, or salvation by continence.

Just as the sexes needed each other for balance sexually, mentally, and morally, to be single was to be unbalanced. Masturbation, "the solitary vice," could cause the male animal juices to dry up by age thirty-five, leading to idiocy or impotence. In a female, unnatural stimulation might develop into an unnatural craving for sex that could lead a woman to prostitution.

The development of character depended upon moral, mental, and physical balance or equilibrium between the sexes. The "solitary vice" in intellectual form was considered dangerous because self-reflection in excess could also lead to madness. Late Victorian writers were critical of the Puritan practice of spiritual self-examination because they viewed self-examination as a form of intellectual masturbation.[18]

The physiological base of faculty psychology explains Victorian abhorrence of any kind of sexual deviancy. It was a biological and moral necessity that the sexes become one in marriage. Either sex alone was incomplete and a biological and social abnormality. The complementarity of the sexes in marriage was a theory that implied that some of the faculties were more developed in and natural to one sex than the other. In women, friendship, parenthood or domestic love, religion, intuitive ability, and aesthetic faculties were naturally more prominent. Men complemented the domestic and religious faculty of women with the more developed faculties related to the "sex passion," work, and justice. The complementarity of the sexes, resting on the faculty psychology, explains why in the Victorian world-view the home and church were considered the natural spheres of women, while the world of work and society was the sphere of man.

All Social Gospel figures and most religious thought of the post–Civil War period assumed the progress of human reason and moral progress in history. They used the barbarian-civilization distinction to designate groups that contributed or failed to contribute to the progress of the nation. Their understanding of sexual complementarity and the family as essential to progress deviates little from the position expressed by Alcott. However, Alcott and Combe both developed their progressive social theories over against social events they perceived as contributing to the forces of animalism and barbarism in their day. The positive tone of their theorizing tends to conceal the fact that their objective in writing was to stimulate and strengthen the moral judgment of the reader in a day when there were choices to be made.

There are references in Alcott that suggest he was writing against a Fourierite theory of sexuality in the sense that the self-sacrificing Christian love of which he wrote was opposed to the Fourierite socialist theory of marriage. A "free love" communal theory of marriage was part of Charles Fourier's *The Passions of the Human Soul,* published in America in 1851. During the 1840s the Fourierites had founded a small but well-known number of utopian communities dedicated to the principles of "familistic" socialism. Whether it was true or not, the communes and socialism were associated with holding wives and property in common.

Like Alcott, Fourier was concerned with problems of sexuality and family created by changes in social circumstance. Both men sought solutions yielding more love, peace, and social harmony. While Fourier's response to changed social patterns, *The Passions of the Human Soul,* was written after the French Revolution (1789), he addressed the same questions raised by industrialization in America after the American Revolution. His criticisms of postrevolutionary France expressed the discomfort of a man who disliked competition and commercialism. He attributed family conflicts to the social and sexual pretense of French women. Commercialism and competition in the economic order caused unnatural family relationships, as well as the economic dependence and materialistic ambitions of women. Where Alcott and other mid-Victorian social theorists had praised the purity of woman, Fourier stated that since women were not distracted by other interests they had more sexual desire than men.

Fourier was bluntly hostile to "civilized morality," which he said was based on the unnatural deference of the female to the male in the family. Civilized morality was "supremely vicious" because "our obscene customs refer everything to the material realm." "Civilization imposes a pecuniary traffic on love."[19] The Fourier phalanxes—the communes— were an attempt to free women from sexual pretense, greed, and boredom. A communal economy, in theory, should relieve men of the pressures of economic competition. Without the economic motive influencing mate selection, men would be relieved of sexual and economic competition. Love would then be pure because sexual partners would be chosen for personal attributes rather than economic success. Ultimately, Fourier envisioned sexual relationships in the commune as "spontaneous association without permanent obligation, except for good breeding and unbounded devotion to group interest."[20]

Nothing could have been more antagonistic to the high standards of sexual temperance and family loyalty of the Victorian ideal than the "free love" communes of Fourier. The communes were a threatening but unlikely alternative to social patterns taking form in America after the Revolution. "Civilized morality" was becoming an American way of life. Social philosophers like William Alcott provided a rationale for emerging social patterns that filled the vacuum left by Calvinism in providing convincing answers to the existential questions created by social change in the mid-nineteenth century.

Although the socialist alternative to civilized morality and the capitalist economy was seriously advanced in the 1840s and again at the end of the century, thinkers like Fourier never appealed to the emerging middle class. The general public, influenced by evangelical theology and faculty psychology, held a view of the potential goodness of human nature that required a less drastic solution to social ills than the communes advocated by Fourier. In Social Darwinism they found a philosophy and promised not only material reward for those who demonstrated civilized morality, but also an even better future for their children and the nation.

Natural Evolution and Theology

The theological crisis precipitated by the 1859 publication of Darwin's *Origin of Species* centered around the validity of the Bible as God's revelation, as compared to Darwin's account of the origin and development of species. Biblical interpretation was a lifelong absorption for William Newton Clarke, who titled his autobiography *Sixty Years with the Bible*. Clarke's first exposure to Darwinism came during the years of his first pastorate in Keene, New Hampshire, between 1863 and 1869. During those years Clarke met regularly with a group of pastors in a futile attempt to reconcile the doctrine of biblical inspiration with Darwin's theories.

Darwin's theory was devastating to men like Clarke because their concept of biblical inspiration rested on an analogical method of proving the reasonableness of religion using natural evidence of design in nature. The method, used by William Paley in his *Analogy of Religion* (1736), was appropriated into American theology early in the nineteenth century. The method of the English rationalist differed little from the epistemology of Scottish commonsense theology. Both commonsense and natural theology claimed that, like natural theology, the revealed religion of the Bible was eminently reasonable. Reason was considered an adequate judge of the meaning, the morality, and the evidence of biblical revelation. Moral law found in Scripture simply added to the truth that could be discovered in the facts of a harmonious universe.[21]

There were two reasons that clergy trained in natural philosophy and commonsense theology were devastated by Darwin's theory Paley's evidences of God the designer of the universe were tied to a theory of a static, unchanging universe. Once Darwin suggested the possibility of evolving species and challenged the biblical creation story, which had been thought quite reasonable as factual information concerning the origins of the world and mankind, it became apparent that a great deal of the biblical record was, in fact, not at all reasonable. Before 1859 only the Unitarians had made an issue of the unreasonableness of the miracles and resurrection of Christ. With Darwin, the house of cards built on Paley's evidences came tumbling down when Darwin undermined the foundation of the method. If the universe was not evidence of a creating, purposeful God, then the analogy between the moral truth in nature and the moral truths in Scripture was also called into question. What was the nature of moral law, of moral truth? Was man a moral being by nature?

The evolutionary hypothesis left intact the possibility, even the necessity, for a God who is the First Cause. But how this God was related to man, if at all, was a new question for evangelicals. Was this God related to life and an afterlife? If God was not personal there was no point to prayer and personal piety. If there was no afterlife men might cease to be moral without the stimulus of such anticipated reward.

Darwinism sharpened questions that had been under discussion for at least fifty years. It provided obviously different and, to some, more satisfying answers to questions previously answered exclusively from biblical resources. The evolutionary hypothesis as an explanation of natural phenomena came as quite a shock to adherents of the theology of natural evidences, who took the Christian view of creation to be the static belief that every species then existing was exactly what always had been.

For those who accepted the biblical account of the creation and fall of man as a literal, historical event, Darwin's suggestion that man might have evolved from an ape seemed a degradation of human nature. In the creedal controversies of the 1830s, Nathaniel Taylor (1786-1858) had softened the Calvinist doctrine of imputed or inherited sin and guilt by saying that men had an "inherent tendency" to sin.[22] Even this was different from the implication of evolutionary theory that men sin because the essential nature of man is not spiritual but animal. This suggested to some that, if Darwin was correct, human life had no particular meaning whatever.

Further, if human existence was explained simply in terms of physical generation, this tacit denial of soul or an eternal element in man implied that there was no afterlife. Man, like any other animal, would be born, grow to maturity, and die. Like a fruit, he would ripen and fall off the tree. It was feared that if man was no longer considered a moral being such a conception of the nature of man would attack the very foundation of society.

While the evolutionary hypothesis raised uncomfortable questions about the origin, nature, and destiny of man, the doctrine of natural selection provoked an even stronger reaction because it suggested that there was no ultimate purpose or design in the universe or in man. Darwin and Spencer were both criticized for naturalizing the creative power and design formerly attributed to God. Spencer's statement that the cause of the universe was unknowable opened him to charges of materialism and atheism. Darwin's conception of evolution by natural causes was seen as fate or determinism concerning human life. It implied that the world and man are products of an unalterable and impersonal mechanism. It seemed to leave man standing helpless before the universe. Natural selection was interpreted as ruling out the doctrine of final causes, or teleology. What would happen if men ceased to believe in the controlling purpose of God in the universe and of man in society?

All the "new" liberal theologies of the 1890s resolved the Darwinian challenge to biblical inspiration and theology by using evolutionary theory to explain why some Scripture was unreasonable and to reinvest the universe and mankind with moral purpose.[23] From the evolutionary perspective, Reason was a trustworthy judge of the truths of Scripture, of morality, and of human nature that had evolved beyond the truths known to Scripture writers of the past. The evolutionary theologians shifted the evidences of nature to the arena of history and looked for evidence of human progress in the increasing prosperity and morality they believed signified an almost Christianized nation. They looked to history, society, and good men for an analogy of the nature of God. They replaced a static universe with history, society, and a race that was ascending not descending. The Social Gospel men were part of a general development in liberalizing theology. They adapted the "old" analogical method of theology to the "new" evolutionary interpretation of history as their defense against Darwinism.

This transition from the evidences of nature to the evidences of history was eased by two prominent theologians, whose major work was completed before the Darwinian furor. Nathaniel Taylor, theology professor at Yale and friend of Lyman Beecher, worked out a theology of moral government that supported evangelical "new light" developments in the church. Taylor, a professor of Horace Bushnell, died in 1858 just before the Darwinian challenge to theology. But he influenced Bushnell (1802–76), who hoped to mediate between the four parties to the pre–Civil War theological disputes. Bushnell never responded directly to issues raised by the evolutionary hypothesis, but there was in his theology enough hint of progress in history that he inadvertently mediated between "old light" Calvinism, "new light" evangelical theology, and evolutionary theory for the men of the Social Gospel.

The major life work of Taylor was his two-volume _Lectures on the Moral Government of God_ (1859). In the introduction, Noah Porter, then president of Yale Divinity School, described Taylor's analogical method. Taylor studied the intellectual and moral nature of man in order to understand God's moral government. He studied human government and laws, that they might tell him of God's government of men. "He reasoned, that man being the subject of all societies, duty being the obligation common to all, and law the expression of the authority by which they are sustained, they must furnish analogies to the moral government of God which comprehends the universe within its dominion."[24] In the period prior to the introduction of Darwin's theory of evolution, theologians had defended Christianity by using observations of design in the universe as evidence of God's activity in the world. In Taylor's era the argument from natural design was transformed by analogy into seeking knowledge about God's design from the moral universe of man.

Horace Bushnell, claimed as a mentor by Gladden, Abbott, and Strong, wrote a book of essays that exemplified the proposition that God governs the world by using "dark" events or circumstances to serve the good. In the preface of *Moral Uses of Dark Things* (1869) Bushnell wrote that moral uses are the last end of God in everything, including "physical uses." Bushnell had used the same principle earlier to justify the Civil War. As a leading proponent of the "vicarious sacrifice" of the war, Bushnell anticipated a glorious future for the reunited nation, in which moral and cultural progress could be expected as the result of the national "sacrifice."[25] God could use even the most tragic of events, with reference to individuals or nations, to serve the good in an immediate and reasonably accessible way. "Old light" Calvinists had always affirmed that the last end of God was ultimate good. But, unlike Bushnell, they never claimed the ability to decipher God's mysterious purposes in such concrete detail.

With clues from Taylor and Bushnell and the work of pre-Darwinian social theorists like Combe, men like William Newton Clarke slowly resolved the question of biblical inspiration. Once that issue was resolved the theological implications were obvious.

Clarke's autobiography provides a chronology of the difficult transition from "traditionalism to reality" in his changing attitudes regarding biblical inspiration and theology. His account provides insight into the struggle for freedom from "old light" theories of biblical dictation waged by a whole generation of evangelicals faced with the same issues. They developed the new theory of inspiration over against "old light" Calvinists like Charles Hodge, a Princeton Seminary professor who insisted that the Bible was a divine revelation because God had dictated it to men word by word. According to men like Hodge, the Bible had to be internally consistent because it was divinely inspired. Therefore biblical truth was self-validating. The theory of dictation involved an unreasonable supernaturalism no longer acceptable to liberal, "new light" evangelicals.

According to Clarke, his initial breakthrough concerning biblical interpretation came in the 1870s, when he realized that the Bible was not a textbook of life, whole and complete in itself, to which life's questions could be addressed. Nor could the Bible be interpreted solely from within itself. The truth of the Bible was not verified by its own claim to truth. "God doesn't dictate to me an explanation of his gracious work. . . . I must search it out in the light of God himself."[26] The individual must interpret the Bible for himself in the light of the revelation of God in Christ. It was the ethical principle in the character of Christ that pointed the way to eternal truth in the Bible. This meant "going behind" dictated principles from the Bible or from the church to find the universal principles present in the divine character. Using the ethical approach to biblical revelation, Clarke was relieved to discover that the ethical propositions of the New Testament "sweep away" the "ancient truth" of the Old Testament.

By the 1880s Clarke no longer hesitated to discard "old light" doctrines that depended on Old Testament sources. He stopped preaching exegetical sermons and preached instead to "inspire" his congregation. The Bible was no longer his starting place for preaching. It was a source book for illustrative material to be used as "a spiritual guide to life."[27] Clarke's belief in the pervasive power of "the spirit" to guide his choices, and his acceptance of the Bible as a spiritual guide to ethical principles, part of which had already become obsolete, led him to conclude that the Bible was not God's final revelation "for setting forth the meaning of what Christ wrought." Although he did not say that the Bible itself might no longer be necessary as the source of the revelation of Christ, Clarke was saying that modern theologians should be able to surpass the biblical revelation in their comprehension of the meaning of Christian salvation.[28]

The theory of inspiration Clarke used for his principle of biblical interpretation was salvation understood as inner light. This led him to affirm that the continuity between the Testaments lay in the "religion of inwardness" displayed both by the Old Testament prophets and by Christ, who was the perfect representative of the "religion of inwardness." By the 1890s Clarke concluded that the Bible served very well as a source for theology without any theory of inspiration. Theology itself was inspired by the same "spirit that inspired the Bible."[29] The question of epistemology no longer mattered.

Ultimately, the standard of choice Clarke used in his biblical interpretation and in writing *An Outline of Christian Theology* (1904) was an evolutionary theory of the progressive development of human reason applied to the question of revelation. He claimed that there was no conflict between theology being written by enlightened men and the Bible, correctly understood, because the same Spirit inspired the theologian in his interpretation and in his contribution to continuing revelation. In relation to this discovery, Clarke passed lightly over the New Testament books attributed to Paul, because Paul was the beginning, not the end, of theology. Because of its ancient origins, Paul's theology was true neither to the nature of man nor to the nature of truth.[30]

Although Clarke's theology contained more evidence of biblical scholarship than the writing of Gladden, Abbott, and Strong, he was not a biblical theologian. Once he freed himself of the notion that the Bible was literally God's word to man and was instead one record of many continuing revelations of God to man, he was free to drop any part of the Bible offensive to the modern mind.

George Combe had claimed that men in the past had misunderstood the Bible because they believed that the natural order was essentially disordered, the world was a wilderness, and salvation meant to be saved from the world. But that interpretation simply reflected the dark, disordered reason of an earlier age. When discreditors claimed that Combe's doctrine of natural law was irreconcilable with biblical revelation, Combe replied that this was impossible because the Holy Spirit and the human mind emanated from the same source. They could not contradict each other.[31] Clarke had to relegate Paul to "old" theology no longer valid because human nature as Clarke understood it was better explained by a faculty psychology of the higher and lower nature of man than it was by Paul's theology. Each liberal theologian disregarded whatever knowledge of past generations failed to fit his own theology. The choices differed but the method was the same. Moral law could be known by studying the evidences of history and the progress of the race. Nature, as well as Scripture, provided supporting evidence for moral law as well as inspiration to the higher—more spiritual—nature of man.

Social Darwinism and Evolutionary Theology

Between Reconstruction and the late 1870s, Abbott, Gladden, and Strong acquired a new vocabulary in which "civilized" and "barbarian" became organizing categories of thought. References to Reconstruction at the time reveal that Gladden and Abbott were not yet thinking in the language and terms of Social Darwinism. Their concern with man as man, antagonism to sectarian division, emphasis on work and thrift, belief in the efficacy of education, and the importance of face-to-face relationships were all themes found in the prewar writing of Horace Bushnell. The same themes continued in Gladden and Abbott in the 1880s, but with one major difference. They moved out of Bushnell's theological frame of reference into the social-historical structure of Social Darwinism.

The fathers of Social Darwinism—Darwin and Spencer—both assumed the faculty psychology concerning the higher and lower faculties of man. In his autobiography Spencer reported that he became a "believer" in phrenology as a child. He also indicated that at the time he wrote his earliest "papers" his "faith in phrenology was unshaken."[32] Throughout his career, Spencer used the peculiar vocabulary of the faculties from phrenology. More important, he was conceptually in debt to faculty psychology for the concept of "moral sense" that was central to his social philosophy. Darwin had been influenced by the writing of Spencer, to whom he referred in the introduction to *Origin of Species* as "our greatest philosopher."[33] Although many of the same arguments for social progress in history are present in both Darwin and Spencer, Spencer's early work, *Social Statics,* was more influential in shaping American Social Darwinism.

The social theory of both Darwin and Spencer provided an evolutionary rationale for the moral superiority of the Victorian family. Both men assumed that the family was the building block of society necessary to the future progress of civilization. *Social Statics,* published in America in 1850, included a social history of the progress of mankind from barbarism to civilized forms of social institutions and individual morality. In *On the Origin of Species by Means of Natural Selection* (1859)

Darwin carried on a dialogue with Spencer's theory of the survival of the fittest. Because Darwin's theory of natural selection was primarily biological, when he applied the theory to man he compared humans with animals. Following Spencer's outline of the social progress of civilization, Darwin thought his biological observations were complementary to Spencer's psychology. Darwin's theory of natural selection reinforced Spencer's theory of the progress of human reason by demonstrating "the necessary acquirement of each mental power and capacity by gradation."[34]

Spencer's moral theory was more humanistically oriented than the work of Darwin because his subject was man and society. Spencer cited Coleridge as the source of his basic assumption that "morality is essentially one with physical truth—it is, in fact, a species of transcendental physiology." He also credited Coleridge for his assertion that human life naturally moves toward "the progressive realization" of moral law and moral behavior.[35] In Spencer these assumptions took the form of a strenuous emphasis on individual character development through conflict as instrumental to civilized progress.

Although Spencer and Darwin differed in their descriptions of human life and morality, they used the same method of empirical observation to substantiate their theories. Both took it for granted that moral law could be discovered, like natural law, by empirical observation. Spencer assumed that moral law was an objective body of truth and that his own social theory was a contribution to that body of truth.

American receptivity to the social theory and social history of Darwin and Spencer was related to the presence of the family ideal, the faculty psychology, and the theory of the progressive development of reason present in American thought before the Civil War. Although Darwin's books challenged all the basic doctrines of classical Protestant Christianity, a transformation of "old light" Calvinism had been well under way in America for a half century before Darwin's work was published. Although the evolution of species was a relatively new idea, progress in civilization was less shocking to Americans. All 1,250 copies of the first printing of *Origin of Species* sold out on the first day of publication because a public receptive to Darwin's scientific verification of progress in nature and history already existed.

Darwin's work caused a furor because it was deemed a direct attack on the Bible and religion in a way that was less evident in Spencer's work. Instead of challenging a world-view, as *Origin of Species* seemed to do, Spencer's *Social Statics* flowed more smoothly with American intellectual currents when it was published in 1850. Spencer's contribution to Social Darwinism is usually attributed to his monumental *Synthetic Philosophy,* a series of books treating various scientific disciplines.[36] But the earlier book, *Social Statics,* was a social interpretation of history that integrated psychology, sociology, and political theory and was written in a style accessible to the general public. The center of the social theory was what Spencer called "transcendental physiology."

Spencer's transcendental physiology depended on a faculty psychology view of "moral sense." He transposed the biological theory of evolution by adaptation to environment into a "moral physiology" of the adaptation of moral sense to social circumstances. At the level of social theory he stated that mankind was evolving toward a perfect equilibrium in the future. He expected social cooperation to occur without forfeiting individuation because the moral sense of individuals could be expected to accommodate both the instinct for self-preservation and personal rights and sympathy for others that would respect their freedom and personal rights.

Moral sense, as Spencer used it, was the center of the faculties because it balanced desire with duty. Like Combe, Spencer assumed that every desire had a positive purpose as a stimulus with a matching reward if properly used. The passion of the human sentiments, or desire, accounted for movement in history and progress in the moral nature of man. The adaptation of individuals to social circumstances depended on the opportunity to exercise the faculties, especially moral sense, the faculty that judged and balanced desire and duty. Otherwise, as was the case with the idleness of the Negro, an unused faculty would atrophy. Spencer advised providing assistance in learning self-discipline for the American Negro so the faculty inclining men to work could develop naturally.[37]

Social evolution from barbarism to civilization depended on the ability of individuals to adapt to social circumstances, since "progress is not an accident, but a necessity."[38] In civilization, most of the necessary adaptations of the human organism had already occurred. Although there was still scattered evidence of barbarism in those who responded only to the "rudimentary" instincts of self-preservation, on the whole America was the leading civilization because of the principle of democracy. Spencer saw in the American democracy the same combination of "sympathy" with "personal rights" that he considered the hallmark of a perfectly evolved personality.

In every historical period, and in a civilized nation, there is a diversity among individuals in the degree of civilization present. Those most civilized are the people who express the most individuation and are conscious of "personal rights" but also "sympathetic." Those not yet conscious of individuation are the least civilized. All "backwater Americans," such as frontiersmen, struck Spencer as "uncivilized."[39] By lack of individuation he meant that they did not have the ability to defer gratification because they had no opportunity to develop the faculty of moral sense.

Spencer's "first principle" in *Social Statics* and in his later work was the thesis that every man has the right to do all he wills, provided it doesn't infringe on the rights of others: "Every man may claim the fullest liberty to exercise his faculties compatible with the possession of like liberty by every other man."[40] All evil represented the nonadaptation of the human constitution, the faculties, to social conditions. Put another way, all evil was related to an incongruity between the faculties of an individual and the sphere of action.[41]

Oddly, the social equilibrium Spencer projected for the future depended on social dynamics. Before the "social statics" of his title could occur, Spencer expected necessary social convolutions during an interim before equilibrium. Social dynamics would be the natural selective process by which people who were less adapted to modern society would cease to exist. Only the best adapted, most civilized people—the fittest—would survive to reproduce their own kind.[42]

Like Bushnell, Spencer saw good purposes in apparent evil, both in individuals and in social history. At the level of individual development, social dynamics are the influences that make people fit to obey moral laws. In periods of social convolution, individual virtue is learned by resisting temptation and vice. At the social level, individual virtue required adaptation to the status quo of society, which Spencer took to be the mean degree of civilization already present in a given society.

The role of government, a necessary but temporary evil, was to interfere as little as possible with social convolutions. Less government is better because it allows individuals the freedom needed to develop and perfect their faculties by use. The Spencerian assumption behind laissez-faire economic theory in America is the belief that civilization will necessarily progress as every individual has the opportunity to develop the faculty of moral sense.[43]

The family and schools were the social units in which individuals learned to adapt to both natural law and the social order by experience. Spencer assumed that children learned by example and by experience which followed a natural order of development. In *Education: Intellectual, Moral and Physical* (1860) he developed a theory for permissive parenting and progressive education. Like his psychology, it had a biological basis for learning by experience. Parents and teachers should permit children to make mistakes, such as burning fingers with matches, so that the child could strengthen the intellectual and moral faculties by drawing his own conclusions. Parents should avoid all coercive discipline such as slapping, spanking, or lecturing. This was not necessary because children would naturally follow and emulate parental attitudes and practices of kindness and mutual cooperation. In the family, self-control and self-sacrifice could be learned without conflict because altruism between parent and child was natural.[44]

The principle of learning by experience also explained why Spencer opposed any legislated form of aid to the poor. Like children, the poor could only learn good judgment and self-control from experience and from use of moral judgment. From the perspective of social evolution, then, the principle of natural selection should be allowed to take its course because protective legislation would only artificially keep the poor alive and retard progress. For example, there should be no laws against quack medicine and false advertising because the poor should learn to judge between true and false. They would learn this by experience, such as the immediate pain resulting from taking quack medicine. A wrong choice resulting in some form of pain or personal suffering would discourage a repetition of the act.[45]

In an 1894 letter to the American Transcendentalist Moncure Conway, Spencer wrote that legislation cannot be used against moral conduct because it enslaves free will just as enforced religious dogma had once retarded religious progress. "Among our faculties the moral sense alone claims absoluteness. The moral sentiment is now borrowing the enthusiasm of religion and should use scientific methods to do so."[46]

Although he believed that legislation was tantamount to moral coercion, Spencer believed that the acceptable way to permit the development of the individual faculties was through the power of public opinion. Although the individual personality was the carrier of culture, public opinion represented an aggregate of personalities. Assuming that moral sense never errs, Spencer placed unquestioned faith in the rightness of public opinion prompted by the moral sentiment of each individual. Government should never initiate any legislation unless public opinion, understood as a vehicle of eternal truth, so dictated. Men in society would progressively develop laws in closer harmony with the absolute natural laws in this fashion. Until that time, they would continue to make mistakes in legislation unless they restricted themselves to passing only laws that embodied social practices already well established as customary procedures. Any law not already established in practice would inevitably interfere with the freedom of the individual to develop his faculties. Therefore opinion, not legislation, was the proper agent of social change. And opinion was prompted by moral sentiment.[47]

Spencer's work was greeted with more enthusiasm in America than it generated in England. His system promised a future peace, "a glorious future," and explained temporary social disorder. It told middle-class Americans that they were the most civilized people in the most civilized nation, and that adaptation to the status quo of society was a virtue in times of social convolution.

Spencer's philosophical method and his psychology were congruent with American modes of thought. The use of natural and physical laws to explain human nature, society, and history was considered scientific. His historical conclusions drawn on the basis of empirical evidence from the whole of human history differed little from the practice of Americans like Bushnell. Spencer gave content to a mode of thought already familiar to American theologians.

There were, however, issues raised by the theory that account for the presence of two schools of Social Darwinism in America. Spencer's method attended to the macrocosmic in history, the whole rather than the parts. His social theory explained the role of social disorder in progress and legitimated insensitivity to people who suffered as a result of the necessary convolutions of historical progress. The question that divided Henry Ward Beecher from his friend Lyman Abbott was that of the social responsibility of the privileged and "civilized" middle class for the less "civilized" in the interim between social convolutions and social equilibrium. Like William Graham Sumner, Beecher was a conservative on government policy and followed the Spencerian argument that buttressed laissez-faire economics. The men of the Social Gospel were more concerned with the plight of the uncivilized in the interim.

Beecher agreed with Sumner that men should not interfere with the natural evolution of society. Both opposed all social intervention, because in eliminating the poor and the immoral by the gradual genetic process God was purifying the race.[48] Beecher transformed the old Calvinist doctrine of predestination into a theory of election by social class.

The Social Gospel men refused to interpret the doctrine of natural selection as a social, temporal form of predestination. The aspect of Social Darwinism from which they most clearly deviated was that of natural selection. The liberal camp of Social Darwinists accepted the fact that the "social" nature of man was the major distinction between men and animals. Although virtue was acquired through conflict and temptation, they claimed that social interaction had to be harmonious to be productive. Although competition, aggression, and violence might serve the social good of progress in the historical process, the men of the Social Gospel intensely disliked the implications for the present of Spencer's laissez-faire version of the survival of the fittest.

All Social Darwinists believed in the survival of the fittest if it implied that social change almost of necessity means progress. But not all agreed with Darwin's biological theory of evolution by sexual selection or Spencer's theory of progress by natural selection.

In 1871 Darwin published *The Descent of Man and Selection in Relation to Sex,* in which he claimed that the moral progress of the race depended primarily on the biological process of sexual selection. Darwin assumed, in addition, that a good family was necessary to the normal unfolding of the conjugal and parental elements in the individual. Like Spencer, Darwin assumed that moral progress depended on the continuing development of moral sense in individuals, but because he believed that virtue was inherited he granted priority to sexual selection as the means of moral progress.[49]

Darwin's theory of sexual selection was accepted by some Americans as a law of progress. It was one source of the Victorian interest in eugenics. It implied that the choice of a mate was a crucial decision because Darwin had associated mate selection with the progress or decline of civilization. Whatever the reservations may have been about Darwin's theory of sexual selection, in general terms both Darwin and Spencer provided scientific verification of the importance of a good family.

In *The Descent of Man,* Darwin verified the common distinction between civilized and barbarian cultures with his observations of the natives in primitive Terra del Fuego. He concluded that they were sexually intemperate because their weak reasoning faculty was incapable of projecting the future consequences of present actions. Therefore they were unable to restrain the immediate gratification of their animal impulses. The native lacked the intelligence to see that the "self-regarding virtues" of chastity and temperance would serve the general welfare of the tribe. The licentious habits of the natives and their commission of unnatural crimes resulted from insufficient moral instruction, failure to develop good habits early in life, and unenlightened reason.

Darwin was morally outraged by the nudity of the natives. His observations of barbarism among the natives led him to reflect on the evolution of civilized standards of morality. Drawing upon his observations of chimpanzees in the London zoo and his observations of Victorian culture, he concluded that sexual jealousy prevented both men and monkeys from indulging in promiscuous intercourse. His basic premise concerning the rising moral standards that seemed to accompany progress in civilization was stated in the law of sexual selection. Sexual selection in any age meant that rival males competed for the favor of a female. Granting the power of male sexual desire, monogamous patterns of sexual selection in the nineteenth century must mean that men had learned to control their thoughts, for "the soul is dyed by thoughts."[50] This distinction between barbarian and civilized men was an underlying motif in late Victorian social thought.

Although male chimpanzees competed for the female on the basis of physical prowess, civilized males competed on the basis of economic success. Survival of the fittest men would mean the physically and morally fit. Weaker types—moral barbarians by Darwin's standard—would select themselves out of the race because immorality was almost automatically self-punishing. "Violent, quarrelsome men often come to a bloody end." The promiscuous would die young of venereal disease. The melancholy would commit suicide.[51] Although facts did not support his thesis that "the vigorous, the healthy and the happy supply and multiply," Darwin did his best to support the existing ethos. While claiming that married men had regular habits and lived longer, he admitted that sometimes the reckless, degraded, and vicious reproduced at a much higher rate than the "vigorous" part of the race.[52]

Darwin concluded that certain factors in modern civilization were necessary to ensure continued moral progress. Drawing on Scottish anthropological literature for information about savage tribes, he stated that domestic stability depended on owning property because it kept people in one place. Other components necessary to civilized standards of morality were "a fixed abode, the union of many families under one chief, and the necessity of cultivation."[53]

Although the Victorians found many of Darwin's assertions unpalatable, particularly the ignoble view of human motivation and marriage, his version of civilization was perfectly acceptable. It included all the allegiances of middle-class morality: moral purity, economic success, home ownership, patriotism, and hard work. American middle-class morality was like Darwin's idea of "civilized" morality, and civilized morality meant progress. Darwin used his own experience of civilized morality as the criterion of civilization. His list of necessary components of civilization—property, one-family homes, and regular work—appears in all Social Gospel thought.

While liberal Social Darwinists like the Social Gospel men agreed with the components of civilized morality, they disagreed with the means of natural selection described by both Darwin and Spencer. Instead they followed the line of reasoning advanced by Henry George in *Progress and Poverty* (1879) for the purpose of challenging the Malthusian proposition that natural selection occurred through wars, plagues, natural disasters, and intemperance. George challenged Darwin's theory of moral evolution through sexual selection and Spencer's theory of the natural survival of the fittest by emphasizing the instrumental role played by moral man in the whole evolutionary process in history from barbarism to civilization.

Spencer and Darwin cited aspects of the cultures of Rome, Greece, and the Middle Ages that had contributed to both progress and decline in history. But when they argued for long-range progress in history they minimized elements of barbarism and decline to substantiate the point. George also saw history as a linear process of progress that included temporary periods of decline. But he emphasized the decadence rather than the contribution of ancient people to history in order to demonstrate that the cause of progress was the human effort to facilitate the development of the mental and moral powers inherent in human nature.[54] It was a difference in perception and emphasis.

Ultimately, George argued against Spencer's social theories of total nonintervention in the social evolutionary process on the basis of the higher priority he placed on the positive achievements and moral powers of modern man. The total effect of George's perspective was to imply that modern men taken as a whole were much more civilized than ancient men, who were much more barbaric. He shifted the emphasis of Spencer's theory of growth by conflict to say that conflict and violence belong to ancient history. Modern civilization should have much less conflict and violence. Both men expected that eventually warfare would cease and human perfection would emerge. But George repudiated Spencer's conclusion that utopia would emerge solely by natural historical processes in which men had no role. George argued that a land tax would ameliorate present social disorder by giving every family unit an equal opportunity at economic stability and prosperity.

The land tax would facilitate progress because the mind as "the motor of progress" cannot develop naturally in social conditions of warfare, violence, conflict, and aggression. Development of mental power in children depended first on the gratification of the animal nature and later on the development of sociability and equality. Gratification of the animal nature meant the fulfillment of basic physical needs including food, shelter, clothing, and the sexual instinct.[55]

Civilization, for George, meant "progress in man's powers and conditions." He assumed that since the family performed the social functions of procreation and the socialization of children, society, meaning all other social institutions, existed to support the family in that task.

George's plea to abolish poverty by means of the land tax was based on his conviction that, given the opportunity to fulfill the physical and social needs in the family unit, all families would then contribute to the continued progress of civilization.

Although Darwin and Spencer had granted formative powers to the family, George added a peculiarly American twist in asserting that all other social institutions existed to support the family in the socializing task. For George, the family was the means of natural selection. His was a theory in which the selective process seemed harmonious and not violent, cooperative rather than competitive, rational rather than irrational.

Progress and Poverty was published in fifteen languages and had a circulation numbering in the millions. When George ran for mayor of New York on a land-tax platform, Walter Rauschenbusch campaigned for him. Each of the Social Gospel leaders acknowledges George's influence on their social thought. George was indebted to Spencer's *Social Statics* of 1850 for his proposition that the solution to the poverty problem lay in a land tax. When Spencer later repudiated the land-tax concept, George countered with another book in which he spent three hundred pages denouncing Spencer.[56] Although George invested his energies in an unsuccessful attempt to see the land tax become law, he influenced social philosophy and politics in a more general way through *Progress and Poverty,* which assumed most of Spencer's "principles."

The Social Gospel figures moved with relative ease from the perspectives of commonsense theology and natural philosophy to the evolutionary concept of Social Darwinism. Because of personal predilections to avoid violence and conflict, George's version of Social Darwinism, denuded of the implied violence of the natural selective process, was attractive to them. His continuity with the Victorian family ethos further enhanced the power of his social theory. Like most postwar Victorians, the early Social Gospel men were eager for "scientific" laws concerning society and history that supported a hopeful expectation of peace following the Civil War.

The doctrine of American manifest destiny so central to Social Gospel thought was a direct product of Social Darwinism and an indirect product of the theological methods and psychology of "new light" evangelical Christianity of the pre–Civil War period. The faculty psychology of prewar social and religious thought provided a common ground for the late-Victorian conviction that the destiny of the nation was irrevocably linked to the destiny of the family. The similarity of content in Social Darwinism and liberal theology was taken by the Social Gospel men as evidence of the coming kingdom of God, in which distinctions between religion and culture would no longer exist. While the Bible continued to be a source for moral inspiration, Social Darwinism provided the content of the Victorian world-view that explained the massive social change experienced by the Victorians.

The Victorian social revolution was experienced most dramatically in the family. Faculty psychology explained and rationalized changed roles for men and women, parents and children. The family ethos of Social Darwinism and of the Social Gospel was a social justification of the self-sacrificing behavior required by the new era in family relations. The direct connection between virtue and reward justified obvious middle-class prosperity. The deferred gratification of civilized middle-class America produced prosperity for the present and expectations of an endless spiral of economic and social progress in the future.

Middle-class Victorians, with their voluntarist doctrine of freedom and the urgent demand for self-control, fervently believed that they deserved their material rewards. By their own standards those roomy white houses had been honestly earned. It was natural that they would be attracted by a social philosophy and a social gospel that anticipated equality of opportunity for all, yet for the present justified the social status of the prospering middle class.

PART TWO

THE SOCIAL GOSPEL MOVEMENT: AN ELLIPSE WITH A DOUBLE FOCUS

There is reason to believe that twentieth-century churches will look upon duty as represented by the ellipse described around the individual and society as the two foci.

—Josiah Strong,
The Twentieth Century City

4

Social Change
and Applied Christianity
(1865–1900)

"Progressive" Social Darwinism was a social philosophy that made it possible for Josiah Strong to discuss evangelism to individuals and society simultaneously. All Victorian evangelicals influenced by evolutionary thought envisioned the kingdom of God as the goal of history. While socially conservative evangelicals trusted the future to the "natural" social processes, the men of the Social Gospel were influenced by the "progressive" Social Darwinism of Henry George. Social Gospel support of limited forms of "progressive" legislation earned them a reputation as social and political liberals. However, their expectations concerning the assimilation of nonwhite, non-Protestant, and immigrant Americans to standards of civilized morality reveals a social conservatism related to both Social Darwinism and their evangelical roots. Early Social Gospel commentary on nonwhite Americans, labor relations, the city, and manifest destiny was influenced by a liberal interpretation of Social Darwinism.

Liberal Social Darwinism and the
Early Social Gospel

The convergent concepts of Social Darwinism from Combe, Spencer, Darwin, and George form a general, though not uniform, pattern as they were used by Social Gospel figures. The key concepts of their social commentary were moral categories. For the race to progress meant moral progress from slavery to freedom, from the external coerciveness and violence of a military society to the natural harmonious cooperation which made an industrial society possible. They found democracy the only form of government suitable to a civilized society because freedom was an opportunity for moral development in individuals. Democracy, however, was working because the middle class possessed the self-restraint necessary to peace and progress.

This did not mean that there would be no conflict between different interest groups in a pluralistic society. It did mean that a conflict of liberal and conservative opinion was necessary to the historical dialectic of progress. Although differences of opinion served a necessary purpose, in a civilized society harmony would prevail because people with conflicting interests would voluntarily cooperate with one another. The ideal of the "social state" would be fulfilled when all social institutions reached the stage of development found in the family—the triumph of altruism over egotism, the deference of the stronger to the weaker.

The Social Gospel men assumed that the faculties of mankind had developed progressively through the course of human history. The animal instincts, or lower nature of man, remained constant, but the upper nature of man, the faculties of reason and moral sense, had become more powerful and were capable of keeping the animal instincts in equilibrium. Middle-class living standards were proof that the primary instincts of food, shelter, and clothing were being fulfilled.

The question of the age—"the social question"—converged around obvious moral and cultural differentiation. There was a painfully large gap between the living standards of a "captain of industry" and those of an Irish immigrant. Did this mean that the captain of industry had been so handsomely rewarded because he was the finest and most moral specimen of the human species ever to walk the earth? Or did this mean that something was terribly wrong with a social organism that granted so little in tangible rewards to the ever-increasing poor? Both answers could be supported from within the framework of Social Darwinism.

It was on this issue that the Social Gospel men departed from the middle-class consensus. Although they accepted the theories of natural evolution of the species, they refused to accept the Malthusian theory of social equilibrium achieved entirely by natural selective processes. They followed Henry George in the liberal form of Social Darwinism that emphasized the instrumentality of man in the social processes. Man was not a passive observer but an organism capable of intervening in and ameliorating the social processes, though in a limited way. The Social Gospel men conceptualized the role man could play in terms of family relationships. They believed that family patterns of altruism were transferable to all social relationships.

The language and concepts of Gladden and Abbott in books written before 1880 were those of faculty psychology and evangelical Christianity. After 1880 their thought has added dimensions from Social Darwinian influences. Strong quotes Charles Darwin and Horace Bushnell more often than other sources. This accounts for differences in emphasis between Gladden, Abbott, and Strong.

The social activism of the early leaders of the Social Gospel consisted more of efforts to influence public opinion than of direct participation in the political process. Their books, preaching, and public-platform appearances were intended to ameliorate social conflict and accelerate moral progress by influencing the opinions of individual readers and listeners.[1] They were counting on the influence of the middle-class family and their own influence on good men in the church and in the world to be the means of "the ascent of man." Their social activism was a form of evangelism in which they expected their influence on individuals to be the means of social change and progress.

Changing social circumstances and the faculty psychology combined to place the family theoretically and concretely at the center of the universe of the Social Darwinism of the Social Gospel. Although the individual was the carrier of culture and the most basic social unit, his mental, moral, and physical development were dependent on his parents in both the genetic and behavioral sense.[2] The whole future of civilization and the continuation of patterns of civilized morality seemed to depend on wholesome mate selection and successful parenthood. Any individual lagging behind the present level of civilization was perceived as retarding progress and labeled "a barbarian." The pressures to conform to accepted patterns of middle-class morality, linked as they were with the world-historical process, were intense.

For the Social Gospel, "civilization" meant that all Americans should adapt to "social" circumstances to maintain the existing social order. "Social," in this instance, meant the development of altruism, the highest potential of the faculties of each individual. The "social state" would be achieved by means of the natural organic development of individuals which would simultaneously fulfill the moral law and contribute to the progress of civilization.

The attention of the Social Gospel men was divided between the amelioration of social conflicts in the present and the continuation of the standards of the family unit as they knew it. The net effect of this double focus was that the Social Gospel men held views that were associated with "progressive" politics, while their activities were socially conservative insofar as they worked to conform all men to the image of the middle-class family. To the Social Gospel, "progressive" legislation was not a means of social change. Legislation was progressive if it contributed to the progress of civilization over barbarism. Because they believed that a law could not be enforced unless it was supported by public opinion, they directed their activities toward the institutions responsible for educating moral sense—the church and the family.

Reconstruction: Nonwhite Americans and Civilized Progress

After the Civil War, Americans had an immense need to affirm the goodness and purpose of life in the face of the national tragedy. Some, like Walt Whitman, turned to extreme forms of cosmic idealism for reassurance that the deaths of so many men were not meaningless. But it was more common to adopt the theory of the progress of civilization over barbarism. Horace Bushnell was the source of the moral interpretation of the war used by the Social Gospel pioneers. Although the Social Gospel men later integrated Bushnell's moral interpretation with Social Darwinism, Bushnell had hinted at the possibility of progress in history.

Bushnell suggested that history was a succession of the old giving way to new eras. More concretely, he thought that the changing ideas of the nineteenth century were a preparation for the "reign of the spirit." The "spirit" he had in mind was the germinal force working out God's will in history according to an inner law of development. Although the "spirit" was unconsciously present in groups as well as in individuals, "progress" meant that the inner law, or "spirit," would become known to man in a manner analogous to the discovery of natural laws and would be visible in the historical process. He pointed out that human history represented stages in the "Great and Divine Future." Bushnell's point was the reliability of the power of God working through men. To him history was God's plan for mankind. His Social Gospel disciples used the concept of inner law, or "spirit," to explain the source of progress in history achieved through the instrumentality of virtuous manhood.[3]

Bushnell's interpretation of the "vicarious sacrifice" of Northern soldiers on behalf of the glorious future of the reunited nation contained the seeds of the Social Gospel hope for a kingdom of God on earth. The Northern ethos, according to Bushnell, represented order, law, liberty, and right emerging victorious against a morally degraded South that had fought to uphold faction, conspiracy, "madness," and "the defiant wrong of slavery."[4]

This view of the Northern victory involved a set of attitudes about work, government, family, and sexuality that contrasted Northern and Southern morality. In Southern literature, the use of "blood," unlike Bushnell's concept of blood sacrifice, denoted family ancestry and affection as the source of the sense of historical continuity. The Southern preoccupation with "blood" relatives and inherited family land was, to the Northern mind, an obsession reminiscent of ancient feudalism with echoes of heraldry, chivalrous but immoral knights, and feudal chiefs living off the work of serfs.

The heart of the Northern objection to Southern culture was contained in this view of the South as a hierarchical paternalistic aristocracy, where the strong literally ruled the weak. The implications of Southern culture, tied as it was to inherited land and income, were offensive because the aristocratic plantation owners lived off the work of others. To the Northern evangelical, work was a necessary component of mental and moral growth.

This attitude toward Southern culture was not restricted to evangelicals. Henry Adams's characterization of his first encounter with a Southern male, a Harvard classmate, reveals Yankee presuppositions about the lasting effects of Southern culture on character. Roony Lee, a son of Robert E. Lee, had two virtues according to Adams—the habit of command learned from his slave-owning experience, and the social graces.

> The habit of command was not enough, and the Virginian had little else. He was simple beyond analysis. . . . No one knew enough to know how ignorant he was: how child-like. . . . As an animal, the Southerner seemed

to have every advantage, but even as an animal, he steadily lost ground.... Strictly the Southerner had no mind: he had temperament.[5]

To Adams, "temperament" meant "blood." It represented the dominance of the natural animal impulses of sexual desire and family affection, carried to an extreme at the expense of mental and moral maturity necessary to the advancement of civilized standards of life.

The Northern mind was fascinated with the image of the South as a warmer and more sensual climate and environment than the harsh, cold North. The sexual implications of the Northern view of the South are related to the suspicion that too much leisure, and an accumulation of material wealth separated from work, automatically leads to sensuality and lasciviousness. The Northern victory was seen as a victory of an "industrious civilization" against a nonworking Southern aristocracy.

The Northern victory provided a historical example of the survival of the fittest—the morally fit. Vicarious sacrifice carried two implications for the Northern evangelical. It would eradicate the evil in Southern culture. Equally important, sacrifice in the North would regenerate the Northern moral climate, which was being weakened by prosperity. Washington Gladden wrote that the depression of 1873 was the price to be paid for war. The war, taken as a whole, was a force for good in the universe, but the waging of war was evil, and as such extracted its own price.

While the moral interpretation of vicarious sacrifice prevailed in Gladden's response to the war, his immediate concern in 1875 was unemployment:

We had a battle to fight with the false philosophy of a former generation, in order to maintain the dignity of work. There were those who insisted that labor was dishonorable and degrading; that the laboring classes ought to be the servile classes. That fallacy we have pretty effectually exploded, though it took not a little gunpowder to do it. It is now generally admitted in all parts of the land that labor is honorable. . . . Now we must make it equally clear that labor is not optional but imperative . . . that it is not only respectable to work, but that it is not respectable to be idle.[6]

The imperative to work was the line of continuity in Gladden's approach to Reconstruction and, later, to labor problems. All men must work because work was the indispensable condition of character development. In 1876 Gladden wrote that it was the design of the Creator that the natural comes first, then the spiritual development of man: "Mind steadily gains on muscle, and will continue to gain until the spiritual or immaterial part of man shall gain a complete ascendancy over the natural forces of the world in which he lives."[7]

During Reconstruction, Gladden and Abbott both participated in the Northern-based Congregational home mission board effort to educate the freedmen for citizenship. Among Northerners there was a difference of opinion concerning the extent to which the "negro" was educable. While many Northerners favored only manual training for the "negro," the Social Gospel men assumed that uplifting the "negro" involved educating all the faculties. Viewing all men as potential manhood material, they argued that head and hand training for the "negro" would develop both mental and moral faculties. Gladden interpreted the desire of some Northerners to keep the "negro" intellectually retarded as a threat to civilization, which would regress if the South was permitted to enslave the freedmen intellectually.

Both Gladden and Abbott had doubts about the equality of the "negro" with white men, but both men were willing to give the "negro" the opportunity to rise out of the state of animalism. Looking back at the failure of Reconstruction forty years later, Gladden concluded that it might take the "negro" another one hundred years to rise to the level of the white man. In the interim, neither man questioned the wisdom of keeping the races separate as "nature's way" of avoiding miscegenation. The black community, though separate, would need to be equal in every way to the white community. Such institutions as Hampton and Fisk were a source of great pride to Gladden and Abbott, as were men like Booker T. Washington, because these developments indicated that the "negro" was capable of becoming the business and professional man in his own self-sufficient community. Abbott opposed all legislation that would grant the "negro" rights for which he was not yet ready, on the grounds that it would not serve to advance the "negro." No good could come from an incongruity between the level of development of the faculties and the environment. Such laws would not change white prejudice toward the capacity of the "negro" either. Abbott assumed that white prejudice would eventually be eradicated through years of education.[8]

Gladden was certain that retribution would be swift if the white race failed to discharge the obligation to educate the "negro," for "this is a moral universe." Gladden feared the retrogression of civilization if the North failed to carry through the full moral implications of the vicarious sacrifice. The penalty of such disobedience to moral law would mean a humanity degraded and weakened and a manhood despoiled. The full range of personal and immediate recompense for moral disobedience was included in his list. Instead of experiencing the health, wealth, and vigor of virtuous Christian manhood, the North was in danger of being "pauperized"—morally, physically, and intellectually.[9]

Every fall between the years 1883 and 1916, Lyman Abbott attended a three-day conference on Indian affairs at Lake Mohonk, New York. The nonsectarian conference, funded by two Quakers, was instrumental in the writing and passage of the Dawes Act of February 1887. The act embodied their belief that in order to educate the Indian for civilization and home ownership the tribes should be relieved of their collective land and the reservations destroyed. Individual Indians were to be given land allotments. The presupposition of this radical proposal was the belief that Indian reservations perpetuated a tribal form of barbarism that had to be eliminated in the most civilized nation on earth.

The major mark of the barbarism of the Indian was his failure to cultivate the land. He was seen as a nomad, with no fixed abode, who roamed the commonly held land and contributed nothing to it. Accordingly, the most direct way to assimilate him into American civilization would be to give him private property and train him in nationally operated schools. Mission schools, because they were sectarian, would only retard the process of assimilating the Indian to the "social" state.

It was the whole indigenous Indian culture that the Dawes Act aimed to destroy. Abbott distinguished between the rights of man as man and the rights of cultures. He respected the rights of the "negro" and the Indian as individuals. He was more liberal in relation to the freedman than to the Indian because he assumed that the "negro" lacked the well-established culture represented by the Indian tribe. The assimilation of the Indian seemed more difficult because of the strength of tribal culture. "Barbarians have rights which civilized folk are bound to respect; but barbarism has no rights which civilization is bound to respect. In the history of the human race nothing is more certain than that civilization must conquer and barbarism must be subdued."[10] It was obvious to Abbott that no man had a right to property unless he earned the right by his own labor. The Indian, to become civilized, would have to earn the privileges of democracy by demonstrating the ability to cultivate the land and live with his family in one place.

Abbott was impressed with his success at influencing major government legislation. The enactment of the Dawes Act was evidence of the power of public opinion working for the good of society. Public opinion, as he understood it, was a major force in accelerating the progress of democracy and civilization by upgrading the level of all men. If the Indians were too barbaric to deserve the rights of civilized men, then the government was justified in taking whatever action was necessary to educate them for citizenship. It never occurred to Abbott that a powerful segment of the public opinion behind the passage of the Dawes Act represented land interests eager to obtain the valuable acreage of the Indian reservations.[11]

The attitudes of Gladden and Abbott toward Southern culture, the "negro," and the Indian reveal presuppositions about character development found in faculty psychology. Intellectual, moral, and mental development were understood as correlative to the proper socialization of human beings. Civilized morality was their standard of character; work and self-discipline were the means of character development. The destruction of indigenous cultures was justified as a contribution to individuals, to democracy, and to civilization.

Labor Conflicts: Social Darwinism and Social Gospel

As participants in social reconstruction after the Civil War, Gladden and Abbott developed definite attitudes about nonwhite Americans. Strong expressed similar attitudes about Mormons and Catholics in *Our Country* (1885). Social Darwinism provided the Social Gospel men with their standard of distinction between white middle-class Protestants and those of other races and religions. The theory of the equilibrium of the faculties was also their way of distinguishing between the middle class, the upper class, and the lower class. While they favored equal opportunity for all people to develop character through work appropriately rewarded, those who were too wealthy or too poor were probably unbalanced. Too much income could lead to moral disintegration as easily as too little income gave no opportunity to develop self-discipline through work.

As early as 1875, Gladden responded to industrial conflicts. His participation in the public debate concerning labor relations, unions, and strikes continued through the 1880s. At the time it seemed to many Americans that the violence of the strikers was as potentially threatening to the future of the nation as the Civil War strike had been. It was no accident that Gladden's 1886 address to workers, "Is It Peace or War?" was then, and remains, a paradigm of the issues of the period. Gladden was alert to the complex of problems signaled by labor conflicts well in advance of the general public, the church, or the government.

Gladden's address repudiated the application of the doctrine of natural selection to industrial problems. Presented three times in May of 1886, the month of the Haymarket Square riot, it established his public reputation as an activist in labor warfare. In the address, Gladden said that the adaptation of natural selection to an industrial society was an unfair battle between men of trained faculty and men of low intelligence. Industrial warfare was the natural result of competition, but the competition was uneven, and in war the strongest always win.

Gladden criticized the wages system because it provided unsteady employment for the worker.[12] While Gladden supported the right to strike, which won the workers' attention, he condemned their violence as barbaric. He advocated altruistic methods of settling disputes. First, employers should identify the goals of the workers with their own goals. Employees, for their part, should make an effort to view employers as people who might not be as greedy as they supposed. Gladden urged outside arbitration to settle disputes because it had been used successfully by a member of his congregation.

Pitting altruism against egotism as the ruling motive of the "social" state, Gladden assumed that industrial cooperation in the form of profit-sharing would be the next step in the evolution of "our industrial system." Although he had become critical of the wages system, he still expected employers to initiate voluntarily the change to a profit-sharing system.

> You can have hell in your factory, or you can have heaven there, just which
> you please. If it is hell that you want, build your business on the law of hell,
> which is simply, "every man for himself and the devil take the hindmost!"

Out of that will come wars and fightings, perennial and unrelenting. If it is heaven you want, then build your business on the law of the kingdom of heaven, which is "Thou shalt love thy neighbor as thyself." That will put you on the path of peace.[13]

Employers were, after all, better educated and more reasonable than "men of low intelligence." His final appeal was to both labor and capital to view one another as "brother man," "all children of one Father," in order "to bring the day when between Labor and Capital there shall be no longer war, but peace for evermore."[14]

The distinctive contribution of the Social Gospel men to the public discussion of labor conflicts was their ability to place men above commodities in importance. As Gladden put it, "It is not commodities we want so much as men. The main question for the people to ask is not how fast the aggregate of their products is increasing, but rather how it fares with the multitude of their producers."[15] The corollary to Social Gospel concern for the individual was concern for the nation. Men were more important than commodities because the vigor of the nation depended on the vigor and independence of its citizens.

Gladden and Abbott disliked the implications of competition, aggression, and violence in the laissez-faire version of survival of the fittest. They never abandoned their respect for man as man, and they were consequently unwilling to accept any political-economic theory in which human beings were dispensable in the process of letting nature take its course. As early as 1879, Lyman Abbott advocated laws to control the power of corporations over the individual, on the grounds that corporations were not people.[16]

Gladden disagreed with Spencer that children and the disadvantaged adult should learn self-control by hard and unpleasant experiences. He reasoned that the stronger must protect the weaker until the weak were mature enough to understand the relations of cause and effect. Applying the family model—deference of the stronger to the weaker—to the American democracy, both Gladden and Abbott supported social policies that accorded equal opportunity for all, while noting that not all citizens were equally qualified to participate in government processes. Among those not yet qualified by reason of development of their faculties were Indians, "negroes," Mormons, and women.[17] The Social Gospel men opposed laissez-faire economic theory because they believed that mature human beings were capable of assuming responsibility for the less mature members of the race.

To a man, the Social Gospel figures abhorred violence and social disorder. Although they accepted labor conflicts as the last necessary conflict before the millennium, they worked for nonviolent settlements of labor disputes. They interpreted Spencer's observation that civilization would fall if government was controlled by one class to mean that capitalist domination in America might precipitate a worker revolution. They were mildly critical of the wealthy and fearful of the poor. The possibility of another war was alarmingly real to them.

Because Gladden believed that employers were morally mature men, he expected them to take the initiative in resolving labor conflicts. Civilization would rise not by competition alone but by material and moral progress, which would occur only when all men had an equal opportunity to grow through properly rewarded work. Although competition and struggle were a source of character development, this would occur only under social conditions in which every individual would rise or fall as the result of his own work or lack of it. If opportunities were equal, then everyone would get exactly what he deserved. Moral struggle was necessary to individual development, but competition must not be so fierce as to discourage the acquisition of self-control by overcoming obstacles. Self-assertion was necessary to growth, but without the balance of self-control it would become the vice of selfish competition.

Gladden could accept the theory that the moving force of history was the conflict of conservative and progressive ideas. He accepted the role of struggle in personal development, but he could not accept the physical violence and riots produced by the wages system which brought labor and capital into open conflict. In *Working People and Their Employers* (1876) he finally concluded that the wages-fund theory based on the law of supply and demand was a new determinism, as detrimental to the free will of man as Calvinism had been. He said it was an excuse used by capitalists to avoid accepting their share of responsibility for labor conflicts.[18]

Conservatives like Sumner believed that laissez-faire economics should not be tampered with because the morally fit would prosper and the immoral would eventually cease to exist. Sumner's fans were people who saw the hanging of the Molly Maguires and the Haymarket Square "anarchists" as evidence of the working out of natural selection in society. They assumed that the poor who were not immoral would rise by profiting from their own work. Those who did not would be no loss to civilization. Competition and violence from this point of view were acceptable means to the end of producing a thoroughly civilized humanity. According to Henry Ward Beecher, this was God's way of doing things.[19]

Competition held no such positive connotations for the Social Gospel men. They believed that work properly rewarded was the stimulus to both personal character development and social progress. The proposition that the faculty of acquisitiveness would develop only if properly rewarded led them to view material reward for work well done as a necessary incentive contributing to social order and progress. Stated negatively, improperly rewarded work could activate the negative potential of the acquisitive faculty. The rage and envy of a frustrated worker class, denied a living wage, could result in a class war. If the desire to possess was thwarted, the animal instincts of the laborer class could be unleashed against the capitalist class.

The Social Gospel men criticized the laissez-faire system of economic competition because it appeared that the most aggressive, egoistic, and self-seeking men would always succeed at the expense of the less competitive and less able worker. Competition, operating like a natural process of elimination, was a violent process that rewarded "vicious, weak, wretched" men, in the moral sense. Laissez-faire competition failed to encourage industry, thrift, and purity in either the worker or the capitalist class. There were too few incentives to encourage the development of the acquisitive faculty of the worker.[20] The employers were becoming a morally weak class of men because they lived off the work of others. Acquisitiveness, in the underdeveloped form, could lead civilization into decline either from lack of incentive or from moral weakness and effeminacy induced by luxury and materialism.[21]

Just as the Social Gospel men loathed the self-seeking egoism implied by Sumner's maxim that the individual should "take care of himself," the word *competition* also meant selfishness to them. "Competition" and the "survival of the fittest" carried both sexual and economic implications. Darwin's doctrine of sexual selection stated that the most economically successful men would attract the most beautiful women.

Social Gospel reaction against competition, because the egoistic man would prosper most, was also a reaction against Darwin's theory of sexual selection.

The nonviolent, peace-seeking men of the Social Gospel disliked competition in any form. Darwin's theory of sexual selection implied that the economic and sexual ramifications of competition in the male work world would be social acceptance or rejection according to a man's capacity to display his wealth. The Social Gospel proposition that the rich man might decline into moral weakness meant that idleness led to moral deterioration and sexual indulgence. Either way, as a sexual reference or an economic reference, "competition" meant "selfish" to the Social Gospel men. The egoistic or selfish motives carried sexual overtones and suggested the sexual intemperance of men who dominated their women. Social Darwinism provided the Social Gospel men with a theory that promised material and spiritual rewards for the moral superiority of the middle-class male while giving them intellectual grounds to suspect that both the wealthy and the poor were sexually indulgent.

Thorstein Veblen, a Spencerian economist, expressed his outrage at the "barbaric nature" of conspicuous consumption in *The Theory of the Leisure Class* (1899). The book is a classic in American economic theory. Neither Veblen nor the Social Gospel men would accept the logic that the largest consumers were the best men. The Social Gospel men argued that consumption could become insatiable desire as capable as economic deprivation of producing "weak, vicious" men. The appearance of wealth might mean only that the best competitor had taken care of himself, at the expense of everyone around him.

In *The Pit* (1903), Frank Norris attributed the character disintegration of a broker on the Chicago Board of Trade to fascination with accumulating money by gambling on the exchange. Norris used the metaphor of the pit to convey the vortex of circumstances that engulfed the broker like a blinding whirlpool. Norris's point was the commonly accepted one that man is at the mercy of the laws of supply and demand. Norris portrayed economic law as a natural force with the terrifying power to destroy human beings. According to Josiah Strong, competition could lead to moral vice, physical decimation, and mental disequilibrium or despair.[22] But Strong championed the moral autonomy and responsibility of the individual against the prevailing view of laissez-faire Social Darwinism that attributed moral failure in the individual to circumstances beyond his control.

Urbanization: The City and
Manifest Destiny

Josiah Strong was a social theorist of both the city and the manifest destiny of the nation. In his mind, if the city could be regenerated by revitalizing the church and the family, the American nation would set an example of Christian civilization for the world. By the 1890s the "universal synthesis" of Christianity had captured the public imagination. In secular language it was "manifest destiny" and it represented a nationalistic form of social and historical evolution. In religious language, it was the kingdom of God on earth. To the Social Gospel men, it mattered little whether the goal of history was expressed in sacred or secular language. Like a good marriage, the sacred and the secular were correlative terms which were as intimately related as "the two become one."

In *Our Country* (1885) and *The New Era* (1893) Strong outlined the historical dialectic that led him to believe in the supremacy of the Anglo-Saxon race. The three great races of antiquity each had their own genius. The Romans had excelled at physical development and law. The Greeks possessed an aesthetic and intellectual superiority. The genius of the Hebrews was their monotheistic religion. Hebrew spiritual superiority, expressed in monotheism, directly affected national character and life. The Anglo-Saxon genius was that of a "universal synthesis" of the intellectual, social, and spiritual genius of the three great races. As such, American manifest destiny would mean that the plan of God for the race—for all human history—would culminate and be made manifest on American soil. For the first time in history the greatest race would occupy the greatest home.[23] Strong was conscious of the role the land played in the Anglo-Saxon accomplishment. He acknowledged the importance of the natural resources of America as a necessary incentive to the development of American thrift and industry.

The spiritual development of the Anglo-Saxon race would mean that for the first time in history, religion and culture would be correlative rather than antithetical. Quoting Bishop John Ireland, Strong praised Ireland's recognition of the glorious American contribution to the brotherhood of man, the balance of self-respect, and respect for the rights of others. Ireland had reiterated Strong's own thesis that the American genius was the synthesis of "civil liberty" and "pure spiritual Christianity."

Bishop Ireland was an acceptable Catholic because he was obviously a civilized man. Although Strong devoted a chapter of *The New Era* to the "perils of Romanism," it was the lower-class Catholic immigrants, a group representative of barbarism, that Strong considered a threat to manifest destiny. Using Darwinian language, he predicted that there would be one last competition before the "fittest" men would rule the earth. Although Strong meant the final struggle to establish Anglo-Saxon hegemony in America, the term *manifest destiny* could be used to support any future conflict—and it was.

Strong saw a need to control domestic factors that he considered detrimental to Anglo-Saxon purity. If Catholicism could be contained as a minority group, if immigration were restricted before the Anglo-Saxon American was outnumbered, the only force left to fear would be "devitalization by alcohol and tobacco." Adapting natural selection to his own purpose, the means to the end of the manifest destiny endorsed by Strong was "the out-populating power of the Christian stock." This might be God's final solution to heathenism among inferior races. Strong had transformed Darwin's assertion that the healthy, happy, and vigorous would survive into moral eugenics. The problem, as Strong saw it, was the need to limit the sexual productivity of non–Anglo-Saxons so that virtuous and morally superior Anglo-Saxons could out-populate the barbarians.[24]

The intensity of Strong's conviction that the future of the race depended on American moral leadership rested on his belief that spiritual evolution would result in the millennium. Evolutionists generally assumed that man as a species was the highest and final product of natural evolution. There would be no higher physical development beyond the species Homo sapiens. Moral evolutionists like Strong expected the continued spiritual evolution of man to be the last stage in the historical dialectic. The "new era" for mankind would be the first time in human history when the individual (the principle of progress) and the social organism (the principle of conservatism) would both flourish. In the "new era" the perfection of the race would mean the perfection of both body and soul by the eradication of sins against the body.

The Truth, shining and visible in the universe, would mean that men as individuals and men in groups were in harmony with God's moral and natural law. Like Combe and Spencer, Strong believed moral law was the spiritual counterpart of the natural laws of the universe. In the coming kingdom, moral law would be clearly defined by observing the behavior of moral men as the natural inner goodness of man was externalized. Knowledge of moral law was acquired by a method analogous to the scientific search for inner laws of the universe. The most valuable characteristics of moral goodness, according to Strong, were the Anglo-Saxon qualities of acquisitiveness and self-control then visible in New England. In short, it was the old New England ethos of individualism that constituted the genius of American moral leadership.[25]

Darwin's theories of natural selection provoked an interest in various forms of genetic planning or control as a means of guaranteeing the survival of the fittest. Strong's faith in the "out-populating power of the Christian stock" was a faith in the spiritual power of the moral purity of Christians to influence the morality of the less pure. This would be possible only if the "Christian stock" managed to out-populate the barbarian element flooding America. The answer to city slums, those masses of "venomous filth and seething sin, of lust and drunkenness, of pauperism and crime of every sort," was to remove causes that produced slums.[26] The home was the weakest institution in the city. The churches lacked influence over the poor, who refused to attend city churches. In order for spiritual influences to penetrate the squalor of life in the city, Strong endorsed the use of legislation to control the corrupting influences of gambling, saloons, prostitution, and the endless stream of new immigrants.[27]

Unlike other Social Gospel figures, Strong proposed a definite program for social reform in response to the social disorder of the 1880s. His twofold approach to eradicating evil in the cities involved lifting up the sinful poor by education and putting down moral temptation by legislating it out of existence. Like Gladden, Strong assumed that the poor were inferior to the middle class both mentally and morally. Observing that the middle class was reproducing less than the immigrant class, he concluded that a better developed brain would reduce immigrant fecundity. Further observing that the more highly developed, finely tuned, and sensitive nervous system of the middle-class body type was more susceptible to alcohol, he proposed that the inferior moral standards of the lower-class slum-dweller could be raised by improving the quality of his mind and his body. The poor would then be more naturally resistant to the "alcohol evil." He intended to use both education and legislation to develop the self-interested virtues of chastity and temperance among the poor.[28]

Strong invited Gladden, Abbott, Graham Taylor, and Richard Ely, among others, to a Congress on Cities in 1885. Although Abbott and Gladden were concerned with city problems, it was Strong, as secretary of the Evangelical Alliance, who initiated a series of meetings in 1885, 1887, and 1893 in which the "challenge of the city" was the priority item on the agenda. Coincidentally, 1893 was also the year of the World Congress of Religions and the reappearance of nativism with the rise of the American Protective Association.

Abbott shared Strong's anxiety concerning the city. It was the unharmonious, dirty, noisy press of the conglomerate people of the city that distressed the middle-class consciousness of men like Strong and Abbott. Abbott blamed city problems on the free competition of the political economy, which was part of the industrial system. In *Christianity and Social Problems* (1896) he borrowed a quote from Thomas Carlyle to convey the misery of the city:

> This general well and cesspool, once bailed and clear, today will begin again to fill itself anew. The universal Stygian quagmire is still there, opulent in women ready to be ruined, and in men ready. Toward the same sad cesspool will these waste currents of human sin ooze and gravitate as heretofore. Except in draining the universal quagmire itself, there is no remedy.[29]

Abbott saw no point in supposing that giving money to the poor would cure "pauperism." The solution to the problem was individual regeneration. The situation called for people with the will to stay out of the quagmire.

With character reorientation his first concern, and social circumstances second, Abbott designated the family as the source of social change. He declared that marriage was the one permanent social order in a world in which all other institutions were subject to change. Since the family was the fundamental social organization on which all other institutions depended, Abbott saw the purification of the family as the key to solving social problems. The future of Christendom depended on the permanence and purity of the American family.[30]

There was a strain of nature romanticism in Social Gospel reflections about the city that is most apparent in the division of the world into natural and artificial, or unnatural, categories. The Social Gospel men spiritualized the created order of the universe and designated as natural that which was not the work of human hands. Human products and the human social order, by comparison, were artificial. The pastoral innocence of the country as a natural environment was moral, while the city, the work of man, was an artificial and, by implication, an immoral environment.

Gladden, for all his concern with urban affairs, turned to nature and the nature poetry of Wordsworth for peace and reassurance.[31] The romantic view of the permanence, continuity, and benevolence of the natural order present in romantic thought colored Social Gospel views of the city. Like the English romantic poets and the American Transcendentalists, the Social Gospel men saw in the beauty and harmony of the natural order the reassurance they needed that the natural and the good would prevail in the social order as well. "Natural" connoted law and order, permanence and stability of an aesthetic, not a militant, variety. They still relied on natural evidences of the Designer of the universe.

Strong identified the natural virtue of the country with living habits that were conducive to the hard work and thrift that produced material rewards and civilized progress for all. Living circumstances in the country encouraged the interdependence and social cooperation necessary to the social development of men. The city, as the antithesis of natural goodness, was organized on the basis of competition and encouraged conspicuous consumption. In Strong's rationale, everything about the city was artificial, and the artificial interfered with the natural unfolding of goodness possible in small-town America.

The natural-artificial antithesis was a recurring motif from Ralph Waldo Emerson and Horace Bushnell through Henry Ward Beecher and a host of evangelical ministers.[32] Using that dichotomy, Strong capitalized on a whole range of middle-class prejudices and fears concerning the urban "cesspool." He linked the concept of barbaric behavior with the sins of the city—sex, slums, tenements, political corruption, and the liquor industry. The city, as he saw it, was a modern Sodom, destined to corrupt the nation if drastic measures were not taken by the church to regenerate the city. He preyed on middle-class fear of a workers' revolution.

Using Darwin's components of civilized life, Strong contrasted the stability of the middle-class home to the tenement environment. Tenements were hothouses of physical and moral disease. The crowding together of people in small hot, stuffy rooms encouraged "morbid passions and appetites." "Darkness means the devil's deeds." The foreign element brought crime. Ignorant peasants mistook American freedom for license.[33]

Homeowners, however, contributed to stability in society. Non-homeowners moved more often, which meant a decrease in social stability and fluctuating church membership. Strong experienced nostalgia for the more stable, dependable, slower moving atmosphere of country life, where self-control was easier and temptations were fewer.

Strong was fearful for the middle class. Public response to his polemics against the city came because he had evoked and expressed middle-class anxieties. His readers were tempted by the anonymity of city life. The stereotype of the slum-dweller as a beast indulging uncontrolled animal passions contained the fantasy and the fear of the middle-class male. Social Gospel preoccupation with a sliding-scale interpretation of history, and the possibility of decline and fall, had its subjective counterpart in middle-class morality. The middle-class evangelical dreaded nothing so much as the possibility of being out of control. This dread activated his complicity in the temperance movement and the purity crusade. When he supported "progressive legislation" he was protecting his own moral standard as well as attempting to "elevate" the lower classes.

The Victorians assumed that alcohol and sexual license were intimately linked, although that was rarely stated explicitly before 1900. Integral to Gladden's support of the labor movement, Abbott's championing of the purity of the home, and Strong's drive to wipe out the saloon was a shared sensitivity to the plight of helpless women and children. Their own sense of self-sacrifice in deference to wives and children reinforced their prejudice against the lower-class man, who they assumed was vulgar and sexually demanding because he was not properly civilized. Alcohol, as they understood its effect, added to the woes of the "weaker" women and children.

The force behind the temperance movement lies in its relation to the Victorian concept of temperance as the golden mean, to self-control as the road to individual goodness and civilized progress. Evangelical male hostility to the immigrant male was further intensified by the presence of large Roman Catholic populations in the city slums. All individual Catholics were not barbarians, but the Catholic church retarded the moral development of its members because of the authoritarian nature of the priesthood.

Harold Frederic captured the essence of evangelical racial and religious attitudes in his portrayal of Theron Ware:

> He had never before had occasion to formulate . . . this tacit race and religious aversion in which he had been bred. . . . The foundation upon which its dark bulk reared itself were ignorance, squalor, brutality and vice. Pigs wallowed in the mire before its base, and burrowing into this base were a myriad of narrow doors, each bearing the hateful sign of a saloon, and giving forth from its recesses of night the sounds of screams and curses. Above were sculptured rows of lowering, ape-like faces from Nast's and Keppler's cartoons, and out of these sprang into the vague upper gloom, on the one side, lamp-posts from which negroes hung by the neck, and on the other gibbets for dynamiters and Molly Maguires; and between the two glowed a spectral picture of some black-robed, tonsured men, with leering satanic masks, making a bonfire of the Bible in the public schools.[34]

To the evangelical male, the "negro," the anarchist, and the priest had one thing in common—animalism, or the perpetuation of an authoritarian religion which permitted or encouraged animalism.

Although the Social Gospel men rarely stated a connection between alcohol and prostitution, they assumed that the two problems were related. Supporters of the temperance movement like Strong assumed that the control of alcohol would diminish prostitution. In *The New Encyclopedia of Social Reform,* W. D. P. Bliss was explicit in his treatment of "the social evil":

> Careful observers believe it [prostitution] to be a more constant and fundamental cause of degeneration than intemperance . . . Intemperance is, however, all but universally the companion of prostitution. It has been

87

frequently said that girls rarely can, and men rarely do, continue in a fast life without a drink. If the saloon is often literally the entrance to a brothel, the brothel as frequently leads to the saloon.[35]

Strong fully expected the closing of the saloon to improve all social conditions in the city.

Gladden and Abbott came late to the support of the temperance crusade. With the exception of Strong, the other Social Gospel figures opposed the legislation of morals for the same reason that they objected to Roman Catholicism. External coercion, either by positive law or by church authority, would prevent—not aid—the development of the self-control necessary to solve the alcohol problem. Writing against the "prohibitory laws" in 1902, Abbott held out for the principle of self-government of the individual as "the essential principle of a democracy, which is founded upon local self-government." The function of law in a democracy was confined to the protection of person, property, family, reputation, and liberty. "Any other use of law would be a violation of the fundamental principle that every man is to be left free, in a self-governing community, to regulate his own conduct, provided he does not impair the rights or injure the well-being of his neighbor."[36] While the Social Darwinism of Gladden and Abbott contributed to the crystallization of middle-class anxieties that emerged in the temperance movement, they never endorsed the movement until it appeared to embody public opinion. Only then did they grant it legitimacy, because the prohibition law would embody an already established custom.[37] After years of opposition to any kind of moral legislation, Gladden finally supported prohibition on the grounds that it would protect innocent women and children. He further rationalized his changed opinion by reasoning that when lower-class men were unable to squander their slender incomes on alcohol, they would then be able to save their income and move out of the slums. Indirectly, prohibition might promote the virtue of thrift.[38]

The ethos of the new middle class was the link between solving the social ills of the city and achieving the manifest destiny of the nation. Just as the mother was the source of social order by her moral influence over members of her family, the Christian citizen would inspire the poor to rise above the immoral circumstances of ghetto life. Then the nation as a whole would serve as a light of inspiration to the nations of the world.

Following the decade of social disorder in the 1880s, the mood of the country took an optimistic upswing culminating in the "Gay Nineties." Strong's *Our Country* anticipated either the great triumph of a "universal synthesis" of all nations assimilating American democracy and Protestant Christianity or the tragic fate of social revolution. The possibility of revolution was drowned out in a climate of universalist hope graphically symbolized for the nation by the World's Columbian Exposition held in Chicago in 1893. The World Congress of Religions, held in conjunction with the exposition, seemed to symbolize the spiritual superiority of Christianity as the one, complete, and final religion.[39]

In *Our Country* Strong unified a series of related concepts. The doctrine of "the Fatherhood of God" was central to the "new" theology; virtually all middle-class evangelicals preached the Fatherhood of God to the near exclusion of other divine attributes. The judging, punishing God of "old light" Calvinist theology was still attractive to the lower-class premillennialists, but the relegation of that God to less-developed peoples and earlier stages in human history was an important aspect of the new middle-class world-view. "The Fatherhood of God," "the Brotherhood of Man," and "the Kingdom of God" were more than central affirmations of the "new" theology; they were publicly accepted slogans that served to integrate the "new" world-view of a large and ambitious American middle class.

Our Country was one of several popular sources of the powerful religious-patriotic ethos expressed by manifest destiny. Whether applied to domestic problems or to foreign affairs, the correlation of religion and culture appealed to an unsettled middle class threatened by the coincidence of the great immigrations of the nineteenth century, the social displacement of the middle class, and the scientific challenge to religion as a viable explanation for life in all its forms. Americans had always been susceptible to the vision of the nation as a "city set on a hill" for all the world to see. Manifest destiny was that vision in the concrete form of democratic and Christian universalism.

Austin Phelps of Andover Seminary, who wrote the introduction for *Our Country,* caught the thrust of Strong's endeavor. Phelps identified it with the sense of urgency expressed from the public platform by Lyman Beecher in the 1840s concerning the mission enterprise on the western frontier. At that time Beecher had popularized the expression "Now is the nick of time." Phelps saw that Strong, the church bureaucrat, had expanded Beecher's urgency and vision to the frontiers of the world. The obstacles to success in this endeavor called for the force, courage, daring, and vigilance of "powerful manhood" to Christianize "metropolitan centers and virile races." The "martial virtues" should rule Christian missions and, used properly, would crown its success.

Strong did share Beecher's urgency. He also shared Beecher's anxiety about Christian manhood. According to the Victorian bifurcation of characteristics by sex, ministers were associated with weakness and effeminacy because religion was the province of women. Strong's appeal to the universalist, inclusive imagery of the Fatherhood of God, the Brotherhood of Man, and the manifest destiny of the Anglo-Saxon race was the antithesis of the sexual-economic aggression implied by Darwin's theory of sexual selection. For middle-class men overwhelmed by the experience of the savagery of the work world of supply and demand, manifest destiny, expressed in the Christianized form of family imagery, promised success to the civilized. Christian love would be the ultimate weapon in the world arsenal, and civilization would triumph over the evils of the city, the virile races, and the sexual potency of barbarians.

In 1893, when the American Protective Association publicly circulated "Instructions to Catholics," a fraudulent document ordering Catholics to take any steps necessary to "secure control of cities, railways, mines and the press," Washington Gladden took immediate measures to counteract the "astounding outbreak of religious bigotry that followed." Gladden blamed the outbreak on the "ultra-Protestants" of the Middle West, where the movement was strongest. He and Theodore Roosevelt were the two most prominent Protestant leaders to repudiate the new nativism, which was reportedly seventy thousand members strong. Gladden surmised that the conservative Protestant sectarian spirit might have been aroused by the "fraternization of religion at Chicago. . . . It is possible that some small souls were disturbed by what seemed to them a dangerous lowering of barriers between religionists, and may have been spurred to dig deeper the chasms which sympathy and good will were filling up."[40]

Social Change and Applied Christianity (1865-1900)

Unlike the fictional Theron Ware, who was relieved of his "race and religious prejudices" by contact with Catholic laborers, Gladden had little experience with the "immigrant hordes." His distinction between cultural barbarism and "the barbarian" led him to believe, and to act upon the belief, that he had no prejudices against Catholics as persons. In his autobiography he praised "our Roman Catholic fellow citizens . . . for bearing their part in the promotion of thrift and order and intelligence. Any attempt to disenfranchise them on account of their religious beliefs ought to be resisted by every intelligent American."[41] Gladden failed to see that nativism was not simply a religious prejudice but involved class and racial hostility as well. Theoretically, Gladden, Strong, and Abbott valued individuals while condemning the groups to which they belonged. In so doing, they unwittingly fueled the fires of the nativism they found so repugnant. Nativism was in part a protest against the evils symbolized by the city.

The evangelism of the Social Gospel was, as Josiah Strong put it, "the ellipse described around the individual and society as the two foci."[42] The humanitarian concern of the "new light" evangelicals of the early Victorian period was directed toward the "negro," the Indian, the laborer, and the immigrant by the Social Gospel leaders. Like earlier revivalists, they wanted to change individuals through the power of personal persuasion—their own and that of church members.

Under the impact of the Social Darwinism of the Social Gospel, home missions moved from the western frontier to the city. In addition to their own self-conscious efforts to influence public opinion, the Social Gospel men exhorted their congregations to undertake missions of personal evangelism. They believed that cultural progress depended, in part, on more civilized groups inspiring less-cultured groups by personal influence and contact. Befriending the poor was an appropriate means of raising slum living standards, but gifts of money would discourage the habit of thrift. The stewardship of self was potentially more valuable than the stewardship of money. Strong urged church members to give generously to the denomination, but not to individual charity projects.

Gladden and Strong were not enthusiastic about the institutional churches, city missions, or settlement houses, such as Graham Taylor's Chicago Commons. Though aware that the poor were uncomfortable in middle-class churches, they continued to believe that theoretically the Christian church should know no barriers. Their objective in the evangelism of the poor, the "worker class," was preventative. From a historical point of view, such evangelism would prevent the retrogression of civilization. Stated positively, it would contribute to American manifest destiny. From a political point of view, converting the poor would prevent a revolution and lend stability to the social order. The assimilation of the worker class to civilized morality, whether considered as individuals or as a class, remained the constant objective of the men of the Social Gospel.

The actual outcome of the Social Gospelers' evangelism was full of contradictions. While championing the rights of the worker, they reinforced middle-class confidence in the right to success and prosperity. While stirring the social conscience of the church, they discouraged church members from charitable activity on behalf of the poor. While establishing public reputations as political and social liberals, they proposed very limited forms of legislation to remedy social ills. While taking a public stand against the doctrine of natural selection, they were instrumental in the crystallization of a world-view dependent on the psychology and social philosophy of Social Darwinism.

It was through such popularizers as Henry George, and the men of the Social Gospel themselves, that Social Darwinism entered the mainstream of American thought. The power of the Social Gospel men was in their expression of the concepts of the new social philosophy in terms of family images. Although Henry G. Lloyd is said to have used the terms "the Fatherhood of God" and "the Brotherhood of Man" in print for the first time in *Wealth Against Commonwealth* in 1894, these slogans encapsulated the thrust of the religious language in use among the Social Gospel figures for twenty years before the Lloyd book was published. The Social Gospelers had been thinking, preaching, and writing in terms of family relationships and family analogies long before *Wealth Against Commonwealth* was published.

The source of Social Gospel success was also the source of the contradictions between their social objectives and their influence on the middle class. Social Darwinism, in either conservative or liberal form, became the shibboleth of the middle class against both the upper and lower classes. Only the middle-class family exhibited the equilibrium necessary to the socialization of children to standards of civilized morality. The idle rich were suspected of keeping mistresses in their New York brownstones. The animalistic poor could not possibly be living normal, moral family lives all packed together in city tenements.

According to Strong and other Social Darwinists, the genius of democracy was in accommodating both "personal rights" and "sympathy" for all men. In the "new era" of civilized progress to come, Strong expected both the individual and the social organism to flourish without conflict or contradiction. For the present, the men of the Social Gospel and the middle-class public saw in the altruism of their own families a microcosm of the promise of the American democracy.

5

The Social Problem and the
Kingdom of God
(1890–1924)

The productive working years of William Newton Clarke, Francis Greenwood Peabody, and Walter Rauschenbusch were years of social unrest and reform after the turn of the century. Theirs were the years in which unquestioned acceptance of "civilized" progress became impossible. Some socialists expected civilization to progress beyond democracy, the family, and Christianity. Whereas Abbott, Gladden, and Strong had articulated the role of the Victorian family and Christianity in bringing in a "new era," Clarke, Peabody, and Rauschenbusch became defenders of the faith, and of the family.

The socialism that loomed as an alternative to democracy in 1900 appealed to people who doubted that social equality could be achieved voluntarily in a democratic political system. The social reformers and feminists who advocated socialism offered it as a cooperative approach to government designed to relieve the pressures of competition brought on by capitalism. Their social criticism made it clear that the roles assigned to the sexes by the Victorian family ideal were not equal and were not satisfying to either sex. Indirectly they were attacking the most sacred institution in the middle-class world: the family.

Public debates between socialists and defenders of democracy touched on questions of war, the martial virtues, manhood, work, and womanhood. Social Gospel contributions to the dialogue about the Spanish-American War, manhood, feminism, and socialism were influenced by their unquestioned allegiance to the Victorian family ideal. Although Clarke, Peabody, and Rauschenbusch differed in their responses to war and socialism, not one of them deviated from the basic assumption that the sexes were complementary to each other in carrying out their separate but equal social roles. According to all three men, the social equilibrium depended on the stability of the family and the balance of the sexes.

Social Darwinism and the Later Social Gospel

Walter Rauschenbusch looked back on the first, restless decade of the twentieth century as "the awakening of the nation." In *Christianizing the Social Order,* published in 1913, Rauschenbusch interpreted public campaigns for new voting procedures, the public discussion of sexuality, and the American victory in the Spanish-American War as evidence of "a national religious energy coming out of the depths of God."[1] The American people were suffused with a new sense of self-sacrifice, a new sense of duty, and a new openness to ideals. America was a nation almost Christianized. Like Strong before him, Rauschenbusch enumerated the reasons for his optimism. The church, the family, the schools, and the political life of the nation were the "almost" Christianized sectors of the social order.[2] Only the economic order was open to criticism. Like Strong, he challenged the church to fulfill its "historical destiny" in Christianizing the world.

The social milieu of the nation had changed considerably between the 1885 publication of Strong's *Our Country* and the Rauschenbusch book of 1913. Like the Social Gospel pioneers, the later men were hopeful about the possibility of the coming of the kingdom of God. Yet, the naive optimism of the pioneers concerning implications of evolutionary theory was giving way to an awareness of more complex issues raised by the dynamic theory of the universe. If society was constantly evolving through the clash of conservative and progressive forces, what were the limits of social progress? If the physical law of the rate of acceleration was applied to social institutions, that could mean that the social order would "move beyond" democracy, Christianity, and the Victorian family. Francis G. Peabody, Professor of Christian Morals at Harvard University, questioned the moral implications of the principle of acceleration. Concerned with the restlessness of spirit that the new age seemed to impart to the American character, he saw in his students a lack of purpose and a lack of moral fiber:

The Social Problem and the Kingdom of God (1890-1924)

The future for them is a kingdom of elevators, telephones, motor cars and flying machines. . . . The principle of the Universe is Acceleration. . . . We do not know whence we come, or whither we go, and what is more important, we do not care: what we do know is that we are moving faster than anyone ever moved before.[3]

The earlier Social Gospel leaders had articulated an almost unquestioning faith in the progress of civilization, both moral and technological. The invention of the steam engine, telegraph, railroad, and daguerreotype had revolutionized daily life for the average Americans in their lifetime. Early industrial developments had opened worldwide avenues of commerce as well. By 1900, Americans were engaged in commercial and military adventures abroad, and in foreign missions as well. William Newton Clarke challenged the popularly accepted notion that all American foreign involvement was a form of the "spirit" of Christianity. He questioned the optimism of men, like Strong, who advocated Christianizing the world "in our lifetime."

The invention of the automobile, the airplane, and the elevator early in the twentieth century brought a dizzying sense of acceleration to Americans. The jazz and ragtime music of the era vividly expressed a sense of living in "a nervous hurry." Middle-class Americans became increasingly anxious about the possibility of a revolution of the proletariat against the bourgeoisie. Socialists, Marxists, labor leaders, and social reformers were all suspected of being "anarchists." The public drew few distinctions between social theorists, social activists, and social reformers. Among the most radical-sounding "anarchists" there were few social activists.[4]

Improvement in methods of communication and a growing educated class by 1900 meant that more Americans than ever before were aware of the undeniable movements of unrest among people denied access to the prosperity of the new middle class.[5] A "new social consciousness" emerged in the middle class amid fears of socialist anarchy and the consciousness of the accelerated pace of life. The "social question" was a term commonly used to express acknowledged social inequality. The later Social Gospel leaders were one of many groups proposing solutions to "the social question."

That "the social question" was the question of the twentieth century is evident in the titles of the books published by the second-generation figures between 1900 and 1924. That their answer to the question was to be found in the social principles of Jesus is also evident. Rauschenbusch published *Christianity and the Social Crisis* (1907), *Christianizing the Social Order* (1913), *A Theology for the Social Gospel* (1917), and *The Social Principles of Jesus* (1916). Peabody published *Jesus Christ and the Social Question* (1900), *Jesus Christ and Christian Character* (1904), *The Approach to the Social Question* (1909), and *The Social Teachings of Jesus Christ* (1924). *The Ideal of Jesus* (1911) was the only book in which William Newton Clarke explored "the social question." Clarke, the most conservative second-generation figure, summed up "the new social spirit" of Christianity. "The Kingdom of God" was not personal religion or the church; it was a social ideal. "We mean national when we say social hope."[6] The "civilized" Christianity of the pioneers was being transmuted into a new form: "social" Christianity.[7]

Biographically, the later figures differed in education, professional orientation, and self-image from the men who first articulated the social application of the gospel. Clarke, Peabody, and Rauschenbusch were professors during a short interlude in the development of modern social institutions when academics held status as social critics and activists. For a brief time between 1880 and 1910, the source of much social criticism came from the pulpit and the university. After 1910, opinion-makers were less likely to be found in the university community. Academics like the second-generation Social Gospel men Thorstein Veblen, Richard T. Ely, and William James were replaced by a new genre of well-educated journalists like Walter Lippmann, Van Wyck Brooks, and H. G. Wells.[8] Because of the respect accorded the intellectual community, the three seminary professors possessed a self-awareness concerning their task as theologians and social critics, which the earlier Social Gospel figures did not have.

Although Clarke associated himself with "social" Christianity and wrote all his books after the turn of the century, his life work addressed intellectual issues posed from early Darwinism through the social questions of the early twentieth century. An example of the transformation of "new light" evangelical Christianity into the social gospel is found in the sequence in which Clarke's books were written: *A Study of Christian Missions* (1900), *An Outline of Christian Theology* (1904), *The Use of the Scriptures in Theology* (1907), *The Ideal of Jesus* (1911), and *The Christian Doctrine of God* (1923).

With reference to evangelical Christianity, Peabody and Rauschenbusch were each the antithesis of the other. They responded differently to a reawakening of the revivalist tradition in the late nineteenth-century campaigns of Dwight L. Moody. Rauschenbusch clearly wanted to dissociate himself from that kind of anti-intellectual evangelical emotionalism. Peabody, coming from an emotionally austere Unitarian background, was warmed by the enthusiasm of Moody. He also greatly admired the sophisticated English evangelical, Henry Drummond.[9] Drummond had relieved the anxiety of many evangelicals by transforming the threat of Darwin's *Descent of Man* into the hopeful *Ascent of Man* (1894).

By 1900 the theory of evolution no longer provoked heated public debate within the intellectual world. The evolutionary principle was taken for granted by most religious liberals. Although expectations of human progress were widely shared, the doctrine of natural selection became ever more suspect to the middle class as an explanation of the means of progress. In second-generation Social Gospel thought, the terms *civilized* and *barbarian* were used primarily as the basis of a social ethic and as a principle of historical interpretation. Rauschenbusch and Peabody were social theorists and social ethicists. As such, they were critical of the individualism of earlier forms of Social Darwinism. They thought that the Spencerian philosophy lacked an adequate sense of the spiritual nature of society.

> The conception of society as a biological organism, which was confidently announced a generation ago, has proved insufficient, and social evolution turns to psychology for its interpretation. These aspects of the world and its affairs—a spiritual significance within the machinery of nature, a demand for the spiritualization of material life, a renaissance of ethical idealism—find unprecedented recognition as a new century begins. The nineteenth century had for its subject the social body; the twentieth century has for its subject the social soul.[10]

The social orientation of the later Social Gospel men came primarily from ethical idealism. Gladden, Abbott, and Strong had been influenced by natural philosophy, commonsense theology, phrenology, and early Social Darwinism. Consequently, their subjects were the individual as a part of the social whole, and the natural order as a model for society. They saw the "progressive development of the Spirit" in man and in the natural order of the universe. Clarke, Peabody, and Rauschenbusch, influenced by Social Darwinism and German ethical idealists, took man and society as their subjects. They saw "the spirit of Jesus" being revealed progressively in society and in man.

The different intellectual orientation of the two groups results in two different theories of society. The earlier leaders conceptualized society as organic in a biological sense. The later men described society in the anthropomorphic sense of a person possessing both body and soul. Gladden and Abbott thought of society as a sum, or collection, of individuals. Each individual counted as one element of the nation in the same way that votes represented the will of the majority. Social institutions served to evoke and complete the social nature of the individual, and they used the word *social* to denote the social nature of the individual. The Social Gospel, during the early years of the movement, meant that Christianity had implications for the social whole, as well as for individuals.

Peabody and Rauschenbusch granted more complexity to the social order, viewing it primarily as a sum of interacting institutions. The individual existed as a part of a national whole, ideally for the purpose of serving the whole. Christianity was the source of the spiritual energy needed by the social organism for social regeneration. The Protestant church was needed to channel the "spirit of Jesus" into the American democracy. If Christian social ideals were embodied in American social institutions, then social justice would exist for all members of society.

The later Social Gospelers sought the establishment of "social" Christianity. The primary reference point for the term *social* was social institutions, or the state as the sum of social institutions. The kingdom of God would come on earth when social institutions were Christianized.

Despite the different emphasis in the two Social Gospel generations, there is considerable continuity in their hopeful expectations of the coming kingdom. Both groups interpreted present social disorder as temporary but positive contributions to the kingdom. According to Rauschenbusch, "the Kingdom of God" was the evolutionary concept in the form of religious faith.[11] Although all the later Social Gospel men spoke the language of ethical idealism and were critics of Social Darwinism, there was more Social Darwinism in their thought than they were aware of. Rauschenbusch, Peabody, and Clarke wrote social commentary and social ethics from a philosophical perspective which assumed that the sexes were complementary, that the faculties needed freedom to mature by proper use, and that social progress depended on the family.

There was also more personal piety in the second-generation practice of Christianity than a reading of the books of these men would indicate. Clarke and Rauschenbusch were known as "mystics" because of the intense spirituality of their prayers. Rauschenbusch was convinced that individual piety was being "socialized" and that it resided in groups and institutions. He wrote of the social forms of the Christian spirit in the belief that in the future the practice of piety would not be necessary.

Although Rauschenbusch wrote little about spiritual intuition, Clarke considered subjective intuition of the spiritual world to be the source of the religious nature of mankind. All three of the later figures exalted the progressive power of reason and believed that men in their generation were closer to God's simple "truth" than ever before. Although they were all influenced by German theology, the combination of rationalism and spiritual intuition found in their thought is an American development that occurred under the impact of the evolutionary theory of progress. The combination of reason as the source of religious knowledge and the semimystical elevation of personal spirituality and prayer is peculiarly American.

Taken as a whole, the Christianity of the second-generation Social Gospelers was closer to evangelical piety than they would have admitted. The combination of rationalism and personal piety is, for all its Germanic allusions, not very different from the evangelical Christianity of the Second Great Awakening. Charles Grandison Finney's description of conversion techniques reveals a recognition of the power of a group akin to the emphasis in Rauschenbusch concerning the social group as a channel of the spirit. Both men knew that the emotional power generated in a group was more powerful than that usually experienced in a one-to-one encounter. And both were intent on the sublimation of the erotic impulses into acceptable patterns of social morality. Rauschenbusch was highly critical of the individualism of such earlier American evangelicals as Finney. Yet he considered a conversion experience a necessary prelude to participation in "social" Christianity.

In *Christianizing the Social Order* Rauschenbusch presented a hopeful social analysis and prophecy concerning the future of the nation, the church, and the social gospel. If Christianity would fulfill its "historical destiny" to be the soul of the nation, then a new epoch in the evolution of the human race would follow. If the church refused to participate in rebuilding the economic order of society, it could mean the decay of Western civilization. His intent in *Christianizing the Social Order* was to challenge the Protestant churches to fulfill their social function lest the social order crumble in class warfare.

The church did not become the soul of society. The social movement in the churches never became the social force envisioned by the proponents of Social Christianity. The social order did not disintegrate. There was no socialist revolution in America. But the social thought and theology of the second generation of the Social Gospel was written under circumstances in which these possibilities seemed very real. Their interpretations of and attitudes toward three social issues—war, socialism, and feminism—reveal their role in the Social Gospel movement.

Internationalism: War and Christian Manhood

Throughout the Victorian era there were two competing and overlapping models for manhood: the moral purity of the Christian gentleman and the virility and aggression of the male-achiever ethos associated with the "captain of industry." Because the conversionist and faculty psychologies linked tangible reward to virtue, the Christian-gentleman image was associated with the prosperity of the middle class. Up to the 1890s the middle class looked to the captain of industry for their model of success, even though that success was associated with selfish egotism. Although there was ambivalence in middle-class admiration for the success of the captain of industry, and suspicions of immoral behavior, the attraction of the male-achiever ethos was in the association of his success with virility.

The question of manhood was related to the two forms of Social Darwinian reaction to laissez-faire economics. The male-achiever ethos encouraged an aggressive attitude toward work and unlimited success at the expense of others. Until illegal practices of business tycoons were exposed by muckrakers in the 1890s, the public stood in awe of the success of the best competitors. As the Social Gospel men had challenged laissez-faire economics because of the effect it had on individuals, they had suspected that too much prosperity could lead to sexual immorality and lack of moral fiber. With the general prosperity evident by 1890, they became concerned with the moral fiber and possible effeminacy of middle-class youth as well.

The Spanish-American War raised issues that called for a critical appraisal of two forms of laissez-faire expansion: the business practices of the captains of industry, and war and internationalism. The meaning of manhood was integral to both issues. The Social Gospel men differed in their responses to the war and international expansion, but there was a common thread of agreement in their attitudes toward manhood. They all held an image of a Christian gentleman who was both moral and virile. This was the kind of manhood that would permeate business, industry, and the state with the spirit of Jesus.

Despite public enthusiasm for the war in 1898, two matters that commanded well-publicized differences of opinion were raised. The first was the disturbing recognition that the war contradicted the expectation that war would cease with the progress of civilization. The second was the question of how American men would acquire the "martial virtues" of courage and aggression if not through military training. Between the Civil War and the Spanish-American War, the "military virtues" had been attributed to the captain of industry as the epitome of male success, power, and morality. In the period of the Spanish-American War, public admiration for the self-made "captains" of the industrial war had begun to wane.

The most famous justification of the Spanish-American War came from Theodore Roosevelt, who claimed that soldiers, statesmen, businessmen, and missionaries were all agents of the Anglo-Saxon destiny to carry civilization to the world.[12] This posed a problem for the Social Gospel men, who like most evangelicals had equated the virtues of civilized morality with Christianity. It also tested their ability to define Christian manhood in terms that were moral without being effeminate and weak. Roosevelt's justification of the war was all the more engaging because he represented the epitome of "the Christian gentleman" to evangelicals. Roosevelt was a man of courage, boldness, and obvious public success, yet he was also a man of highest virtue, given to praising the sanctity of the American family.[13]

Sentiment for and against American involvement in the Philippines filled the columns of the popular and religious press in the months before war was declared. Those who favored the war saw it as an acceptable means of extending the ideals of democracy and Christianity. Beyond that, war taught men social solidarity and group loyalty. The line of reasoning taken by Stephen Crane in *The Red Badge of Courage*, a Civil War novel published in 1895, was typical of this attitude toward war and manhood.

Crane's hero, Henry Fleming, went to the Civil War a callow, cringing youth. He emerged a "man" from his confrontation with the terrors of war and the fear of death. No longer did he fear the terrors of war or his own inadequacy before the overwhelming forces of nature. He had acquired the virtues necessary to face life with "quiet, nonassertive manhood." He had learned the necessity of "cooperative action." War, a characteristic of barbarism, was ultimately glorified by Crane as a lesson in courage and social solidarity. From the Social Darwinian perspective, the ultimate test of womanhood was childbirth. The only commensurate test of the courage of manhood was war. Both were confrontations with the possibility of death.

The war was also defended on the ground that it provided a career for young men lacking vocational ambitions or opportunities.[14] Washington Gladden, a minority voice amid the war furor, rejected all war on principle as a barbaric form of evil. He was appalled to hear "an eminent statesman" say it was time for another war because war created work opportunities unavailable in peacetime. Gladden found such "an atrocious sentiment" uncivilized.[15]

Not everyone agreed that military experience was a valid training ground for the manly virtues. The best-known proponent of an alternative to war as manhood training was William James. His famous essay "The Moral Equivalent of War" addressed the question of how to make men of "our gilded youth" without waging war. James's concern reflected the dread of the educated middle class that the life of ease and luxury would render their sons flabby and effeminate. A related concern was the need of lower-class youth to learn self-discipline. War was considered a training ground for masculinity as well as self-discipline.

In the essay, James relegated the origin of the martial virtues to dark, barbaric periods of history but affirmed the continuing need for the virtues of the "war-function." He proposed that the virtues of the "war-function" be transformed into the "virtues of the civic-function."

> To the coal and iron mines, to freight trains, to fishing fleets in December, to dishwashing, clothes-washing, and window-washing, to road building and tunnel-making, to foundries and stoke-holes, and to the frames of skyscrapers, would our gilded youth be drafted off, according to their choice, to get the childishness knocked out of them, and to come back into society with healthier sympathies and sobered ideas.[16]

James's alternative was compulsory military service for young men enlisted in a war against nature. The war against nature would provide an equal opportunity for all young men, the privileged and the under-privileged, to acquire "the military ideals of hardihood and discipline." This would be an army disciplined by physical labor.

> We must make new energies and hardihoods continue the manliness to which the military mind so faithfully clings. Martial virtues must be the enduring cement; intrepidity, contempt of softness, surrender of private interest, obedience to command, must still remain the rock upon which states are built.[17]

The reward James promised to the young man matured by alternative military service was self-respect, the admiration of women, and the right to be the respected fathers and teachers of the next generation.[18]

Social Darwinism of the more deterministic laissez-faire variety had contributed to public admiration for the war hero and the captain of industry as successful and masculine men. The captain of industry represented a self-made man who had prospered by hard work and aggressiveness. This was a male model quite different from the educated gentlemen from Harvard with whom James was acquainted. Until public opinion was aroused against big business, monopolies, and trusts in the late 1890s, the captain of industry was a "civic" hero who embodied the martial qualities of hardihood and discipline. Every philanthropic act of an Andrew Carnegie was applauded as exemplary self-sacrifice, an example of "noblesse oblige."

The Fatherhood of God and the Victorian Family

The controversy precipitated by the muckraker journalists of the 1890s was implicitly a discussion of the manly virtues. One of the muckrakers most favored in religious circles was Henry G. Lloyd. In *Wealth Against Commonwealth* (1894) he provided facts about the business practices of trusts and monopolies, as well as a highly charged emotional attack on businessmen whom he portrayed not as heroes but as immoral barbarians. Lloyd provided useful ammunition for men like those of the Social Gospel, who had never been entirely comfortable with the "virtues" of the captain of industry.

Lloyd's ambition was to be the Harriet Beecher Stowe of the evils of uncontrolled corporate power. He aimed to arouse public opinion against "industrial slavery" and against the new breed of tyrant being created by the trusts. He pitted the virtues of "the people"—hard work, good homes, thrift, and sobriety—against the vices of the monopoly as an economic power threatening the virtues of self-discipline by improperly rewarding honest work. Like the Social Gospel men, he feared for the social order if good men ceased to profit from their self-discipline and hard work.

Lloyd used the language and categories of Social Darwinism to portray the tyranny of the captain of industry as a throwback to barbarism. He charged that a robber baron in the public sphere could not be defended as a good family man or churchman. Unlimited power could corrupt the best of men. He accused the church of harboring thieves among its members and cited the Baptist denomination as a case in point. His target was Standard Oil and John D. Rockefeller. Rockefeller, the founder of Standard Oil, had been converted by Rochester Seminary president Augustus Hopkins Strong.[19] Strong, a Baptist theologian, was the father-in-law of one of the Rockefeller daughters. Strong was also a lifelong friend of the Rauschenbusch family and a seminary professor of Walter Rauschenbusch. Rauschenbusch had traveled in Europe with a son of Augustus Strong and was acquainted with the Rockefeller family through the Strongs. It was not simply idle gossip on Lloyd's part to accuse the Baptists of befriending thieves.

According to Lloyd, the captains of industry were possessed with an insatiable lust for wealth, which was enslaving and victimizing the worker. Monopolies "seduced" the people, used them for their own purposes, then cast them aside. Lloyd exploited the sexual implications of economic theory to imply that group monopolies were like a gang rape of the defenseless but virtuous individual. In his moral drama of the wealth of the barbarian millionaire pitted against the hope for a commonwealth of civilized people, Lloyd wanted to demonstrate that what the "survival of the fittest" produced was monopoly power and businessmen who were the equivalent of the old slave masters. He called for legislation to defend the weak against the strong.

At the turn of the century, the most persuasive and uncritical voice speaking on behalf of the martial virtues of the businessman and soldier was that of Theodore Roosevelt. Roosevelt used national politics as a pulpit for his own "preaching." Like Rauschenbusch, he thought of himself as a social prophet, taking the press for his pulpit when he left the presidency. He was the evangelist of American manifest destiny. To Lyman Abbott, who gave Roosevelt an *Outlook* editorship in 1908, Roosevelt was a combination of the apostle Paul and Saint Vitus.[20] He had the restless energy of the age, but he directed it into the cause of righteousness. His vigor exemplified the ideal of manly righteousness. Theodore Roosevelt could not be accused of "effeminacy." He was the ideal Christian gentleman.

Although Roosevelt was an immensely popular President, enthusiasm for him was not universal. William James's "moral equivalent of war" was offered as an alternative to the militarism so forthrightly defended by Roosevelt. Roosevelt had stumped the country between 1898 and 1901, defending American imperialism in the Philippines as a just war. He placed the Spanish-American War in historical continuity with all American wars of "righteousness." It was another "blood sacrifice." This time the sacrifice was on behalf of civilization, freeing the barbarian from the "chains of slavery."

Roosevelt simply used the major categories of Social Darwinism, similar to the manifest-destiny claims of Josiah Strong, to justify American imperialism and entrance into international affairs. He claimed that the "great law of right" applied to nations as well as to individuals. As an individual could not develop social attributes in solitude, so a nation could not grow in isolation either. America must expand in the cause of international peace. Someday peace would rule on earth, but until it did it was the moral duty of the state to promote peace by maintaining a position of military preparedness and power. Otherwise some barbarian nation might do so first.

In the process of defending the war, Roosevelt portrayed American commerce, military power, statesmen, and missionaries as the carriers of the material, physical, and spiritual progress of civilization to the barbarian. Although approving of the commercial enterprise, he implied that the captain of industry was inferior to the statesman because business was a vocation more material than spiritual. From this point of view, the soldier and statesman were evangelists of democracy who embodied "the Christian spirit" of the nation. Except for times of war, the soldier was otherwise a quiet, nonassertive man.

The moral or physical weakling, either as an individual or a nation, would not survive according to the doctrine of the survival of the fittest. Roosevelt was harsh with those who disagreed with his expansiveness. Those who saw no need to expand the navy or wage war in the interest of peace were labeled weak, selfish, or foolish.[21] Roosevelt was colorful, bellicose, and belligerent. As a national leader, he expressed the self-assurance of his fellow Victorians who believed that the historical destiny of America was God's plan for the race.

Roosevelt made pronouncements on the domestic front with equal certainty. He praised the virtues of the Victorian family and protested the flabby naiveté of the socialists, anarchists, social workers, and reformers. He linked the virtues of the Victorian family with the health of the nation in a classic summary of that point of view:

> When men fear work or fear righteous war, when women fear motherhood, they tremble on the brink of doom; and well it is that they should vanish from the earth, where they are fit subjects for the scorn of all men and women who are themselves strong and brave and high-minded. . . . As it is with individuals, so it is with the nation.[22]

William James and Washington Gladden notwithstanding, Theodore Roosevelt and the Spanish-American War were well received—for a time. Roosevelt transformed patriotism and militarism into the vocation of statesmen at a time when young men were casting about for careers.[23] He invested nationalism with the larger purpose of serving international progress and peace and incorporated the male vocations of statesman, soldier, or family man into one patriotic ethos of service to the state.

Lloyd and Roosevelt both contributed to public doubt about the morality of the captain of industry. New images for male emulation were needed. Lloyd questioned the belief that businessmen were good men. Roosevelt interjected his own version of the survival of the fittest. The soldier, the statesman, and the family man were the new images identified with moral fitness, the survival of civilized virtues, and patriotism. Above all, Roosevelt himself epitomized the ideal of the Christian gentleman as a man both brave and aggressive, moral and hardworking.

The issues raised by the Spanish-American War represented a critical appraisal of two forms of "laissez-faire" expansion: internationalism, and unlimited individualism in business practices. Among the older Social Gospel leaders, Gladden and Abbott differed sharply on these issues. Gladden's version of "the Kingdom of God" was a vision of peace in his time on American soil. He distinguished between foreign missions and national expansion, especially if expansion meant war. If America had an international role to play, it was to bring peace, not war, to the world.

After the fact, Gladden conceded that the Spanish-American War had launched America as a world power and that therefore the nation could not shrink from the task. But the twentieth century was bringing to the doorstep of America a world that the old gentleman from Columbus found burdensome. He accepted the new American role of responsibility for the "well-being of the world" only because it was "inevitable."[24] Gladden lived another twenty years, but by 1898 his most productive years were behind him.

When Gladden died in 1918, Abbott used the occasion to point out that Gladden had never abandoned his pacifist stance. As the editor of the widely circulated *Outlook* magazine, Abbott wrote an obituary in which he noted Gladden's belief that war damaged progress in industrial reform. Abbott, however, believed that war promoted industrial reform.[25] Abbott had been slow to accept the Spanish-American War, but he had less difficulty seeing how war could contribute to progress once the break was made with his principle that "Christianity and war are absolutely inconsistent." Abbott preached a sermon on March 13, 1898, one month before war on Spain was declared, using Gladden's well-known title "Is It Peace or War?" While saying that he had no patience with arguments for war in the spirit of patriotism or heroism, he did think America had an international responsibility to eradicate "barbarism." America would be the "knight-errant" of Cuba, fighting for her liberty from "barbaric" Spain.[26] Abbott concurred with friend and colleague Roosevelt that the war was fitting to the historical destiny of America.

Walter Rauschenbusch was a more subtle thinker than the older men, less given to thinking only in terms of future destiny. His reactions involved the dual perspective of the present as a part of the whole of Christian history, as well as the place of the present in the future. He was deeply ambivalent about war. Although he expected war to cease in the future, he was less adamant than Gladden that it should not exist in the present. He interpreted the American victory over Spain as a triumph, as a sign of national "manhood," and as the birth of democracy for all the world. He hailed the consequent American involvement in Cuba as a positive element in a new spirit of international cooperation in America.[27] His enthusiasm rested on his interpretation of Catholicism as a tyrannical power and conservative force working against the progress of civilization. The defeat of Catholic Spain by Protestant America augured well for the future of civilization.

The enthusiasm accorded the American victory over Spain by Rauschenbusch did not expand to World War I. Rauschenbusch envisioned "the Kingdom of God" on an international scale as the extension of the political democracy and spiritual power of the Teutonic nations. He looked to the joint leadership of America, Great Britain, and Germany to establish "the Kingdom of God," a world social order in which both social justice and individual freedom were present. Rauschenbusch was not ambivalent about World War I. He flatly opposed it.

While the men of the Social Gospel had always been sensitive to the possibility that unlimited self-assertion lent itself to selfish and immoral behavior, they had not condemned the captain of industry. The later figures, as teachers of young men, looked to a virile, aggressive leadership from vital young men as the hope of a Christian nation. Peabody, with this objective in mind, depicted the captain of industry as a man with qualities worth emulating—a "virile and forcible type of man." Men who were to be leaders in society would need to be alert, audacious, and commanding. The industrial order would be transformed by the good character of business leaders and the thrift, frugality, and self-control of all men. Peabody believed in the propagating power of personality. As the honest businessman was the soul of domestic America, the Christian statesman would keep "the soul of the nation alive" in the international realm.[28]

During Peabody's tenure at Harvard, the faculty there had committed itself to promoting a virile, aggressive Christ as a model for young men.[29] Like Peabody, Rauschenbusch advocated the service of virile, regenerated youth as leaders in society. Such leadership was a Christian vocation carried out in the "spirit of chivalry." He too relied on the power of the purified personality to give force and righteousness to public opinion and custom. Turning the male images of the culture to his own purposes, Rauschenbusch wrote that the social service of Christian youth would be the equivalent of the finest spirit of "battle" and the "finest temper of sport."[30] His concept of virile manhood meant morality, industry, and social service.

The later Social Gospel men added a quality of virility to the ideal of the "Christian gentleman" with the use of chivalry images. The Christian gentleman as "knight-errant" was potentially a man of spiritual and material success. The spirit of chivalry was the self-sacrificing motive of the knight-errant fighting the forces of evil out of his love for woman, God, and country. He could easily appear to be successful from a worldly point of view. But he was distinguished from the "Victorian gentleman" of the male-achiever ethos primarily in his motivation, which was not self-serving, although his vocation did demand aggression. The knight-errant was motivated by love, not by a desire for economic gratification and personal power held at the expense of others. The aggression of the knight-errant was moral because it was not economically or sexually motivated.

Socialism: Democracy and the
Spirit of Jesus

Throughout the turbulent 1880s Americans routinely identified socialists with anarchism. Socialism was also commonly identified with free love, communal living, family disintegration, and violence. The identification rested on impressions formed in the 1840s, when the

The Fatherhood of God and the Victorian Family

Fourierites organized a small number of utopian communities. Although they were critical of society, the early Fourierites were not political activists. The "familistic"communes represented an alternative to a society suffering the social dislocations of industrialism. The communal alternative was passive withdrawal, not revolutionary change. But the link between socialism and communal living was firmly forged. From 1840 on, the American middle class continued to assume that socialism implied the abolition of private property and the destruction of family "purity."

Socialism in 1900 appealed to people who doubted that social equality could be achieved in a democratic society. For some, socialism was a constructive form of "progressivism," seeking the limited objectives of public ownership of utilities and home rule for local and city government. Some historical evolutionists expected socialism to evolve out of democracy. For feminists and social reformers who wanted a single standard of sexual purity for men and women, socialism promised a system that would make purity possible. Like the earlier socialist communes, socialism in 1900 offered a cooperative venture to relieve the pressures of competition brought on by capitalism. But this time it had leaders who were social reformers.

In the years around the turn of the century, socialism was seriously advanced as a political and economic alternative to American democracy. In the 1912 election, the year of the defeat of Theodore Roosevelt and the Progressive platform, socialists received 6 percent of the popular vote. That was the high tide of American socialism in terms of popular political support. The years in which socialism was prominent coincided with years of concern about the stability of the middle-class American family. The two events were related.

Roosevelt reflected and stimulated public anxiety about the decline of the family suggested by rising divorce rates, falling birthrates, and a new phenomenon—the childless marriage. His speeches reflect the related values of family sanctity, work, and patriotism:

> The man who will not work hard for his wife and his little ones, the woman who shirks from bearing and rearing many healthy children, these have no place among the men and women who are striving onward and upward. Of course the family is the foundation of all things in the state.[31]

The Roosevelt speeches reveal the heart of evangelical antipathy to socialism. Like the men of the Social Gospel, Roosevelt assumed that democracy depended on self-disciplined citizens, that work and morality were integral to each other, and that "moral betterment . . . usually brings material betterment in its train."[32] From this perspective private property was a necessary incentive to workers to rise by "the law of work." Roosevelt thought that the socialist revolutionary objective of "pulling down" the upper class in order to benefit the lower class had dubious merit. The use of force to take from the rich and give to the poor was unacceptable.

In general, the "progressive" legislation passed in the Roosevelt administration was designed to make possible more equitable opportunities for the "uplift" of the lower class.[33] Roosevelt expected social equality to follow a prudent use of legislation. Given an equal opportunity, all men would then either work or suffer the result of their own failure. The Progressive platform of 1912 represented a large-scale attempt to translate the ideals of economic and social justice into a concrete form. Roosevelt did not fear the socialist alternative. As a politician, he considered it unnecessary, and he aimed some of his most trenchant criticism at the naiveté of the would-be social reformers.[34]

Peabody and Rauschenbusch were considerably less sanguine about the socialist alternative. While the Social Gospel men shared some of the objectives of American socialists, especially with regard to equal vocational opportunities for men, they disagreed radically at one point, namely, the possibility that socialism would damage the family and, in turn, the state. Both men were attracted by the socialist desire for social justice, but they rejected any aspects of socialism that would discourage individual initiative and self-discipline. The socialist solution was unacceptable if it meant the destruction of private property.

Peabody and Rauschenbusch were both sensitive to the possibility that socialism could conceivably replace democracy. Rauschenbusch admired Peabody's book, *Jesus Christ and the Social Question* (1900), because Peabody had paid the socialist alternative the compliment of taking it seriously. In addition, Peabody had refuted the undesirable aspects of socialist theory:

> This unflinching radicalism proceeds to examine the very pillars of social life, and to consider whether they are worth what it costs to buttress and maintain them. Three such social institutions appear to support the fabric

of modern civilization—the family, private property, and the State: and there is not one of these institutions whose continued existence in its present form is not now a matter of active discussion, or whose abolition is not confidently prophesied.[35]

Peabody attacked both socialism and Social Darwinism as philosophies contributing to family disorder by fostering self-interested individualism. He identified Spencer's philosophy with the new "animalistic" utilitarian philosophy of balancing sexual pleasures in marriage. Socialism, as a form of scientific materialism, claimed that marriage was nothing but a "temporary business with laws to protect rights, inheritance and legitimacy." Such a materialistic view of marriage ran contrary to the teaching of Jesus that marriage was "a moral creation designed for the development of personality and the discipline of character."[36] The socialist marriage contract implied easy divorce. To Peabody, divorce was not permissible because marriage was an eternal, indissoluble union.[37]

Peabody condemned laissez-faire economics for contributing to the social unrest that invited socialist alternatives and made it seem plausible. But he never condemned capitalism as a source of human misery. He believed that since Christian ideals were the source of human morality, individual immorality was caused by an absence of high ideals and self-discipline. Indolence bred alcohol problems, poor homes, and child neglect. Since Peabody subscribed thoroughly to the psychology of moral growth through work and self-discipline, his fundamental opposition to socialism rested on the socialist proposal to abolish private property. The availability of private property was essential to morality and democracy. The continued existence of private property was insurance against family disintegration. State ownership of tools and the institutions of production would doom the family and, with it, the moral integrity of the individual.[38]

Despite Peabody's theoretical criticism of the "animalism" engendered by Spencer's Social Darwinism, his own analysis of social problems rested on Darwin's maxims for civilized morality: a stable family living in a home of its own and a man who worked to support his family. Egoism, altruism, and self-interested altruism were his categories for individual motivation. The Victorian family ideal, with the emphasis on female virtue and purity, set the boundaries of Peabody's "social" gospel. His concept of the ideal democratic society was the family ideal: "The Kingdom of God is the expansion of the family into a world of intimate and unconstrained love."[39] The love Peabody had in mind was the deference and mutual service of the Victorian marriage.

The thrust of Peabody's survey of socialist thought was the implication that Christianity needed to defend itself against the possibility of socialism becoming a substitute for religion. He associated socialist antipathy to Christianity with the left-wing Hegelian assumption that "spiritual ideals were the result of economic circumstances, not revelations of absolute truth. . . . Christianity, then, the prevailing spiritual expression of the present economic order, must pass away as a better order arrives."[40] Peabody was puzzled by the socialist tendency in American social reformers to attack domestic relations rather than economic conditions:

> Nothing is stranger in the modern social agitation than this transfer of its storm-centre from the issue with capitalism in which it began, to the apparently remote and tranquil region of the family; and it is not inconceivable that the judgement of history on the program of economic socialism may be determined, not so much by the main issue for which the program seems to stand, as by the effect of the changes proposed upon the integrity of the family.[41]

Socialism offered a comprehensive creed that like a religion touched all aspects of life. Earlier Social Gospel figures had feared a socialist revolution born of the discontent of the poor. Peabody feared a socialist evolution made possible by the "ennui" of the handworker and a failure of nerve in the educated middle class. To the host of social reformers advocating unacceptable socialist strategies for social change, Peabody advanced the claim that "the whole theology of Jesus was a transfiguration of the family." "Jesus finds in the unity of the family that social force that molds all mankind into one great family under the Fatherhood of a loving God."[42] The "theology of Jesus" was the answer and the meeting place for the Christian and the social reformer.

Rauschenbusch considered himself a socialist because he believed that Christian socialism was the emerging stage in history. He devoted his writing to creating enthusiasm for Christian ideals, lest an irreligious form of socialism occupy the world stage. After an early abortive attempt to inspire the worker class, Rauschenbusch turned his attention to the American middle class as the potential source of uplift for the poor.[43] Assuming that the lower emulates the higher, Rauschenbusch concluded that if the lower class could learn morality from the middle class, the middle class could likewise emulate the materialism and greed of the upper class. Assuming that people would never voluntarily curb their wealth, a legislative solution would be required to prevent the accumulation of great wealth.

Rauschenbusch was the only Social Gospel figure to condemn two major elements in the American argument for capitalistic competition: the unlimited accumulation of wealth and the absolute sanctity of private property. With reference to the issue of private property, the socialism of Rauschenbusch was that of Henry George's single-tax proposal as a panacea for all social problems. Rauschenbusch advocated the redistribution, not the abolition, of private property.

Because Rauschenbusch assimilated parts of the socialist critique of society into his own social analysis, his criticisms and solutions differ from those of Peabody in some details. Because he incorporated Christianity, as he understood it, into his socialism, Rauschenbusch also differs from American popularizers of socialist utopias like Edward Bellamy. Bellamy's highly successful utopian novel, *Looking Backward: 2000–1887,* inspired dozens of imitators between 1887 and 1900. The novel was representative of the popular forms of utopian socialism to which Rauschenbusch took exception.[44]

Bellamy was typical of the socialist perspective that viewed the social competition fostered by capitalism as the cause of sexual inequality and unrewarding marriage relationships. His contrast of the Victorian marriage of 1887 with the marriage relationship anticipated by the year 2000 implied that the Victorian marriage was not rewarding to men. His utopian community, Altruria, was a model of social organization which enabled marriage to be equally rewarding to husband and wife because each would have his or her own "healthful and inspiriting occupation."[45]

The imposed socialist state envisioned by Bellamy offered a socialist economy and government that would make altruism possible for both men and women by establishing an equitably rewarded work system for both sexes. The Victorian ideal of the sexes as separate but equal was transformed by Bellamy into two separate but parallel worlds of work and competition for men and women. He differed from the Victorian ideal in his proposition that the family would be enhanced if women worked because they would be happier. He compromised the ideal in postulating two separate work worlds in which male and female did not compete against each other. But his major objective was the creation of a community that demonstrated the wisdom of the socialist claim that the eradication of a competitive economic system would make "pure love" in marriage possible. It would make possible the family love which Bellamy considered necessary to an altruistic, selfless love for the race. Children would be reared out of a sense of duty to the nation. Ultimately, his proposal represented a socialist means of fulfilling the Victorian marriage and family ideal.

Like Bellamy, Rauschenbusch viewed the socialist economic system as preferable to capitalist competition because it would make altruism possible. He envisioned a social order in which both social justice and individual freedom would be assured. The socialist influence in the thought of Rauschenbusch led him to affirm the maxim that society should be reformed so that good men would be able to be good. This suggests a social determinism in assessing the cause of immoral behavior. Yet Rauschenbusch always assumed that individual moral rectitude depended on the "spiritual" power of Christianity. Consequently, he integrated the perspectives of socialism and evolutionary theology concerning the solution to the social problem. His emphasis oscillated between the universalist hope that society would eventually be assimilated to the uplifting power of Christian love, and the degree to which the legislative measures of socialism were necessary to make Christian love possible. The family was the one independent variable in Rauschenbusch's considerations of the means of achieving both social justice and individual freedom in the American democracy. His final standard of judgment concerning political systems was their effect on the family unit.

All Social Gospel figures believed that goodness was strictly an inner, spiritual process. Although they all agreed eventually that some laws should be passed that would protect the weak, the content and purpose of legislation to achieve such an objective was broader in Rauschenbusch. His most radical proposal—and the one which never gained public acceptance—was the socialization of land. He shared the common belief that the ability to acquire some property and wealth was a necessary incentive for work and morality. But he took the proposition so seriously that he considered the availability of land to all the people so important that socializing the land would justify any temporary difficulty involved in the redistribution of private property.[46]

During public discussion of the possibility of an income tax, Rauschenbusch favored a stricter measure: outlawing inheritance entirely. He advocated outlawing inherited fortunes so that every man would start life in a position of economic equality. Assuming that all men would work if rewarded equitably, Rauschenbusch reasoned that equality of opportunity would eradicate immorality because men would learn self-control through work. A new economic order would protect the purity of women by providing job security for men.

Rauschenbusch followed the socialist critique of capitalist competition as a source of social disorder and applied it in terms of the Victorian marriage ideal. Unlike Bellamy, Rauschenbusch favored social equality for one sex only. He expected a socialist economy to reduce the pressures of economic competition on men which, in turn, would ensure the continuing purity of women. Like many other Victorians, Rauschenbusch believed that poverty drove women to prostitution and that alcohol accounted for men who would "ruin" women. From this point of view he saw a socialist economy as the key to the prevention of individual moral corruption, the degradation of the family, and possible national moral decline.[47]

Rauschenbusch never supposed that individual morality could be imposed, although he did think it could be facilitated by legislative means. Just as capitalism caused social problems, socialism would facilitate social cooperation. Even if social amelioration could be achieved by controlling the accumulation of wealth, progress and justice still depended on the voluntary cooperation of "each for all and all for each." Justice depended on the moral autonomy of every individual serving the good of the whole.

> The fundamental virtue in the ethics of Jesus was love, because love is the society-making quality. . . . Love creates fellowship. In the measure of which love holds together any social organism, it will hold together without coercion. If physical coercion is constantly necessary, it is proof that the social organism has not evoked the power of human affection and fraternity.[48]

The Social Problem and the Kingdom of God (1890-1924)

The socialist measures favored by Rauschenbusch for facilitating the evolution of Christian socialism were all moral concerns related to the integrity of the family. The first principle of his social ethic was the necessity of maintaining the standard of civilized morality. The church, the home, and the schools all evoked the "higher relations" of social cooperation. As such, they all served the state. But the family was more basic than the other institutions because it channeled sexual and parental love into the useful function of helpful relationships. Rauschenbusch favored legal restrictions concerning child and female labor for the purpose of keeping children and women in the home.

The second principle of his social ethic was the evaluation of legislation according to its power to protect the weak against the strong. This applied to groups, to society as a whole, and to individuals. The underlying objective of his ethical standard was no different from that of any other Social Gospeler—or conservative evangelical. It was moral autonomy. Or, as he stated it in social terms, since man was a social animal, "freedom is applied Christianity." Freedom was necessary for the development of a Christian personality. And freedom was also the condition of a Christianized social order.[49]

In the second stage of the development of the Social Gospel, the central slogans shifted. "The Brotherhood of Man" replaced "the Fatherhood of God" as the focal ideal of the Social Gospel. The ethical idealists were interested in religion primarily as the inner spiritual power of the individual, and of the state, rather than the sustaining-creating power of the universe. Earlier optimism about an unlimited evolution of morality was no longer accepted without question. God the Father, as the author of natural evolution of the universe and guarantor of moral progress, was eclipsed by the nature of social circumstances, which demanded a power more socially adaptable than that of mere physical generativity. The comprehensive "spirit of Jesus," understood to mean the power of human brotherhood, became the guarantor of social stability and moral progress. The principle of Christian comprehensiveness served as an ideal and as a vantage point from which it was possible to claim that the new and conflicting social movements were really signs that brotherhood would soon be achieved. Peabody and Rauschenbusch considered demands for freedom from so many groups to be evidence that the democratic ideal of freedom was spreading through all levels of society.

The Fatherhood of God and the Victorian Family

Despite the variations between the socialism of Rauschenbusch and the Unitarian evangelicalism of Peabody, three elements in their social thought remained constant and interdependent. The economic order, the family, and personal morality of the individual would rise and fall together. Despite the emphasis on the effects of social institutions on the individual, all the ethical idealists advocated the morality of individuals as the solution to the social problem. Although they were more conscious of the complexity of the social order, like the earlier Social Gospel leaders, they believed that individual morality required freedom from social coercion to flourish and develop.

The Social Gospel defense of Christianity, democracy, and the family against the possibility that socialism might "sweep away" the present social order was ultimately a defense of the social status quo. The objective of the ethical idealists was social justice in order to make moral integrity possible. The socialist vision of Rauschenbusch was the hope of a society conformed to the middle-class view of civilized morality. Socialism was a means to that end. Voluntary Christian socialism would mean endless potential for character growth, and a society in perfect harmony. The materialism and individualism of capitalism would fade away as cooperation gradually replaced competition. In place of socialist solutions involving communal property or "familism," the Social Gospel men saw the solution in an infusion of the "spirit of Jesus." Under the motive-power of love, the nation would become one large, self-sacrificing family.

Feminism: The Family and the Kingdom of God

Clarke, Peabody, and Rauschenbusch all believed that the Victorian family was the apex and epitome of advanced civilization. Their judgment was based on a contrast with what they believed to be the family organization of barbaric societies. Following the family ethos incorporated into Social Darwinism, they assumed that the family was the source of the social virtues of cooperation and altruism.

The Social Gospel analysis of the threat of socialism to the family is not intelligible unless the standard of contrast between civilized morality and barbarism is assumed. Clarke spelled out the components of "barbarism" in writing about the social ills a missionary might encounter in primitive societies, where people were ignorant, superstitious, cruel, and even unclean. The worst part of a primitive society was the family organization: "Woman is degraded, infanticide prevails. The family needs uplifting. Truthfulness has not been there to build up trustworthy order."[50] Victorian family ideals colored the Social Gospel view of the world.

The Victorian family ideal developed originally under the impact of social changes that inevitably accompanied the industrial revolution. It was used later as evidence of human superiority over animals under the impact of the Darwinian evolution. By 1880 what had been a practical rationale for self-sacrifice in *Physiology of Marriage* became a sentimentalized adoration of the self-sacrifice necessary to the purity of marriage and the duties of parenthood. The ideal had always been identified with the good of the nation, because democracy depended on the ability of the individual to handle freedom responsibly. When the challenge to the ideal came from socialist sources in the 1890s, its defenders never questioned their own assumptions concerning the comparative standards of civilized and barbarian morality. It was basically the difference between the morality of a person fit for "the family of God" and that of an animal. For Rauschenbusch, it was identified as the difference between internalized moral control—"the policeman inside you"—and externally coerced morality.[51]

Much of Peabody's career was devoted to preventing "the undermining of the family" by the Marxist prophecy that the family would fade away. A statement made in the Boardman Lectures in 1924 captures the issues involved for Peabody:

> The family, it is now confidently taught, has illustrated a gradual development of type, and is now approaching a period of dissolution. It is pointed out that one important factor in the establishment of the family group has been the desire to control and transmit private property. The family, it is urged, is thus an economic unit, an instrument of the capitalist class. With the transition from capitalism to communal ownership, therefore, a revolution in domestic life is not only probable, but inevitable. Women, it is said, will be no longer domestic slaves of the dominant group. Children will be cared for by the community. . . . Woman will be both socially and industrially independent. She is to be subjected to no semblance of ownership, but to stand over against man, free and equal, the mistress of her fate. . . . Such is the transition in domestic relations freely prophesied as the corollary of economic change.[52]

121

The Fatherhood of God and the Victorian Family

From the point of view of civilized morality, it was impossible to think desirable a social order in which women would be "socially and industrially independent." The family, as the most elementary form of "the moral education of the race," demanded the self-sacrificing model of the mother in the home. Because of the power of the male "sex passion," Rauschenbusch believed that all people should marry. In addition, women must become mothers because children "constituted" the family. Every marriage needed children to evoke the father's vocational devotion and the mother's devotion to her work, the family. Marriage was the only natural channel to control the "sex passion," and parenthood was the source of adult maturity. The self-sacrificing love on which the social order depended was learned as a child in the family and matured during adulthood in marriage and parenthood. The most lyrical prose of Rauschenbusch was devoted to the praise of parenthood:

> The love of fatherhood and motherhood is a divine revelation and miracle. It is a creative act of God in us. Last year it was not; this year it is, and all things are changed. The dry dock of our selfishness has been struck and the water of sacrificial love pours forth. The thorn bush is aflame with a beautiful fire that does not consume. The springing up of this new force is essential for the very existence of human society.[53]

Given such passion concerning the role of the family in society, it becomes more clear why the socialism of Rauschenbusch was so limited. He wanted an economic revolution without a change in the family unit. Against socialist and feminist demands on behalf of freedom for women, Rauschenbusch never changed his basic conviction that a woman belonged at home. He feared the entrance of women into the job market. It was a very real possibility that the "free love" favored by a few radicals would occur if women worked daily with a variety of men. How then could a marriage be pure if a man could not be sure of the "purity" of his wife? Family love, and social order, depended on the continued purity of both male and female.

The purity of woman was the center of the Christian case against socialism. Most Christians, like Peabody, viewed the two attitudes toward the family as antithetical. Socialists held that society shaped the family. The family was subject to change. They blamed virtually all social problems, including the domestic slavery of women, on capitalism. The Christian champions of individual freedom and social justice assumed that the family shapes society, and they refused to grant the possibility that the family was changed by society. With a few exceptions, like Rauschenbusch, they feared that socialism would cause further social disintegration.

The question raised by Rauschenbusch was not in the least trivial. What would happen if men could no longer trust the purity of women? It penetrated to the heart of the world-view of Victorian America, and it explains the religious intensity of American hostility to socialism. To the defender of the family ideal, for women to be socially and vocationally equal to men would place them in the same competitive circumstances that tempted the virtue of the Christian gentleman. What would motivate him to virtue if not the economic dependence of his wife and children? Worse, what if the female did "crave" sex? As long as she was bound in domestic servitude to house, husband, and children, her much vaunted purity was never tested. There was lingering doubt concerning female sexuality in the ideal of the Victorian family. Uncertainty concerning female sexual purity was an unspoken dynamic in the American equation of socialism with free love. Implicit in the Victorian sexual code was the belief that if the amative faculty of the female was overstimulated she could become sexually voracious.

Rauschenbusch, for example, was conscious of the force of community moral sanctions lost as American living patterns changed in the nineteenth century. He did not share the reticence displayed by men like Peabody concerning public discussion of sexual matters. He stated the dilemma posed by the feminist demands for social, economic, vocational, and sexual freedom for women with clarity and forthrightness:

> The freedom of movement in American life and the growing knowledge of preventatives makes sin easy and safe. To anyone who realizes the value of womanly purity, it is appalling to think that the standard of purity for their whole sex may drop and approximate the standard prevailing among men. ... The health of society rests on the welfare of the home. What, then, will be the outcome if the unmarried multiply; if homes remain childless; if families are homeless; if girls do not know housework; and if men come to distrust the purity of women?[54]

Rauschenbusch and Peabody rarely mentioned feminism as such because it was integral to socialism and social reform. Feminism in 1900 included social reformers who favored a diversity of causes: woman suffrage, economic independence for women, freedom from domestic slavery, prohibition, temperance, remedies for prostitution, a single standard of purity for both sexes, and sometimes free love. Not all feminists supported all the issues gathered under the slogan "feminism." Peabody and Rauschenbusch did not sanction woman suffrage, or legislation to control alcohol or prostitution. The only plank in the Republican platform of 1912 that Rauschenbusch refused to endorse was that of woman suffrage. Their analysis of the woman problem differed, but their attitude and response to it did not.

Rauschenbusch abhorred feminism because it was potentially destructive of the family and society. He considered American women to be "free and equal" as compared to barbarian family and sexual standards. Against the radical feminist critique that women were domestic and economic slaves, and as such were prostitutes to their own husbands, Rauschenbusch countered that Christianity had brought a "finer sense of the right of a soul to its own body."[55] His point was that Christianity had brought into the world the final form of religion, the foundations of democratic government based on moral autonomy, and the final form of the family. He wanted a social order in which good men could be good, so women could be fulfilled in the domestic role assigned to them.

With pressure from socialism on the family, Christianity, and democracy, the ideal of "the Kingdom of God" became virtually synonymous with the defense of the Victorian family ideal. Democratic freedom depended on the stability of the family because the family was the source of the internalized standard of morality necessary to the continuation of democratic freedom.

All the Social Gospel men drew their understanding of a well-ordered society from the Victorian family. With the shift of focus from the individual to the social whole in the later group, their ideal of the state was still that of a well-ordered family. A cooperative social order depended on social institutions being permeated by the Christian spirit of cooperation. The "almost" Christianized social order that Rauschenbusch described in 1912 meant simply that the home, the church, the school, and the government served the purpose of facilitating the development of the "social" nature of more individuals than ever before.

The only forms of social "progress" the Social Gospel men could sanction were those that kept the Victorian family ideal intact. They believed that progress depended on maintaining the complementarity of sex roles assigned to the male and female in the family ideal. As cultural standards gradually eroded the family ideal after the turn of the century, the only response available to them was to reiterate the ideal, with the hope of influencing public opinion.

In the 1912 election, Roosevelt and Wilson both campaigned for social justice at home and peace abroad. Wilson's campaign was conducted in a quieter key than that of Roosevelt's "Bull Moose" appeal to moral militarism and an America well-armed for the good of the "barbarian." Roosevelt's theme song was "Onward Christian Soldiers." The victory for Wilson signaled a new mood in the country. A new consensus was emerging out of the complexity of a pluralistic culture.

By 1912 the nations of the world could no longer be easily labeled "barbarian" or "civilized." The old virtues epitomized by the Victorian family ideal were giving way to "new freedom." Theodore Roosevelt and the men of the Social Gospel held a world-view that was becoming dysfunctional. The Wilson victory suggested the accuracy of Wilson's observation that it was "a new era in human relationships, a new stage-setting for the drama of life."[56]

Although Rauschenbusch believed that the early years of the twentieth century were the years in which the social movement and the social gospel had matured, his own form of Christian socialism was more reactionary than new or creative. The earlier Social Gospel men contributed to the intellectual currents of Social Darwinism that culminated in the doctrine of manifest destiny through their use of powerful family images. Where the earlier men had spoken for the individual against the violence and aggression signified by an uncontrolled laissez-faire economy, the later men defended moral manhood, democracy, and the family against laissez-faire expansionism represented by militarism and socialism. All the Social Gospel men held a common belief, similar to the liberal Social Darwinism of Henry George and Henry G. Lloyd, that social progress had to be harmonious to be productive. For both earlier and later Social Gospel leaders the faculty psychology and the family ideal integral to Social Darwinism was the controlling center of their social thought.

The "social problem" that absorbed the attention of Peabody and

Rauschenbusch was the question of how class equality could be achieved. The presupposition that morality was acquired through work properly rewarded led them to favor equal work opportunity for all men. Because they assumed that love of a good woman motivated a man to work, they opposed any legislation that would upset the balance of the feminine domestic sphere with the masculine sphere of work. The Christian socialism of Rauschenbusch was limited by the Social Darwinism implicit in his social ethic.

The source of later Social Gospel opposition to various forms of militarism, feminism, internationalism, and socialism came from the same liberal Social Darwinism that informed the early Social Gospel. The later men were more concerned with the outcome of social progress than they were with questions of the nature and destiny of the race. Their concern for women, children, and the poor, the missionary zeal of Rauschenbusch for Christian socialism, and their hope for the kingdom of God came from evangelical Christianity. Their preoccupation with infusing the inner spirit of social institutions with "the spirit of Jesus" came from ethical idealism and from Spencer's concept of public opinion as a force of social change. Like the earlier men, their mode of thought was that of analogy. They replaced the biological basis of Social Darwinism with an anthropological analogy of individuals and institutions. The paradox in their social thought lies in the belief of Peabody and Rauschenbusch that their work was an advance on the individualistic Social Darwinism of Spencer and a contribution to the evolving "social spirit" of their era.

In *A Study of Christian Missions* Clarke outlined the responsibility of the Christian church for the "social spirit" of the era. As a Christian universalist and a believer in the gradual establishment of the kingdom of God on earth, Clarke claimed that evangelism was still necessary in order to carry the redemptive message of a forgiving God to all people "now, rather than allow evil a longer time to do its work."[57] As a believer in the gradual evolution of the race, Clarke also defended the uniqueness of Christianity against the possibility that history might go beyond Christianity. As the highest and most universal religion, Christianity was the completion of "primitive" and "arrested" religions. Christianity was the religion of brotherhood, God the Father, and the promise of immortality.

Other religions would have their day and fade away, but Christianity must not accept the fatalistic interpretation that it too would fade away. Clarke affirmed the power of human intelligence to guide the evolutionary process of civilization and reaffirmed the responsibility of Christians to take Christianity to the world. His application of "social spirit" to the world arena was consistent with the "spirit" Rauschenbusch sought for the nation.

6

Theology for the
Social Gospel
(1900-1924)

The reconstruction of religious thought, known by 1890 as the "new" theology, was a gradual development that occurred over a seventy-year period.[1] The Civil War is a convenient point of demarcation between the two major challenges that precipitated the need for a new theology: prewar creedal controversies and postwar Darwinism. Creedal controversy before the war resulted in an unprecedented diversity of doctrinal positions. "New light" evangelicals like Lyman Beecher, Nathaniel Taylor, and Horace Bushnell struggled with issues concerning the nature of man and the nature of God raised by the Unitarian revolt against "old light" Calvinism. The predecessors of the Social Gospel movement attempted to mediate the harshness of "old light" orthodoxy with the hopeful optimism of Unitarianism and Transcendentalism.

The pre–Civil War creedal controversies were part of a larger cultural revolt against Calvinism. The predestining God of Calvinism, a central issue in the creedal controversies, emerged as an odious and unacceptable notion to the later Victorians. A sovereign God who would choose to elect some, but not all, men was undemocratic in the extreme. In the postwar period the debates concerning the nature of God, further complicated by the evolutionary hypothesis, emerged as the question of the nature and destiny of man. The men of the early Social Gospel were interested in ideals adequate to moral inspiration, not in creeds. They managed to adapt theology to the evolutionary hypothesis in such a way that both God and man seemed necessary to the evolutionary process in natural history and human history.

William Newton Clarke, Lyman Abbott, and Washington Gladden

faced a different kind of theological issue in the postwar period with demands for scientific research and verification associated with the "scientific" methods of Darwinism. In addition to the creedal difficulties concerning the capacity of human nature and the relationship of God to man, Darwinism intensified the theological dilemma by undermining confidence in the Bible as God's infallible revelation. The question of the authority of the Bible posed new issues for American theology concerning how God was revealed to mankind.

By the time Peabody and Rauschenbusch began writing, the issues of evolution and biblical inspiration had been settled by men like Clarke. Peabody and Rauschenbusch never discussed the problem of biblical interpretation. Like Clarke, they used an intuitionist theory of inspiration. They also assumed that since Reason had evolved, new theology was superior to old theology. Like Clarke, they used the Bible as a spiritual guide to life. Scripture was not the source of theology. It provided supporting evidence to the moral history of civilization. As a source book for moral ideals, the biblical passages cited most often by the men of the Social Gospel were the Sermon on the Mount, the Lord's Prayer, the golden rule, and the parable of the prodigal son.

The possibility of the evolutionary process going beyond democracy, Christianity, and the family gave a special urgency to the theology of the later Social Gospel men. Walter Rauschenbusch believed that theology would die if it could not keep up with the thought categories and progress of civilization. William Newton Clarke's life work was devoted to reworking theology in forms acceptable to the twentieth century. Although both men believed religion was universal and innate to human nature, and that Christianity was the universal religion, they thought that theology was, like man, subject to death. Clarke, as a biblical scholar, was equally aware that "higher criticism" could reduce the Bible to the status of a myth. The theological task of the later figures was more clearly apologetic than were the reconstructions of the earlier Social Gospel leaders.

There were almost a hundred years of intellectual history behind the book that Rauschenbusch wrote to provide a theology for the social gospel. Just as the earlier men had revised "old light" Calvinism, Rauschenbusch was revising the inadequate truth of "conservative" evangelicals. Like the earlier men, his theology depended on the spiritual intuition of "new light" as the source of his theology. *A Theology for the Social Gospel* included philosophical assumptions and theological interpretations forged in the American social context that were unique to American theology and "new" to the classical tradition of Christian theology.

The Spiritual Intuition of
"New Light" in Theology

The leaders of the Social Gospel movement were theologians by necessity rather than by choice. Only Clarke made theology his life work. The others considered social commentary written from a religious point of view a calling more appropriate to their times than that of being a theologian. This was because they distinguished between the Christian religion and Christian thought, ethics, and theology. Although the earlier and later figures expressed the distinction in different terms, the content and objective were the same. They assumed that Christianity, as the universal religion, contained eternal and changeless truth about ethical ideals. But theology, as the expression of that truth, was subject to both time and change. As religious social critics, the Social Gospel men were interested primarily in ideals adequate to moral inspiration, not in creeds or doctrines.

When Clarke, Peabody, and Rauschenbusch referred to "the spirit of Jesus," they were attempting to identify the essential, unchanging element in Christian truth. Although they differed in their estimate of which aspect of the "spirit of Jesus" was essential, their search for eternal truth was motivated by the recognition that all truth, including the Christian religion, could—from an evolutionary point of view—be considered historical, temporal, and therefore relative.

Although it is difficult to distinguish religious thought, social ethics, social commentary, and theology within the literature of the Social Gospel movement because of the mixture of religious language, theology, and social philosophy, by their own standards the Social Gospel men wrote very little theology.[2] Strong chose not to write theology lest it perpetuate theological warfare and prove harmful to the religious spirit of cooperation of "the new era." Abbott published *The Theology of an Evolutionist* in 1897 as the second book in a projected series of five books on Christianity and evolution. He never wrote the other three books. Gladden wrote *Present Day Theology* (1913) to prove that the Social Gospel did have a theology. Peabody's books were social ethics—religious by his definition, but not theology. Rauschenbusch originally prepared the material in *A Theology for the Social Gospel* as invited lectures in doctrinal theology for the Yale School of Religion in 1917. Despite the distinction between religion and theology, the Social Gospel men wrote their books for one purpose only: the inspiration of the reader.

As in their social thought, the religious thought or theology of the Social Gospel men was written in response to different sets of issues affecting the church and their ministry in two different time frames. The earlier men, faced with the challenge of evolutionary theory to the validity of the Bible and Christianity, adapted theology to evolutionary theory. The later men, faced with the implications of a more closely examined evolutionary theory, developed a more consciously apologetic theology in their attempt to locate the eternal, unchanging truth of Christianity that would validate the claim that Christianity was the universal and final form of religion.[3] Although Clarke and Rauschenbusch were known as the "American Ritschlians" of their day, the line of continuity in the theology of all the Social Gospel men lies in their epistemology. Albrecht Ritschl, a German ethical idealist of the late nineteenth century, influenced Clarke and Rauschenbusch, but their understanding of the function of ideals in character formation was that of Social Darwinist philosophy.

The God of early Social Gospel "new" theology was the immanent source and spiritual power of the physical universe and every individual. God as First Cause and Vital Energy was a God immediately and vitally related to the universe and to men. Such a God satisfied the need of the early Social Gospel men to counter Spencer's "unknown force" and the God of Calvinism, who was so transcendent as to appear unrelated to individual behavior. They identified God with the world as the inner power of both physical and moral law.

In Social Gospel parlance, "In him we live and move and have our being" meant that the whole universe represented the unfolding of God's thoughts and energies.[4] With reference to moral law, God as the power of good within was interpreted as "the partner of our better selves." The faculty of "moral sense" was transformed into the God so close to individual consciousness that it should "make every man who can think thrill in every nerve."[5] This was not a logically developed philosophical position. The assumption underlying their religious thought was the belief that the objective, observable world as they knew it conveyed the spiritual realities of God's truth. The Social Gospel men habitually looked at objective phenomena and found evidence of eternal truth.

The early Social Gospel men solved the issues raised by Darwinism by assuming an idealism already present in Victorian thought. The Victorians invested the novel and the autobiography with moral and spiritual power. The Victorian reader expected to be inspired by the personal power of the writer beaming through the pages of personal forms of self-expression. Autobiography was expected to contain a record of the spiritual development of the writer. The novel was expected to lift up a vision or present a moral ideal.

Hamlin Garland criticized a novel written by William Dean Howells in 1888 because "it does not allow his strong, fine, and tender personality to appear in overt fashion."[6] Such expectations reveal something of the idealism present in the Victorian world-view. Any form of the written word was believed to contain the power to shape and change lives by appealing to the sentiments of the reader.

Idealism concerning the inner power of external forms pervaded all forms of middle-class culture from the paintings of the Hudson River school early in the century through the neoclassical architecture in public buildings late in the century. The principle in all was the same. Inner spirit is revealed through external forms. For a religious perspective this meant that the light breaking through the clouds in a luminist painting symbolized the sustaining presence of God in the natural order. For the secular and the religious perspective, plans for Greek-revival city centers represented the best of the Greek "spirit" present in American civilization.

Like Herbert Spencer, the men of the Social Gospel applied the natural analogy to the sphere of history and morals. They too believed that law was the external form of the "spirit" of public opinion. Gladden and Abbott posited reciprocity and mutuality between the categories of reason and the phenomena of the objective world. Nature was the outward, external, observable utterance of God's thought. Moral sense was the internal, invisible but knowable utterance of God's thought to intuition. Both physical and spiritual reality presupposed a cause behind the observed or experienced effect. In each case the cause corresponding to the effect was God. From this point of view the existence of God was verified because there are no effects that do not presuppose a cause. With reference to the natural laws of the universe, Gladden wrote: "We talk about the laws of nature but these laws only express the correspondence of the facts of nature to the regulative ideas of our own reason. It is this correspondence which is the marvelous fact . . . the world within is a perfect mirror of the world without."[7]

The mirror analogy of the correspondence of facts of nature to the regulative ideas of reason had its spiritual counterpart in the faculty of "moral sense." As the physical eye filters just the right amount of light for objects to be seen, so moral sense, used positively, would admit only good ideas. The center of the idealism of early Social Gospel thought was belief in the power of ideas to shape lives. The force of their faith in ideas, or "ideals," involved both the power of the spirit and a willful and habitual effort of the individual to "hold well-formed ideas before the mind."[8]

In urging men to choose Christ and high ideals, Gladden did not make a distinction between the two. The objective of the Social Gospel was to permeate society with Christian ideals toward the end of converting as many individuals as possible. Conversely, bad ideas produced bad people and a bad society. Gladden considered the "old" theology inadequate for changing society because the "old light" Calvinists believed that all men were naturally self-interested and incapable of behavior better than the law of selfishness. From Gladden's perspective, a negative social attitude was incapable of producing a good society.[9] Positive character formation depended on high ideals, good habits, and the freedom to develop the faculties by using them.

According to the epistemology of Gladden and Abbott, men in the nineteenth century were capable of using the faculties of reason and moral sense to know more of God's truth, both natural and moral, than ever before in human history. Man's penetration of natural law was God's way of revealing the mysteries of the universe to man.[10] With the further development of the faculty of moral sense and consciousness of moral law, God would be brought closer to humanity and social change would be automatic. Man, in this view, serves the glory of God by interpreting natural and moral phenomena and by using his powers of causation in the service of good.

Under the special pressures and doubts created by the evolutionary theory, Gladden and Abbott adapted idealism to the demand for scientific verification. For example, God as the First Cause produces an effect: the universe. Jesus Christ as the "cause" of the knowledge that God is the Father of mankind produces an effect: progress in history. The medium of integrating idealism and the scientific methods of empiricism was the "science" of phrenology, source of the idea that the world within is a mirror of the world without.

The same intuitionist theory of inspiration that was used to provide evidence of God's continuing and necessary presence in the natural and historical orders also satisfied the early Social Gospel need to repudiate the "old light" Calvinist theory of biblical inspiration defended so unremittingly by Charles Hodge of Princeton. Admitting that all expressions of religion were related to the culture in which they were formulated, they adapted the principle from "higher criticism" that the Bible had developed over a long period of time. Following the implications of Social Darwinism, this meant that the Old Testament was less exalted and noble than the New Testament because its origins were that of a less cultured age. The "light" of the New Testament was higher and more advanced and, as such, became the standard of judgment concerning the contents of the Old Testament.

The new theory of inspiration made it possible to disregard the judging God of the Old Testament and the "old light" doctrine of predestination. Belief in the moral evolution of the human race made a God who would consign a part of the human race to hell for no apparent reason appear to be grossly immoral. For people who believed that virtue was rewarding and vice was sure to be self-punishing, the God of the Old Testament who punished children and grandchildren for the sins of the fathers was outrageously vindictive. Gladden and Abbott adapted the new inspiration theory in the interest of making continued faith possible for their congregations. Observing that faith had previously been grounded in the church or in the Bible, Gladden concluded that "sacred truths" no longer needed such supports.[11]

When Rauschenbusch remarked in *A Theology for the Social Gospel* that the worst thing that could happen to the God concept would be for

God to remain an autocrat in a democratic era, he was alluding to the punitive God of "old light" Calvinism.[12] Like the earlier men, Rauschenbusch assumed that the ideals people held about God—the God concept—were directly related to the moral standards of those people. Although Clarke, Peabody, and Rauschenbusch reversed the order of the focus in the relation of acts to ideals, their ethical idealism depended on a theory of spiritual intuition. Instead of saying that bad ideals led to bad people, they looked instead to the ethical act to verify the truth of the ideal. But they assumed, like Gladden and Abbott, that spiritual truth was known through an intuitive grasp of unseen reality as the basis of the religious experience of the individual. They used the language of ethical idealism, but the content was that of the faculty psychology of Social Darwinism.

Clarke, Peabody, and Rauschenbusch all held that religious experience was the source of knowledge of Christian truth. Clarke claimed that the "eternal truth" which Jesus brought into history, known to the individual in the spiritual experience of "life" and "love," was the subjective test of the truth and eternal validity of Christianity. The experienced truth was verifiable insofar as it lived in the ethical acts of individuals. The central Christian truth that God is the Father of all men, and its corollary—the brotherhood of all men—was verifiable both subjectively and objectively. The objective verification of the truth of Fatherhood and Brotherhood was obvious moral progress in history. To make this claim, Clarke identified human reason with the power of the spirit within.

> A God who has placed within the race a growing soul is always in communication with that race through the presence of that soul. With the growth of the soul the moral element in life becomes larger and the religious element more full of meaning, and through conscience and religious aspiration God becomes yet more deeply and closely present in the inner life.[13]

Because of his belief in the progressive development of the reasoning power of mankind, Clarke concluded that "the rational power of man" in his era was so well developed that it could be trusted to reveal the truth. Because of this assumption, religious knowledge as Clarke understood it was not an unusual experience but a power of human reason equally available to all men if they would use it.[14]

Theology for the Social Gospel (1900-1924)

It was on the basis of such assumptions about the progressive spiritual power of reason and the ethical act as verification of the ideal that Rauschenbusch undertook to "construct" *A Theology for the Social Gospel.* He described the social gospel variously as "heart religion," "a new social orientation," and "a social movement." The contemporary "social problem," understood theologically, was a special opportunity for the development of faith because it would force men to see their need for the spiritual power to meet the new social circumstances.

According to Rauschenbusch, theology was too abstract to awaken an awareness of a need for God. But "audiences who are estranged from the Church and who would listen to theological terminology with frank scorn, will listen with absorbed interest to religious thought when it is linked with their own social problems."[15] Such religious experience of "solidaristic social feeling" demanded a new theology, one that expressed the new social "spirit." Social problems were a form of "heart religion" because they drove men to seek help "beyond their own strength." "So they cry to a higher Power to help, to forgive, to cleanse, to save."[16] The need for God to relieve the individual under conviction symbolized by the "anxious bench" was socialized by Rauschenbusch. The new solidarity of anxiety about the social problem would make modern men aware of the need for spiritual power from God.

A Theology for the Social Gospel represents a transformation of evangelical concepts of sin and salvation into "social" concepts congruent with "the Kingdom ideal." Rauschenbusch was concerned to "bring the God concept" in line with "our ethical ideals" in order that the new theology would be a vessel adequate to carry the new social spirit.

The stated norm of the theology of Rauschenbusch was the doctrine of "the Kingdom of God," the essential, unchanging Christian truth. "This doctrine is itself the social gospel."[17] He believed that the Social Gospel as a religious experience was creating new ideals. If, in turn, his theology could express and embody the ideals, they would empower and inspire the new social movement. In that sense Rauschenbusch hoped that the theology for the Social Gospel would initiate a new era in Christian history. "The social gospel is God's predestined agent to continue what the Reformation began."[18] As he believed that socialism was an inevitable historical development, so he liked to think that the Social Gospel was its religious counterpart.[19]

The Fatherhood of God and the Victorian Family

The objective of the ethical idealists was to direct men to the spiritual power contained in the Christian ideal. Compared to the activism of the evangelism campaigns of Josiah Strong, the program of an ethical idealist was the more intellectual effort to make men aware of their need for spiritual power and to direct them to the spiritual power of Christianity.

All the later Social Gospel men looked to a time in the future when the gospel would be clear, cloudless, and simple. This was a hope predicated on their belief in the progressive nature of eternal truth and the belief that knowledge of God and the experience of religion were normal activities of the human spirit. They believed that "the pure in heart" were even then coming out into the "pure light" of God. As Clarke put it, the reason of man was coming closer to grasping the whole of eternal truth as more false ideas went into "retirement." However, regardless of the completeness or simplicity of the Christian truth known to men in the future, faith would always demand the trust of a child in man's relation to the unseen.

The Fatherhood of God: God the Absent Father

As the only Social Gospel figure who thought the doctrine of God was a serious problem for modern theology, Clarke attempted to mediate between older "orthodox" and newer "liberal" ideas about God. Although his starting point was the new idea of God that came from the mind of Jesus, he considered it his prerogative to add to this idea, since modern man faced questions entirely foreign to anything known in the time of Jesus. Clarke stated the modern dilemma with clarity. Scientific materialism had given many people the impression that God was an unnecessary and outmoded idea. Clarke was convinced that beyond the question of the existence of God, the central issue raised for Christians by the evolutionary hypothesis was the question of how God was personally related to man.

Clarke thought that the relationship of God to the individual believer was not comprehensible unless the nature of God was conceptualized as both transcendent and immanent. Gladden and Abbott were so enmeshed in the scientific proofs and facts of their era that the God they described had no "unseen reality." Their God was evident in the order of nature and history and was knowable through images taken from human experience. They identified God so completely with the natural processes of the universe and human consciousness that they had no God who was transcendent to the world as they experienced and interpreted it.

While claiming the possibility of "new light" breaking forth in the theological explanation of religious life, Gladden and Abbott took the "new" concept of the Fatherhood of God to be the final revelation about the nature of God. Since images of God were drawn from human experience, they dismissed all earlier images of God the Judge, King, and Ruler as "figures and analogies" and concluded that their image of God the Father was an objective fact. They posited no mysterious God transcendent to human reason and experience because they believed that the eternal was immanent, that the correspondence of inner faculty to experience had given them this "fact" of human history. Men would not seek God if there was no reality that corresponded to the faculty of reverence. The knowledge that God was the Father was the culmination of the revolution of reason.[20] Facts, in both science and theology, were the products of the inductive method. Earlier images of God were discarded as products of an "incomplete induction." Graham Taylor's comment that his father was his theology meant that the content of his "theory" of God came from what he knew of his father. The same is true of all Social Gospel figures. The content of the revelation that God is the Father was consciously descriptive of their own cultural ideals, although it bore little resemblance to relationships with actual fathers.

As the Father, God was conceptualized as a procreator and as the ever-forgiving father of the prodigal son. God as the procreating Father was the immanent God of the evolutionary process in contrast to the God of deism, who created the world once and for all time and left man in the world at the mercy of those natural processes. The immanent God was the First Cause and the sustaining vitality in a world understood as evolving in an orderly, sequential way.[21] Only a God present and acting in all the forces of nature seemed adequate to denying the possibility that the processes of nature were a blind mechanism evolving the universe to no particular purpose. The comfort Washington Gladden found in nature and in nature poetry was related to the identification of God with the continuity seen in nature. For a Victorian with this cast of mind, a pastoral scene was a reminder that God was present and acting in the world.

God as the procreator of the natural world was also the procreating father of the moral order evident in history. To say that God was an objective fact of human history held a double meaning. First, Jesus Christ, as God in history, was the source of the revelation that God is the Father. Second, the revelation of God's Fatherhood was itself continually verified by the evolutionary process of the race. Genetic reproduction in a moral order that was progressing mirrored the orderly, purposeful, chronological sequence of the evolving natural order.

The parable of the prodigal son, used in Social Gospel thought to the exclusion of all other parables, made the point that God was a forgiving Father. When the father was the central figure in the parable, it was the patience, the pity, and the willingness of the father to forgive that were important. The God who pitied the weak never gave up hope of retrieving his lost children. Like the prodigal, the weak were those who lacked resistance to the temptations of the flesh—materialism, the irresponsible use of money, and immorality. "Pig," "mire," and "oozing mud" were images commonly used by Victorians to connote laxity, sensuousness, and gluttony. The "morally weak" had two reference points. The term usually referred to the weakness of the lower class, but it was also used to appeal to the moral weakness of those who belonged to middle-class congregations.

The "true Father" portrayed in the parable gives "the right view of God" in that the disobedience of the son did not cancel the love of the Father. A true father never disowned his children as unworthy and was always ready to welcome them home again. It was the unchangeableness of the God who forgives that was important. Although the individual was free to sin, as in the parable, if he did he dishonored his Father and destroyed himself. Even so, God was always loving and always ready to forgive any prodigal who came to him and sought to love and obey the Father.[22]

The God who pities most resembles the ever-virtuous and pure Victorian mother who pities her children when they fail. Her purity consisted of an almost divine perfection in truth and loveliness, which aroused the passion of reverence, or the pure spiritual love, of the child. Gladden described Dante's Beatrice in terms of a "vision of divine perfection." Dante's vision of Beatrice was spiritual because she was not present to tempt him in the flesh but inspired him to creativity out of his devotion to her "ideal."[23] Like Dante's Beatrice, the forgiving Father of Gladden was more inspiring in His absence than in His presence.

God the Father who creates and sustains and loves and forgives reflects the two halves of a Victorian marriage. He contained the male powers of procreation and sustenance and the female virtues of pure love.[24] The God who creates and sustains the universe was objectively visible to man in the same way that the Victorian father was visibly present to his children in the provision of material sustenance for his family. Like the Victorian father, the God who creates and sustains the universe is a powerful yet personally remote figure.

God the Father who loves and forgives his wayward children is like the pitying, forgiving, inspiring love of the Victorian mother. Christ the friend, or the God within, was associated with feminine, motherly characteristics. It was the loveliness of the suffering self-sacrifice of the God within who entered human history that inspired the reverence and moral purity of the Christian, just as the Victorian mother inspired her husband and children. The mother-father God of early Social Gospel thought was as personal as the Victorian mother and as remote as the Victorian father. Social Gospel rhetoric to the contrary, God the Father differed very little from the impersonal, absent God of deism.

Gladden and Abbott were not logicians, philosophers, or theologians. They were popular preachers and journalists. More than anything else, they reflected the need of a segment of the new middle class to be reassured that they were children of a personal God to whom they could go in prayer for comfort and power amid the hard work, moral demands, and stress of life. In an age when the very existence of God was called into question, when man seemed to be loose in a universe of fate and chance, God the Father held them personally responsible to him. Further, this God loved all his children so much that his capacity to forgive was limitless.

The loving-forgiving Father of Gladden and Abbott contained the evangelical individualism repugnant to Rauschenbusch. He had no inclination to meditate upon the nature of God. While he did not question the existence of God, he considered the conception of God to be an ever-changing "social product."[25] Recognizing that the concept of

God takes on the "properties of the group" holding the concept, his interest in God-concepts was purely pragmatic. Although his purposes were ethical, Rauschenbusch was interested in the manipulation of the symbolic power of the God-concept for the purpose of facilitating social progress.

In an essay written in 1893, Rauschenbusch outlined his understanding of the way in which men express their consciousness of God. First, men are limited in speaking of relations between man and God to terms "borrowed from the relations between man and man." "Our language has no other symbols, nor is our mind capable of conceiving anything else." Second, the terms, "when applied to God and our relations to him, are symbols and only symbols. They approximate the real thing but they are not identical with it." "There are good symbols and bad symbols. To get the best symbols for God's ways, we must go to the best men." "In general, we may say that expressions taken from family life are preferable to those taken from court life . . . because in the family justice and love are blended, and modify each other."[26]

In *A Theology for the Social Gospel* Rauschenbusch was consistent with his symbol theory. He dinstinguished first between "the real God" and the symbols men use to speak of God. The real God was the God who is the common basis of all life. In this sense the God of philosophy and of science is the same God. Beyond that, Rauschenbusch was interested primarily in the "democratizing power" of the symbol of God the Father.[27] God the Father, as revealed by Christ, was the God of democracy. He was the power, the energy, immanent in society and in man. This God hated iniquity and loved righteousness, but he was not responsible for inflicting punishment on whole groups of people. Instead, God the indwelling Father suffered with all men.[28]

For Rauschenbusch the fervor of group experiences of the "Spirit" was a social-psychological process. While he acknowledged that such experience was not "primarily a product of reflection," he interpreted the power of the Holy Spirit in groups to mean that the individual experience of a personal God had been socialized.[29] The "mystic experience" was a transaction among individuals in a group which could make them aware of the religious dimension of the spiritual power already present in life. For practical purposes, Rauschenbusch was interested only in the social uses of the God-concept.

Theology for the Social Gospel (1900-1924)

The only image of God used in common by Peabody, Rauschenbusch, and Clarke was that of "light." It was more potent and convincing than anything any of them wrote in connection with God as a Father. William Adams Brown, another liberal theologian, wrote of Clarke that if he had wished to define God "in a sentence, he would have said: 'God is light, and in him is no darkness at all.' "[30] All three men used light imagery in relation to religious insight to express their own grasping of unseen realities.

Peabody expressed the attraction of light imagery for the Victorian mind. It represented an inexhaustible source of life and light which could penetrate all the barriers to theological reflection erected by the age of scientific rationalism.

> Light is by its very nature comprehensive, transmissible, ubiquitous. There is not too much for one man's needs, and yet there is enough for all.... It is the same with the influence of Jesus Christ. Each new age or movement or personal desire seems to itself to receive with a peculiar fulness its special teaching, and it is quite true that a direct ray of communication and illumination enters that chamber of the mind which reaches no other point.[31]

The attraction of light imagery, used to express both the brightness that illuminates sight and insight, and the warmth of spiritual energy and power, is an index of the unspoken anxiety of the Victorian era—if not the personal sense of being "in the dark" in a cold and unfriendly world. A favorite hymn of many Victorian evangelicals, noted by several of the Social Gospel figures, was "Lead, Kindly Light," written by Cardinal John H. Newman in 1833.[32]

> Lead, kindly Light, amid th'encircling gloom.
> Lead Thou me on;
> The night is dark, and I am far from home;
> Lead Thou me on;
> Keep Thou my feet; I do not ask to see
> The distant scene—one step enough for me.

God as Father met the intellectual need to replace the threatening figure of the undemocratic judging God of "old light" Calvinism. God as Light met a personal need to dispel the darkness.

Clarke's faith, as some of his students knew, was more persuasive than his attempts to express his faith theologically. In his attempt to explicate the content of the revelation of Jesus that God is the Father of mankind, he failed to explain how God as the source of all existence could also be the Father who was personally related to individuals. In identifying moral conflict and the inner operations of moral sense with spiritual power, the moral conflict of an uneasy conscience was identified with the struggle between man and God. The entire dynamic of the spiritual life went into the struggle to achieve moral purity.

The Victorian hostility to self-examination and the double mind led the men of the Social Gospel to seek simple, childlike, unquestioning faith. But it was finally a faith in a God who seemed remote from the world of a Christian gentleman. Like the Victorian father who lived with his family but seemed rarely to interact with them, the God of the Social Gospel was absent from the dynamic processes of life itself.

The Brotherhood of Man: The Spirit of Jesus

The Calvinist doctrine of the nature of man was as dysfunctional for the Victorians as the Calvinist doctrine of God. The controversy concerning the nature of man surfaced as the emotionally charged question of the damnation of unsaved infants early in the nineteenth century. A major change in cultural attitudes toward children is signified by two concurrent developments of that period. The Second Awakening concept of conversion as a moral change made on the basis of a personal decision by the individual coincided with the publication of a large, widely circulated literature on homemaking and child-rearing.

As the implications of the doctrine of election concerning children became less believable, the child was increasingly viewed as the innocent and malleable raw material of Christian "manhood." The Unitarian revolt had contributed to a revised estimate of the capability of human nature; the Transcendentalist movement added to it the idealization of innocent, happy childhood. Older patterns of stern discipline of children by parents and teachers gave way to the kinder educational methods of a Bronson Alcott, who believed the goal of education to be educing the good from within the child.[33] Childhood became a symbol of unfettered and untroubled freedom. Gladden and Abbott thought of childhood as a time of innocent happiness and gaiety in the absence of the moral struggle and self-sacrifice that characterized youth and adulthood.[34]

Theology for the Social Gospel (1900-1924)

In place of the Calvinist assertion that the essential nature of man was self-interested egotism, the Social Gospel men claimed that increasingly the essence of human nature in civilization was the "social" capacity to seek the good of all men. Like many other Victorians, they used the biblical distinction between spirit and flesh to connote the spiritual and animal natures of man, the upper and lower capacity of each human being.

Although the Social Gospel men accepted the arguments of Darwin that some vices were inherited, they did not attribute inherited vices, such as a taste for alcohol, to the middle-class people of their congregations. The anthropology they preached and assumed in writing was the faculty psychology. The social context assumed was that of rearing children in families where altruism was natural because America was the most civilized nation in the world. Character formation involved the positive development of the faculties, especially moral sense, through emulation of parents in childhood and the struggle to overcome sexual temptation in youth and materialism in adulthood.

The Social Gospel men are sometimes characterized as "christological liberals," but their theology contains no consistent Christology. Instead the earlier men talked of "Jesus the friend" and the later men wrote incessantly of "the spirit of Jesus." In both cases, Jesus represented the personal aspect of the Godhead as the friend who inspired man in the lonely struggle against temptation and vice. Although the later men used "the spirit of Jesus" in both an individual and a social sense, when they used it in relation to individual faith they meant the mind of Jesus.

Social Gospel optimism about social change was related to their belief in the relative innocence of children and in the spiritual power of the images of God present in all people. Although they recognized the "kicking egotism" of the behavior of young children, with proper socialization and education chances of facilitating the potential of each child for moral purity and cooperative social behavior were high.

Character development meant the accumulation of conscious, willful choices to do good or evil made by the individual. All people chose their own destiny. Every life was a march from original innocence through temptation to actual virtue or vice. The content of sin, understood as egotism, was that of the moral vices associated with animalism and "bestiality." In the case of a sin which did not immediately and obviously punish the sinner, Gladden held that the sin would eventually become apparent in the suffering of its victims. Spiritual death caused by the quieter forms of egotism bred resentment, antagonism, envy, strife, and malevolence in others.[35] Either way, the result of sin was apparent in the suffering brought upon the self or others.

Sin and salvation meant the contrast between animalism and Christian character. "Character," "personality," "life," and "manhood" were all used as references to salvation, meaning that the image of God within had triumphed over the temptations of the lower, animalistic aspect of human nature. Christian character denoted the control of the animal propensity by reason and choice.

Rauschenbusch believed that some sin was inevitable but that the successful struggle against temptation was necessary to character development. But temptation must not be so great as to overwhelm. His desire to change society was related to his conviction that people do not want to do evil, but that "in a given situation they have to, if they want to survive and prosper, and the sum of these crooked actions gives an evil turn to their life."[36] The social nature of sin, as Rauschenbusch understood it, was related to the effect of social circumstances on the character formation of the individual. Individual conflict to overcome temptation to vice was necessary, but social sin caused unnecessary suffering. His goal for the Social Gospel was to create public guilt about social sin, so that the social situation would be ameliorated to provide an equal opportunity for all people to develop as the individuals God meant them to be.

The Social Gospel men understood temptation as the lure of the flesh against the spirit. The inevitability of some sin, though not caused by God, was a fortunate fall because it was the source of character development. The high tide of the moral struggle occurred at adolescence with the awakening of sexuality. An adolescent conversion experience marked the awareness of temptation and consciousness of the need for spiritual power to overcome temptation.[37] Rauschenbusch, especially, valued a clearly marked conversion experience which yielded a higher view of human worth and enhanced the "social instincts" normal to human nature.

Part of the reason for Social Gospel attention to the potential of young men was the belief that spiritual vitality was greater at the time of life when temptation was greatest. Peabody believed that social service for young men was the modern social form of what had been only an individual conversion experience earlier in the nineteenth century. Rauschenbusch saw social service as the constructive application of a conversion experience. Either way, a religious experience was related to moral growth. The young were the most vulnerable to the pull of the sexual passions, but also potentially the most vital personalities. Youth was the time of high idealism not yet discouraged by "worldly" experience. Rauschenbusch summed up sin and salvation in terms of reinforcement of the spirit.

> Psychology recognizes that the higher desires are usually sluggish and faint, while the animal appetites are strong and clamorous. Our will tires easily and readily yields to social pressure. In many individuals the raw material of character is terribly flawed by inheritance. So the young, with a maximum of desire and a minimum of self-restraint, slip into folly, and the aging backslide into shame. Human nature needs a strong reinforcement to rouse it from its inherited lethargy and put it on the toilsome upward track. It needs redemption, emancipation from slavery, a breaking of bonds.[38]

The essence of sin as related to the "animal appetites," either as insatiable materialism or as unbridled sexual appetites, is a definition applicable primarily to men. If women were as naturally virtuous and self-sacrificing as Victorians believed, they were less tempted and less spiritually developed than men who successfully overcome temptation. Since women did not have to struggle to overcome sexual temptations, their knowledge of suffering came in the birth process. Childbirth and travail reveal the realities of life to a woman more than sympathetic observation.[39] Not only was the female the source of male moral temptation and the occasion of his development, but theoretically her character, though pure, was virtually static.

The spiritual power of salvation came through the God who enthroned himself in the soul to enable a man to "be himself . . . through the normal use of the power . . . available to him."

> And when temptations come, urging the man to destroy the balance of his nature, to put pleasure first, to trample down his fellows, to be ambitious for himself alone, to forget God, to enthrone the brute and not the soul, with these also he may hear the voice of God, warning him not thus to defeat his own being, and bidding him rise upon this opportunity of evil to a new assertion, encouraging and strengthening of his better part.[40]

Although salvation meant overcoming temptation, it did not mean freedom from suffering. Until the kingdom was established, men would continue to suffer the self-punishing results of their own sins as well as the social ramifications of the sins of others.

Jesus Christ, spiritually present to man through his biography, was a friend with whom the faithful could identify. Gladden and Abbott considered the personality of Christ to be the unique aspect of Christianity. As Jesus Christ, God entered history "so we might have One round whom we might put our arms, before whom we might bow in reverence, to whom we might give our highest, supremest, tenderest love."[41]

In his earliest book of sermons, *Being a Christian,* Gladden talked of union with Christ as identifying with Christ in "thought and wishes and purposes." He understood the power of habitual forms of thinking and doing to be the way in which human nature identifies with Christ. Christ, the ideal life, who is "wiser and stronger and more sympathizing than any human being can be," sets the pattern for the follower. Eventually the follower, by habitually doing the virtuous deed, finds himself identified with the mind, the will, and the work of Christ.[42]

Christ was not simply an historical revelation of the past. The immanent God continued to reveal himself through natural law and as the inner power of the moral evolution of mankind. As the power of inspiration in human identification with the life and mind of Christ, the immanent God was also the Christ within. Therefore Jesus Christ was more than the manifestation of God in and throughout history; he was God immanent in the soul of man. Abbott habitually defined religion as "the life of God in the soul of man."[43]

Union with Christ meant identification with the life and mind of Christ. Incarnation, the only doctrine discussed at length by the earlier figures, had two dimensions: individual and historical. Because Christ revealed the true nature of man in relation to God the Father, he was the "type" of the full humanity of the species. Men identified with the life of Jesus because he was the ideal type of what God intended man to be. As a historical fact, he also represented the beginning of human history and of progress in civilization. After his lifetime, Christian manhood meant a "perpetual incarnation" moving mankind toward its ultimate end.

The incarnation was the coming of God to man and the dwelling of

God in man. Christ was the door through which man entered God and God entered man. He demonstrated that all men are sons of God and that the law of his nature was the law of human nature. His life of suffering and sacrificing made it clear that God labors, struggles, and suffers with man.[44] To men who accepted the proposition that man was descended from some dark animal past, the incarnation of God in history was very good news. To men who wanted to think and do the good, the reality of Christ the friend was an important element in the lonely struggle against the temptations of the flesh.

For the ethical idealists, the "spirit of Jesus" meant the ideal of self-sacrificing love necessary to energize the social nature of man. The life events of the man Jesus were less important to them than what the "spirit" or mind of Jesus was able to convey about the nature of God. It was the revelation of the Fatherhood of God, and the moral character of the Father, rather than the life of Jesus, that was a standard worth emulating. The most important aspect of the "spirit" of the Son was that of unbroken "filial" devotion to the Father. All the later figures agreed that "the character of the God a man worships reacts on the man."[45]

The atonement was the central doctrine of later Social Gospel thought because death on a cross was an inspiration and a comfort to men who viewed life as duty, suffering, and self-sacrifice. The "spirit of Jesus" revealed that the power of the "Kingdom of Evil" had been overcome in the life of self-sacrificing love and could be overcome by emulating the single-minded devotion of Jesus to his earthly vocation.

Rauschenbusch was anxious to dispel the older belief that sin was a transaction between the individual and God. Sins were committed against other people, not against God. His term "the solidarity of sin" meant that society is corrupted by human sin because each sinful act automatically affects other men. He interpreted atonement to mean that Christ bore the guilt of the race, not simply the guilt of the individual. That the death of Jesus could atone for the "guilt of the race" meant that his self-sacrifice was capable of inspiring men in groups to oppose and reorder the Kingdom of Evil, a social order built on force and oppression instead of love and cooperation. The knowledge that Christ had suffered for his life of love was an incentive to repentance for the unbeliever and a comfort to the suffering believer.[46]

The Fatherhood of God and the Victorian Family

In discussing the atonement, Rauschenbusch considered the meaning for men of death on a cross. The death of the man Jesus on the cross exemplified the perfect self-sacrifice and dedication to vocation possible for all men. As such, it completed his personality. Like all men, he learned through his suffering. There was no conflict in his devotion to duty. On the cross "his head was up and he was in command of the situation."[47]

The atonement was also evidence that Jesus' death changed the God-consciousness of mankind. As evidence of God's self-sacrificing love for all men, the cross told men that God was reconciled to them. This act was the basis for the Christian view of God as a father, rather than the Jewish view of the judging Jehovah. Above all, Rauschenbusch valued the atonement as a symbol because it had a more powerful effect on the minds of men than just another good life.[48]

Rauschenbusch speculated that the God in Christ evolves in his relationship to men, just as the ideas of men about God also change and evolve. The final result of the death of an innocent man is that it symbolized a new relationship between God and mankind. The new concept of "co-operative unity of will between God and humanity" was available to the Christian, but it was a message of universal importance.[49]

The brotherhood of all men meant that all men were potential children of God. The responsibility of the child to the Father was twofold. First, it meant personal purity, for doing the Father's will meant attaining the manhood that God intended. That would simultaneously fulfill the law of the nature of man and the first half of the great commandment —to love God. Second, it meant to love the neighbor. To love the Father of mankind was to love all his children. The Social Gospel men did not refer to men in terms of believers and unbelievers, the faithful or the unfaithful. They thought in terms of "children of God" and "the brotherhood of all men."

Such a position assumed that humanity was capable of evolving toward perfection. Rauschenbusch noted that the kingdom of God established on earth would not abolish all sin and pride. The perfection envisioned was that of a world which would have become the home of the "love of God." The "spirit of Jesus" was an ideal capable of inspiring the collective conscience through the continuing evolution of the human spirit.

150

The Kingdom of God: Innocent
Children of God

The essential, unchanging truth of the kingdom ideal as Walter Rauschenbusch understood it was that if all men were like Jesus then society would be characterized by cooperation rather than competition, by pure love rather than self-seeking egotism. Faith meant the development of Christian character as the necessary condition for social progress.

> The saint of the future will need not only a theocentric mysticism which enables him to realize God, but an anthropocentric mysticism which enables him to realize his fellow-men in God. The more we approach pure Christianity, the more will the Christian signify a man who loves mankind with a religious passion and excludes none. The feeling which Jesus had when he said, "I am the hungry, the naked, the lonely," will be the emotional consciousness of all holy men in the coming days. The sense of solidarity is one of the distinctive marks of the true followers of Jesus.[50]

The hope to establish the kingdom of God on earth was the dream of a conflict-free society where all citizens would voluntarily cooperate for the good of the nation. The essential nurturing process rested with the family, which in turn depended on the purity and stability of marriage. The power of the spirit in society was very nearly identified with the socializing function of the family. The kingdom of God on earth would mean that every citizen emulated the moral standards and relational patterns of the Victorian family. Until the ideal was actualized, the conversion and nurturing powers of the church would be needed to make the individual conscious of the power of the indwelling spirit.

The problem of the absent Father had been solved by the earlier Social Gospel men by identifying personally with Jesus "the friend." They had stressed the doctrine of the incarnation because that meant God was personally present and, as Jesus of Nazareth, had lived in history. The Jesus who revealed a new "type" of humanity was a person as well as an ideal.

For the second-generation men, the advent of Jesus demonstrated that the man-God relationship had the potential dimension of a perfect "filial relationship" between men. The "spirit of Jesus" was a social principle because Jesus represented the general principles of love and brotherhood among all men which were essential to democracy and social order.[51] For them, the atonement, and not the incarnation, was the central "fact" of the life of Christ because it symbolized the self-sacrificing love necessary to human brotherhood.

For the individual, the importance of Christ's death on the cross lay in His exemplary and singular sense of duty and obedience. Christ experienced no anger or conflict about his own life circumstances. His "unbroken God-consciousness" meant that he was free from internal conflict and single-minded in his devotion to duty. It was this unbroken sense of duty that pulled men up to the high calling of Christ. This quality of power through "assimilation to the mind of Christ" was the perfect fruit of Christian character. Assimilation to the "mind of Christ" was a power capable of conquering the circumstances of life by moving, resisting, or overcoming obstacles. Sometimes it meant transcending circumstances.

Christian character was a demonstration of faith, the result of "conquest by conflict." Good character resulted from habitually choosing and doing the good. Rauschenbusch described religious faith as the ability to defer all minor aims to the long outlook. For all the Social Gospel men, faith was an attitude and an act of individuals, but it also had a social dimension. Faith—meaning the development of Christian character—was the necessary condition for social progress.

Every book Rauschenbusch wrote was for the purpose of stimulating high ideals and social faith in the reader. His hope for a Christianized humanity was a faith statement from a man who feared the possibility of oblivion, both individual and social. His apparent optimism was sometimes tempered by his juxtaposition of the ideal against the present situation. *A Theology for the Social Gospel,* a statement of what is possible for faith, ends with a passionate account of the social prophet as "profoundly lonely and homeless":

> The prophet is always more or less cast out by society and profoundly lonely and homeless; consequently he reaches out for companionship, for a tribal solidarity of his own, and a chieftainship of the spirit to which he can give his loyalty and from which he can gather strength. Then it is his rightful comfort to remember that Jesus has suffered before him.[52]

When Rauschenbusch wrote of faith he related it primarily to conquering evil in society. A chapter of *Christianizing the Social Order* was devoted to isolating one element in the Christian faith "which will inspire the religious minds of our Christian world in the regeneration of society." In the chapter, "Wanted: A Faith for a Task," he criticized the standard evangelical forms of giving a social application to individual faith. Giving the cup of cold water, encouraging stewardship, and appeals to the golden rule as a standard of daily conduct were insufficient methods for social change. Instead, the kingdom ideal of social regeneration was an adequate inspiration for religious faith.[53] He assumed that engaging in the work of social reform would evoke a faith adequate to the task.

For Rauschenbusch a great faith meant a man driven by the power of self-sacrificing love. He wrote more often of love than of faith. In the most general sense he saw love as the social instinct, the basis of all solidarity and fellowship. In that sense, love was the society-making impulse as well as the source of fellow-feeling, family love, patriotism, camaraderie, and human play. Such love was natural to human beings.

In a more specific sense, for the Christian, love to God could be expressed only by love to man. The natural social instinct of love was enhanced under the "religious influence." The special power added by Christian love to the natural society-making impulse was the self-sacrificing love necessary to the society where love, peacemaking, and social sympathy could prevail. To conceive of love only as personal relations between two individuals was inadequate for Rauschenbusch. He conceived of the social power of love radiating from the sense of social solidarity to a national consciousness. In the future, love would extend to an international and interracial consciousness that would represent a new historical stage in the progress of civilization. Essentially, the social nature of man meant the power of fellow-feeling and the ability to defer gratification on behalf of the well-being of the other. Because Rauschenbusch assumed that groups had the same characteristics as individuals, he concluded that the same extension of selfless love was possible for nations as well as for individuals.[54]

The love present in the home depended on both sexual passion and parental love for group cohesiveness. Rauschenbusch did not deny the power of the erotic quality of sexual love. The sexual instinct was necessary to family cohesiveness, but marriage was the only positive channel for the expression of the erotic impulse. The love permeating society and creating fellow-feeling was not the blind impulse of sexual attraction. All love, except married love, was a form of fellow-feeling without the "taint of sexual suggestiveness."[55]

> The fundamental virtue of the ethics of Jesus was love, because love is the society-making quality. Human life originates in love. It is love that holds together the basal human organization, the family. The physical expression of all love and friendship is the desire to get together and be together. Love creates fellowship. In the measure in which love increases in any social organism, it will hold together without coercion. If physical coercion is constantly necessary, it is proof that the social organization has not evoked the power of human affection and fraternity.[56]

Rauschenbusch's hope for social solidarity and personal friendship rested on the belief that love and mutuality are natural in a civilized society.

Christian love, as the Social Gospel men envisioned it, had "no taint of sexual suggestiveness." The individual and social objectives of the Social Gospel represented an expectation of a continual growth of spiritual power over against the temptations of the flesh. Rauschenbusch separated the "sex passion" of marriage from the self-sacrificing love of parents because they were related to two different faculties: amativeness and philoprogenitiveness.

The connection between faith and male vocation was related to the belief that sexual temptation was best sublimated by hard work. Peabody went so far as to say that it was "better to be a dissatisfied man, than a satisfied pig."[57] The reference was sexual. Throughout the Victorian period, the pig was equated with dirty, pushy, squealing intemperance. Over against this horror of the sexual instinct run wild, duty-doing theoretically would produce a Christian character untroubled by double-mindedness, a person who stood firm against the circumstances of life with poise, simplicity, and peace.

The ethical idealists assumed that all men had some assigned vocation to contribute to the good of the social whole. Like Christ's vocation, all work was worth doing because it was God's will; that is, it contributed to personal development and the social good. The new social order envisioned was one in which every man had a place and knew what it was. All work would be meaningful as a part of the social whole, and no man would feel himself to be a victim of circumstances. Living in devotion to the vocational ideal, no man would have to feel powerless or useless. The ideal manhood represented by the "spirit of Jesus" required self-sacrifice. It offered, in return, a sense of purpose.

Although self-sacrificing love was learned most naturally at the breast of a mother, not all people had learned altruism at home as children. This meant that the church had two functions: conversion and nurture. It provided moral inspiration and encouragement to members. For the unchurched, conversion—meaning a change in mental attitude—would be necessary. Gladden explained the nature of the mental conversion that was connoted by the Social Gospel desire to assimilate all people to "the spirit of Jesus." This conversion of attitude was most normally signified by becoming a church member.

> They must highly resolve that henceforth the law of the mind, and not the law of the members, shall rule in their lives, that by God's grace they will become the men and women they ought to be. They went down by surrendering, they must go up by fighting. They must call on Him who has kindled this desire in their hearts to help them in realizing it. And they must put themselves into an environment that will feed and stimulate the better elements of their lives instead of the baser ones.[58]

The changed attitude associated with salvation could occur through the personal influence of a good character in any setting. Since God was the "indweller," all that was required for a conversion was to make the non-Christian aware of the spiritual power already available. Thus Rauschenbusch conceived group awareness of the social problem as a means to convert men to Christian manhood. The lifting power of personality was contrasted in Social Gospel thought to the ineffective evangelical methods of charity and church programs designed to "push up" the poor. Institutional church programs and financial donations did not "change the heart" of the recipient. The poor and immoral would be drawn up to higher ideals by emulating the vital force of good men and women.

"The spirit," a pervasive and essential power available to all men, was "democratized" by the Social Gospel men. "The spirit" was the vital energy of society, the church, and the individual, and in the future it would be embodied in all aspects of society. For the present, any event that served to reinforce social cooperation was attributed to the power of "the spirit." The spiritual power available to all people and all institutions seemed to have no limits. Like the "inexhaustible light" of the "spirit of Jesus," it was all things to all people. From this point of view, the only reason the kingdom of God had not yet come was that all people had not yet become aware of the "the spirit" within. Therefore, for the present, the task of the church was to promote good morals and proclaim the high ideals of the coming kingdom.

For the ethical idealists, the church was not to be confused with the kingdom of God on earth. It was only the temporary vehicle through which spiritual power would flow out into society. Ideally, in a spiritually infused society spiritual power would be disseminated through the psychosocial influence of groups serving the cause of social justice. When Christianity was embodied in society, the church would be obsolete. For the present, the later Social Gospel men viewed the church as a "spiritual power house" providing a source of "power and light" for society. That meant that the church should continue to nourish "the filial reverence and family solidarity . . . written deep into human nature."[59]

While the church was not to be confused with the kingdom of God, the family was virtually identified with the kingdom. The Victorian family and the standards of civilized morality provided the content for the kingdom of God. "The Kingdom of God arrives whenever and wherever the will of God is done by the will of man."[60] The will of God meant the moral code of mutual service and cooperation assumed to be present in the family. The Victorian family was the kingdom of God in microcosm.

The description of faith as childlike trust and innocence was the hope of Victorians nearly overwhelmed by "the spirit of the age." In the "good" society they hoped for, men would be teachable just as children were teachable. Men would adapt themselves to work with a good attitude rather than bitterness. Self-sacrifice would mean a world of unselfish mutual helpers capable of "sweet co-ordination" with superiors. In the future men would need the childlike qualities of simplicity and humility to function in the bureaucratic atmosphere of the early twentieth century.

The Social Gospel vision of the leadership potential of virile Christian manhood was a hope that the burgeoning bureaucracy would be guided by men both manly and moral. The portrait of the Christian gentleman as a virile and commanding, but cooperative, man was an ideal for leaders capable of being the soul of a Christianized nation. It would take high ideals and moral purity to handle vocational success without succumbing to an insatiable lust for personal power. The kingdom of God would come empowered by the quiet, orderly, but commanding presence of leaders with moral integrity, perseverance, and spiritual power.

The childlike qualities involved in the hope for the kingdom of God were the qualities of a quiet conscience. The faith of the Social Gospel was a desire for the unquestioned certainty of a God-consciousness unbroken by sin and untroubled by guilt. It was the hope that the strenuous morality demanded by the Victorian family ideal would result in peace of mind. The hope of holding unbroken fellowship with the Father by avoiding sin is a poignant reminder of the pressured atmosphere in which Victorian men lived. The hope for the establishment of the kingdom ideal on earth must be interpreted as the very human longing for stability and security. It was the hope of troubled men for a society in which life would be ordered and dependable. It was the impossible dream of a child that he will never have to grow up and go away from home.

The issue of death and immortality —the hope for the reward of heaven—was difficult for the Social Gospel men. The hope of heaven was the reward for moral purity in the evangelical conversionist psychology. But the antimetaphysical stance of the Spencerian materialist assumptions used by the men of the Social Gospel ruled out speculations about the "unseen." Although Rauschenbusch refused to speculate on the nature of God, he justified a chapter on eschatology in the *Theology* as "simply the play of personal fancy about a fascinating subject."[61]

Despite the honest admission that nothing "scientific" could be known about the afterlife, all the Social Gospel men believed that immortality meant the continuing development of the soul after death. The continuing upward spiral of development characteristic of the Social Gospel concept of salvation was present in their hope of heaven. Heaven represented the perfection of Victorian ideals—unlimited upward development and continuity, rather than change, decay, and discomfort. Gladden imagined that heaven had direct continuity with life. Since the kingdom of God is within, those with a Christian character must continue in some altered form. The body might be dispensable in the afterlife, but the spirit must go on. Rauschenbusch hoped that in the world to come, those who were underdeveloped personalities in life would then be able to develop their "normal" human potential.[62]

Clarke used the image of childhood potential for spiritual growth as a figure for life as the childhood of the race. One of his poems captures the essence of Social Gospel thought concerning the childlike innocence of mankind, life as spiritual growth, and the afterlife as continuing development. It is the product of a period in which belief in life after death was no longer taken for granted and the meaning of life itself was no longer certain.

> Gone they tell me is youth,
> Gone is the strength of my life;
> Nothing remains but decline.
> Nothing but age and decay.
>
> Not so: I am God's little child,
> Only beginning to live.
> Coming the days of my prime,
> Coming the vision of God,
> Coming my bloom and my power.[63]

The intuitionist epistemology and evolutionary assumptions in Social Gospel theology distinguish it from the Ritschlian theology to which it was likened. Rauschenbusch conceived a new task for theology in expecting *A Theology for the Social Gospel* to inspire the regeneration of the social order. While the task of theology has always been to adjust the Christian method to the spirit of the times, Rauschenbusch displayed little inclination to construct his "new" theology in dialogue with either biblical or systematic theologians of the past. The result was a highly selective, and sometimes unorthodox, interpretation of doctrine and the Bible. Although Ritschl, Schleiermacher, and Hegel believed in some kinds of progress in history, they did not interpret progress to mean that new knowledge and new truth had superseded the wisdom of the Christian biblical and theological tradition.

7

The Paradoxes of
the Social Gospel Movement

The double focus of the Social Gospel ellipse was an equal concern for individual morality and social morality. It does, however, raise puzzling paradoxes about the social and religious thought of the movement leaders. There was a contradiction between the ideals and the experience of Victorian men, both at home and at work. The concept of the Fatherhood of God was an ideal of perfect parents offered to Victorians who believed that the family was already Christianized. The social theory of the Social Gospel sounds like social determinism with an ethic of autonomous individualism. The attitudes of the Social Gospel men concerning the response of a church member to the poor is curiously similar to the attitudes of conservative Social Darwinists.

The Social Gospel Men and the
Fatherhood of God

From 1830 on, early Victorians like Lyman Beecher were aware of changing social patterns caused by urbanization. One major component of the change was increased economic opportunity and a higher standard of living for the middle class moving into urban areas. That movement resulted in a new autonomy for the individual and considerable anxiety about the stability of the family unit as government, churches, and schools acquired new functions that had once been family functions. In particular, many fathers no longer disciplined children, instructed sons in farming or a trade, or led in family devotions at home.

As the new democracy took shape, the social situation demanded individuals who were independent and capable of self-discipline. With the abolition movement and the Civil War, thoughtful people in the areas of the North most affected by urbanization came to abhor any dependent relationship. The premium on moral autonomy, understood as independence and self-government, was expressed in abolitionist literature concerning master and slave relationships. The theme reverberated throughout the nineteenth century wherever personal independence was limited. It is found with reference to the paternalism of the "old" theology, in the family, in the state, in labor conflicts, in white slavery, in economic theory. The term "self-made man" implied rejection of any external force perceived as paternalistic interference with individual autonomy and moral development. The Northern victory over the slave master provided irrefutable evidence that civilized progress meant freedom from paternalism.

In democratic America, being a father and being a son was not easy. In an earlier day the father had been a family disciplinarian. Charles Beecher, the youngest son of Lyman Beecher, commented that his father kept at least one child at home as long as possible so he would have someone to "love and govern." Charles envied the dog who took his place when he left home; the dog experienced more forgiveness than he had.[1]

In colonial New England, fathers had maintained some control over sons as long as there was property to be divided. Near the end of the eighteenth century, as available land disappeared, the frontier movement began.[2] Fathers held little leverage over their sons as a result. By the Civil War era there was nothing of substance that an American father could pass on to his son in a country without nobility, titles, or inheritable property. Instead, fathers tried to give sons educational opportunities and the will to succeed where they had failed.

The economic self-image of the self-made man who succeeded in the fierce competition generated by a laissez-faire economy was related to the inability of early Victorian fathers to aid their children economically. The development of patterns of upward mobility produced a situation in which sons were encouraged to surpass their fathers. In economic terms, the self-made man was a fatherless man.[3] Insofar as the economic vocabulary of the Victorians had sexual implications, there are sexual overtones in the term *self-made man*.[4] The Victorian propensity for adoration of virtuous womanhood suggests the discomfort of sons with the generativity of their own fathers.

During the early Victorian period, when functions once shared by parents shifted to mothers, there was a period when fathers were unusually autocratic toward their children. The absolute rejection of any kind of authoritarianism in the imagery connoted by God the Father suggests that many middle-class men, like the men of the Social Gospel, had experienced fathers who seemed severe, threatening to children, or unforgiving to youth. The insistence on the unbreakable bond of father love in the God imagery suggests a need for some Father who loves and forgives all the sins of the sons.

For moral men born in the early Victorian period, there was the conflict of ambivalence about the father and a need to establish a self-image of moral purity. The sexual ethos of the family ideal set limits on morality in such a way that mothers were highly respected while fathers were nearly superfluous. With the exception of life itself, the mid-Victorian male was very nearly a self-made man. The Social Gospel men were such men.

The difficulty with the Victorian family ideal was that it was unrewarding for men. Work in the new commercial and industrial atmosphere was often not personally rewarding to a man. If he was a moral man, who worked hard and sought success out of devotion to his family, the female dominated domestic atmosphere was not rewarding either.[5] Despite an unrewarding vocational and domestic situation, a man might feel virtuous for doing his duty, but not necessarily masculine.

The western frontier had demanded of a man physical strength and personal valor. Suburban life provided no opportunities for a man to brave the natural elements. A woman could still establish her courage in childbirth. Short of war, where did a man have an opportunity to prove himself? The Victorian ideal of moral manhood, vocational success, and the progress of civilization by continence narrowed the options for masculinity to the aggressive, exploitive behavior of a bully or the self-sacrificing altruism of a "saint."

The new world-view introduced after the Civil War in the form of Social Darwinism further complicated the social changes that had already placed masculine identity in a precarious position. To men whose claim to a place in the world was already insecure, Social Darwinism added the possibility of excusing moral or vocational failure as circumstances beyond human control. To suggest that man might stand helpless before the forces of evolution was unpleasantly demeaning of human potential in general. But it could also be used to rationalize personal moral failure. That was exactly what the men of the Social Gospel were working against, for the Social Gospel was a masculine form of evangelical "new light" Christianity. The Social Gospel provided an image of moral heroism for men who participated in and sought to conquer the forces of adversity present in the world. The "strenuous life" of the moral hero was a prophetic challenge to cultural acceptance of immorality and materialism as evidence of masculine success.

The early Social Gospel figures held moral men responsible to a God who was a loving and forgiving Father. Their antipaternalistic Father was not a tyrant, a slave master, or an autocrat. He neither judged nor condemned. He was not a God of justice who would eventually punish oppressors because the universe was ordered to punish vice and reward virtue. He was a mother-father God who gently encouraged moral purity and hoped for the good of all mankind.

The Fatherhood of God was the most common image for God used by all religious groups in the Victorian period. Not all of them shared the antipaternalistic position of the Social Gospel. The rhetoric of labor leaders between 1860 and 1900 reflected the responsiveness of the worker class to fatherhood-brotherhood imagery. Although labor leaders used the fatherhood imagery as Strong had used it—to reinforce the hope of universal brotherhood—the content was different. Unlike Social Gospel reliance on the New Testament for the concept of a loving-forgiving Father, labor leaders drew on the Old Testament drama of the God of vengeance who punished oppressors. This was the other side of the story of the unjust slave master. The God of the Old Testament punished Pharaoh for keeping the people of Egypt in slavery. To American labor leaders, God the Father was the God of justice. They looked to the power contained in the laws and institutions of the American democracy for the salvation of the oppressed worker and the achievement of universal brotherhood.[6]

The God of the early Social Gospel was the beneficent Father of a prospering but anxious new middle class. The attributes of the fatherhood associated with God were the Victorian ideals of the perfect parent. Biographically, Gladden and Abbott were fatherless sons.[7] Since neither man was reared by his own parents, the ideals they set forth on "the Fatherhood of God" are especially poignant.

The early Social Gospel figures evoked a response among the middle-class public because they responded to the existential situation in powerfully appealing male family imagery. Their religious thought alleviated the anxiety of the self-made man by placing the demand for moral autonomy within the context of a natural and social world created by a loving Father for the benefit of struggling mankind. They disarmed the experience of hostility and competition among men with the hope that all men would soon become the loving brothers intended by their common Father. The Social Gospel men dispelled doubts about democracy and freedom by identifying the American nation with the kingdom of God on earth. Although fatherhood-brotherhood imagery appealed to both the worker class and the middle class, the content of the images was different because it was related to two entirely different sets of life circumstances. The common element in both was the importance of the family in the American experience.

God the Father was the father of the lower class and the middle class. Both classes lacked fathers so economically stable that they could assist their sons in "moving up." The middle class as a group was moving up. They experienced a standard of living entirely different from that of their fathers and grandfathers. The variety of home furnishings available in Victorian America was in striking contrast to the humble homogeneity in appearance of older New England village homes. The process of achieving success in the man-made world created a crisis of consciousness for the conscientious. The middle-class attraction to a God who was forgiving as well as loving is a curious contradiction to the Victorian sense of optimism and self-assurance.

What had they done to merit the need for forgiveness? In addition to genuine sins of materialism and immorality, "moving up" in America—social and economic evolution—involved the sons in going beyond the fathers. The family ideal and the faculty psychology of Social Gospel thought made it possible to be both a moral man and a success in the world of men. The forgiving God of the Social Gospel was the creation of men uncomfortable with their own success. The Social Gospel was preached by men of good intentions who genuinely wanted to include all men in their own success. But success, as they defined it, was costly. To be both a strong man and a saint was almost impossible.

Stated in the categories of historical progress and universal salvation, the ideal of unlimited social and moral progress seemed possible. The ability to interpret social change as progress, and social disorder as contributing to progress, without ignoring the plight of the unsuccessful made the early Social Gospel a gospel of both strong man and saint. It demanded both personal morality and attention to the social situation. It was this-worldly Christianity for men of this world.

The early Social Gospel rationalized middle-class discomfort with success in an era when material success suggested possible immorality. In an age of public adulation of the brilliance of the captain of industry, there was present in Social Gospel thought the nagging suspicion that excessive wealth might not denote the natural ability of the fittest men. The Social Gospel advocated temperance in every aspect of life, including the accumulation and use of wealth. It provided social objectives for individual and national morality by proclaiming the manifest destiny of America. It made family stability and loyalty absolutely essential to individual moral development and to the nation, at a time when social change made family solidarity increasingly difficult.

Faced with a different social situation in 1900, the later figures retained the content of the fatherhood image but shifted the emphasis in the father-son relationship to the responsibility of the son. Peabody and Rauschenbusch were also fatherless sons, in the sense of having fathers unworthy of emulation.[8] They wrote almost exclusively of Jesus—the son. The goodness of God was less a problem to them than the goodness of men. The earlier alienation of fathers and sons created by the social and economic revolution was giving way to what they viewed as a lack of "filial piety." A father who could lavish his sons with the benefits of economic security was as problematic for the self-made man model of character development as the guilt created in the successful son had been. With the establishment of new patterns of inherited wealth, Social Gospel sensitivity to the perils of materialism became more overt.

A man's vocation and his family devotion were the related means of his spiritual development and the marks of his obedience to God. The earlier linkage of hard work, thrift, and virtue was ingrained in the middle-class consciousness by 1900. The fear of moral degeneracy among the sons of the established and pampered middle class resulted in a renewed emphasis on the manly duties of devotion to family and vocation. The "Christian gentleman" of 1900 was a model of manhood demanding strenuous habits of continuing self-sacrifice.

Like the ideals of the Victorian family, the ideals represented by the God-concept and by the hope for the brotherhood of all men were meant to inspire moral purity and social cooperation in men. The "Christian gentleman" of the Social Gospel was a masculine religious orientation designed to assert the inspirational power of a good man in the worldly sphere of work, just as a good woman was an inspiration in the domestic sphere.

Social Gospel thought incorporated the Victorian admiration for female purity into a theology written by, for, and to men. The Social Gospel description of conversion as related to moral self-discipline and worldly vocation is oriented almost entirely to the world of the Victorian male. Social Gospel emphasis on public service, church vocations, and statesmanship as suitable goals for virile young men provided careers that included moral purity and social service in the most public sense. The active orientation to social problems in the Social Gospel was a way of making church leaders feel more "worldly." This was especially true if the middle-class church was, as James implied, in danger of degenerating to the level of a glorified ice-cream social. Under those circumstances both the theology and the objectives of the Social Gospel men were predominantly masculine in nature.

During the period in American industrial development when men felt themselves to be lacking the virility of their ancestors, a variety of manhood models developed. After the Civil War it was not economically viable to sire a dozen children, but a man could display sexual and economic success by keeping a mistress or frequenting brothels. The moral code of the Victorian gentleman required only private virtue—that he be good to his wife and children. The code of the Christian gentleman demanded temperance with reference to matters both spiritual and material, and morality in both public and private spheres.

Upper-class Victorians displayed economic success through the notoriously wasteful conspicuous consumption of the Gilded Age. Against the strong tides of the ambitions of the Victorian middle class to move up economically, the Social Gospel delivered the prophetic demand for social consciousness and responsibility. The moral heroism of the knight-errant was as strenuous a demand as any of the alternatives offered to men in search of manhood.

Christian Manhood and Manifest Destiny

The distinguishing mark of the Social Gospel is the integration of the "new" theology with the impulses of "new light" evangelical Christianity: humanitarian concern, moral purity, church renewal, and missionary zeal. The major paradox of the social gospel is the fact that, at the level of its effect on church members, it differs so little from the evangelical piety that Rauschenbusch so disdained in the "conservative" evangelical. Although the social gospel was theoretically the application of humanitarian concern to the social order, in practice the salvation of the social order depended on the influence of individual Christians as the primary mode of evangelism. This was not significantly different from the practice and methods of the conservative evangelical tradition.

"The spirit of Jesus," or the power of the spirit within, was the answer of the Social Gospel to the philosophical materialism generated by Social Darwinism. The spiritual power of personality and the emphasis on personal evangelism in the Social Gospel was related to the moral-influence theory of atonement propounded by Rauschenbusch in *A Theology for the Social Gospel.* Vicarious sacrifice and identification with the mind and life of Jesus was also the proposition demonstrated in the religious best-seller *In His Steps* (1897). In that novel the characters take a pledge to live by the standard of asking themselves what Jesus would do in every situation in their lives. It never occurred to them that they might lack the power to enact the response called for in a given situation, or that it might not be obvious what, in fact, Jesus would do. The virtuous Victorian, as portrayed in the novel and in the mind of the Social Gospel, was quite literally the perpetually incarnated Christ. The Christian knew what was correct behavior in any situation and acted on that knowledge.

The Jesus of the evangelical Christians, who received *In His Steps* with enthusiasm, and the "spirit of Jesus" of the Social Gospel, was finite, historical, contemporaneous, and identified with the mind and times of the nineteenth century. The knowledge of what Jesus would do in any given situation was provided by the "power of the spirit." From the Social Gospel point of view, being a Christian meant following the example of Christ's self-sacrificing love. This kind of assurance about ethical behavior meant freedom from self-doubt or spiritual self-examination. The Jesus of the Social Gospel never experienced uncertainty and never had to reflect on moral contradictions or compromise.

The attraction of the "unbroken God-consciousness" of a Jesus who was in command of his life, even on the cross, was as a model of assurance and certainty for Christian character. Like the ideal parents represented in God the Father, the "spirit of Jesus" represented the certitude that Victorian men longed to possess. When Rauschenbusch talked of the "mystic union" and "mysticism," he meant that union with the mind and spirit of Jesus would yield intuitive knowledge of the meaning and content of living the Christian life.

The men of the Social Gospel expected to regenerate the social order through the power of personal persuasion carried into the world by the individual church member and through their own ability to influence public opinion through pulpit, press, and platform. They never advocated ecclesiastical participation in the political arena, in the sense that the church as an institution might influence public opinion through lobbying efforts. Their model of public influence was that of mission through personal evangelism. This mode fit their hope for social regeneration without violence or undue conflict. The clash of opinion and will, the uncontrolled bargaining and vote-buying of Victorian politics, was repellent to their view of social change.

The ecclesiastical developments related to the social gospel led to social concern without a commitment of church or individual to any kind of social activism. The social gospel made middle-class affluence acceptable without damning the less fortunate. Church buildings acquired an opulence suitable to the new social status of the middle class in the late Victorian era. Worship services were suitable to the Victorian sense of propriety yet made the worshiper feel a part of the congregation. The emotional pressure of preaching for conversion was transferred to the personal power of the pastor to influence his congregation. Lyman Abbott considered himself to be a dull little man compared to Henry Ward Beecher, who preceded him at Plymouth Church.[9] Abbott was mystified when a woman confessed to being "so electrified" by his sermons that she could no longer attend his church.

People were receptive to any authority figure who spoke to their circumstances. They were hungry for the sense of belonging offered by a community that reinforced the moral code without demanding a public conversion experience. The voluntarism of the psychological model of the self-made man contradicted the viability of the church playing a role in social reform. The middle class was comfortable with the worship and impersonal forms of fellowship fostered by the liberal church community.

Josiah Strong dreamed of a church made strong and prosperous by the voluntary stewardship that would represent giving more than the legalistic "tithe" of the Old Testament. The wealth being amassed by the middle class would be channeled through the church, which Strong envisioned as the organizational center of social service to the community. Church members did not respond to his appeals for generous contributions for the purpose of evangelism and the progress of civilized morality. Instead, they followed the line of thought also advanced by Strong that providing direct charity to the poor was not advisable because it would further degenerate them. No self-made man disliked being told that the government and the church should not give direct financial assistance to the poor.

There was little likelihood of church members actually undertaking programs of personal evangelism to "raise up" the unwashed poor to middle-class standards of morality. But the assumption that the middle class served as a model of Christianity to be assimilated by others reinforced the middle-class sense of being the best people in the most civilized nation. It also encouraged church members to keep the moral code, lest they be unworthy of emulation. The Social Gospel version of evangelism depended almost entirely on the voluntary goodwill and personal service of church members. Ultimately, this form of mission activity increased the comfort of the already comfortable in an economic sense and reduced earlier evangelistic fervor of movements like abolition to nothing but high-minded ideals and good intentions.

Although Social Gospel leaders flirted with political activism, they finally preferred the indirect mode of personal influence in writing, preaching, and speaking to participation in the rough-and-tumble political arena. Their ideals made comprehension of the political processes of trade-offs, bargaining, and compromise to achieve objectives difficult. Washington Gladden wondered why he found so few allies among his fellow clergy on the Council of Congregational Churches when he condemned the church for accepting the "tainted" money of John D. Rockefeller.[10]

In a day when the church and ministry were associated with the feminine faculties and the domestic sphere, the social concern and worldly orientation of the Social Gospel provided a masculine model for ministry. As Rauschenbusch observed, the Brotherhood of the Kingdom "made men of us." The brotherhood, which Rauschenbusch called the "Holy Chivalry," served two purposes that counteracted cultural patterns. First, it provided an atmosphere of men working together to achieve a common objective when competition among colleagues was more usual. Second, the brotherhood made men of its members in the sense of helping moral men gain public recognition and respect in the public sphere.[11] The Social Gospel movement provided a way in which moral men could feel manly without being immoral. The lonely and courageous stance of a Washington Gladden on behalf of an unpopular cause provided an acceptable outlet for the energies of a man who "loved a good fight."[12] As Rauschenbusch had noted, service to society was the equivalent of the finest spirit of battle, and "the finest temper of sport," for the regenerate man.

The antagonism of Rauschenbusch to evangelical piety and individual conversion was a reaction against what appeared to be increasing feminization of religion and the church. The evangelical objective of converting only individuals segregated the church from society at large in the same way that the Victorian woman was cloistered in the home to protect her purity. The Social Gospel objective to convert society was a masculine concept of the church and church leadership in seeing the church and churchmen as vitally related and necessary to society.

Because the later men believed that the nation and the family were permanent institutions, while the church was a transient institution, they saw the long-range hope for the nation as more dependent on marriage and the family than on the church. The viability of democratic freedom depended on the ability of the family to nurture the social instincts of future citizens. The Social Gospel men were so bound by the concepts of moral autonomy that they were incapable of imagining the possibility of spiritual development outside a good family. While socially conservative evangelicals warmed to the possibility of using legislation to improve the social order, the Social Gospel men maintained their belief in the ideals of a voluntary socialism motivated by Christian love that would naturally create a society in which justice and equality would be available to all men.[13]

The knight-errant of the chivalry image of Rauschenbusch was an attempt to make male influence in the social order the equivalent of female influence in the domestic order. The Christian gentleman as knight-errant was conceived as fighting the forces of social evil in the worldly sphere to make the world a place fit for women, children, and any who lacked opportunity for self-development. Insofar as motivation was concerned, this deference of the stronger to the weaker in society was inspired by the love of woman, God, and country. Service to the family was for the good of the nation. Service to the nation would undergird the family.

The paradoxical result of the double focus of the Social Gospel is that it was instrumental in the development of two parallel movements that gave cohesiveness to the emerging middle class. Strong's use of the slogans "the Fatherhood of God" and the "Brotherhood of Man" helped catalyze public opinion behind nationalistic fervor in the name of Christian civilization signified by manifest destiny. With reference to the spiritual power of the nation, Strong wrote that Christ was the revelation of the fatherhood of God which makes possible the brotherhood of man.[14] Gladden used the same ideals to describe the Christian religion.

Paired Paradox: Complementary
or Contradictory

The convergence of cultural and Christian ideals in the "spirit" of manifest destiny can be interpreted from the Social Gospel point of view as evidence of the Christianizing of the nation. The leaders of the Social Gospel movement had claimed that church and society, theology and science, religion and culture were complementary, not contradictory. However, the divergence between the stated social objectives of the movement leaders and the actual history of the church and the nation suggests that their thought-form contradicted their good intentions.

The Paradoxes of the Social Gospel Movement

The mode of thought used in the Social Gospel made the antithetical pairs of categories running through the leaders' social commentary and theology seem complementary. Insofar as the Social Gospelers treated the sensible world of experience as "just like" the unseen reality of ideals, their thought depends on identifying the real with the ideal. The discrepancy between the father-son experience and the ideal Father seems to disappear if analogy is confused with identity. The thought-form in which Strong expressed the double focus in the ellipse was more like a circle with a single center than an ellipse with two foci. The equal focus on individual and society in Social Gospel thought consists of identifying the terms rather than asking what is similar and what is different in the two sides of the analogy.

The God-concept, as Rauschenbusch understood it, reduces a religious symbol to a metaphor. In the Christian theological tradition it had long been recognized that the language used by men to express the nature of God was insufficient to capture the reality of God, but, even though inadequate, language could point to a reality larger than the symbol itself.[15] Rauschenbusch, however, concluded that since all images for God are taken from human experience, reflection about God is limited to what is known about the best men. Consequently, contradictions between the nature of God and the nature of the best men seem to disappear when analogy becomes identity.

The Social Gospel men also used family imagery in the sense of an identity rather than as an analogy. They gave concrete content to the theological concepts of fatherhood and brotherhood that was just like the content of their family ideal. This resulted in an uncritical identification of God with man, history, and the natural process, which led to an easy optimism concerning the kingdom of God and American manifest destiny. It also made it theologically impossible to speak of a God who was related but also transcendent to man and the world as it was known to man. In Social Gospel theology there is no qualitative difference between God and man. The Social Gospelers thought in terms of quantity and likeness and rarely asked about quality and unlikeness.

The epistemology of George Combe in the faculty psychology involved an unquestioned reliance on the power of human reason to know the truth. Combe reasoned that since God's creation is naturally harmonious, so, by analogy, is the social order. Therefore, if man simply

171

knew that the moral order of society was also naturally harmonious, then civilization would progress if all people had the opportunity to develop their faculties. In so doing Combe assumed that knowledge of the moral order of society is acquired just like knowledge of the physical laws of the universe—by empirical observation.

In the theological tradition, biblical revelation had been distinguished from the knowledge of God available to reason. The discipline of natural theology was limited to knowledge that could be acquired without the aid of biblical revelation. Influenced by the faculty psychology, the men of the Social Gospel no longer distinguished between natural and revealed truth, neither did they retain any of the more traditional doctrines that claimed that the reason of fallen mankind was prone to illusion about the goodness and power of human being. In the theological tradition, biblical revelation had been used as a way to distinguish between God's truth and man's illusions.

Because of the faculty psychology epistemology, the Social Gospel men believed they were coming out into God's clear, cloudless, simple truth. They were able to focus equally on society and the individual only because there was no conflict between the two terms in their undialectical mode of thought. There is no conflict or inevitable contradiction between the individual and society if they are conceptualized as being alike. Just as the natural analogy of Paley was tied to a static universe, the moral universe of the Social Gospel was theoretically static.

Men like the Social Gospel leaders attributed their epistemology to Immanuel Kant, the German philosopher of the late eighteenth century. Gladden and Abbott believed that this was the source of the marvelous fact that the world within is a perfect mirror of the world without. Kant, however, had posited carefully drawn distinctions between sensible entities (objects that are present to the senses) and the intelligible entities (objects present to thought which are not visible and available to the senses).[16] He had further cautioned that, in seeking the laws of the physical universe, the scientist works "as if" the laws of the universe are intelligible and harmonious. Such philosophical distinctions and caution about what is knowable were unknown to the men of the Social Gospel, who took Kant's term "transcendental philosophy" to mean spiritual intuition.[17]

The difference in assumptions about what kind of knowledge is available to human reason, and how truth is known, accounts for Social Gospel misreadings of the German philosopher-theologians Hegel, Schleiermacher, and Ritschl. Rauschenbusch listed the convictions that influenced modern life and theology as including "belief in the universal reign of law, the doctrine of evolution, the control of nature by man." Kant had developed moral philosophy, in which he claimed that there were moral laws universally known to all men. But he did not conclude that the universal reign of law was therefore imminent. Hegel and Schleiermacher were both progressive thinkers in the sense of believing in an inner dialectic of the historical process that was in a general sense progressive. But they did not confuse all human history with their own national history. Ritschl organized his theology around the principle of the kingdom of God as the central ideal, but he did not suppose that the ideal would literally be fulfilled in his time because of the moral evolution of the race.

Despite the fact that Rauschenbusch had been partially educated in Germany, philosophical distinctions in German theology eluded him as they did less-well-educated movement leaders like Gladden. Rauschenbusch cited Schleiermacher and Ritschl as the source of his "solidaristic concept of sin."[18] The term as Rauschenbusch used it meant the knowledge of social ramifications of sinful acts, and the guilt engendered by becoming aware of social injustice. He assumed that groups were capable of experiencing guilt. To support the concept of social sin he quoted from Schleiermacher concerning "the sinfulness that precedes all other sin." Although the perspective of Schleiermacher concerning the origin of guilt and consciousness of sin was a reference to individual consciousness, Rauschenbusch interpreted "sinfulness" to mean that actual visible deeds in history are the cause of experienced group guilt about wrongdoing. Rauschenbusch was apparently unaware that Schleiermacher distinguished between original and actual sin, a distinction common to the theological tradition.[19] He also failed to note that Schleiermacher's point of reference was individual and not social.

The so-called American "Ritschlians" used much of the language of Albrecht Ritschl, but their understanding of his concepts owed more to Social Darwinism and an intuitive epistemology than it did to Ritschl. Ritschl pointed out that an ideal represented a heavenly quality that drew men up toward the kingdom of God. But he distinguished between the finite circumstances of human life and the infinite quality of ideals, which sometimes contradicted each other. With reference to "eternity" as an ideal that inspired ethical behavior, he made it clear that "eternity" was a quality of life that could be experienced partially in life by the Christian believer. But eternity did not mean endless time.[20]

When Rauschenbusch speculated on the afterlife, he disavowed the belief that heaven and hell were spatial categories. Yet having denied that they were geographical locations, he went on to envision a heaven open to all men that offered endless time for character development.[21]

The classical tradition of Christian theology utilizes a highly paradoxical mode of thought in the dialectical weighing of the contradictions of life and thought, finite and infinite, real and ideal, time and eternity. In that tradition visible reality is never identified with "the unseen." The ideal is used as a standard with which to discern God's intentions for mankind as compared to the human experience of contradiction between real and ideal.

In his dilemma concerning World War I, Rauschenbusch applied the historical distinction between civilization and barbarism in so literal a sense with reference to America and Germany that he finally had no way to distinguish between his dual national loyalties if they became antagonists. Since he judged both nations to be equally civilized, he lacked an ethical principle that would apply to the German invasion of Belgium. His understanding of the long-range world-historical process destroyed his ability to distinguish between social good and evil in the immediate present. There was no room in the Social Gospel world of ideals for the genuine contradictions of life or for willful, deliberate acts of aggression. Paradox, after all, did mean "contradictory" rather than "complementary." If the "spirit of Jesus" did not infuse the social-historical situation, Rauschenbusch had no option except to interpret the Great War as social disintegration.

The lonely prophet of the Social Gospel wrote his *Theology* only two generations before the renaissance of social activism in mainline Protestant church support of freedom movements and liberal politics during the 1960s. A grass-roots rebellion against clergy and denominational leaders of the new social concerns movement followed. Dean Hoge, a sociologist of religion, surveyed the relationship of theology to the response of church members to social activism in the church. He tested the theory of church historian Martin Marty that Protestant churches are divided between private-party conservative evangelical and public-party social allegiances. Marty defined "private party" much the way Rauschenbusch had in the *Theology*. Protestant churches had seized the name "evangelical" and accented individual salvation out of this world, a personal moral life congruent with the life of the saved, and reward or fulfillment in the life to come. The "public party" was more exposed to the social order and the social destinies of man.[22]

Hoge found that belief clusters supported the two-party theory. In general, conservatives defined themselves as supporting evangelism but not social action, and liberals defined themselves as supporting social action but not evangelism. However, the basic factor regarding lay resistance to social action in both parties was whether "the particular action seems to uphold or disrupt a middle-class way of life."[23]

The major surprise in the survey was the discovery that the basic commitments of persons in both parties was identical. Religion and the church are not ends in themselves but are instrumental to attaining the goals of family, standard of living, and career. Those middle-class values serve as the standard by which particular church actions are judged. Commitment to the church is drastically reduced if any action is seen as undermining the "Big Three basic American values."[24]

In *A Theology for the Social Gospel* Rauschenbusch intended to use the "Kingdom of God" ideal to enlarge the orthodox conception of the scheme of salvation. Unfortunately the thought form and categories of Social Darwinism undermined his theological objective. Like the Spencerian philosophy, the theology of Rauschenbusch was a social philosophy that functioned on the basis of individual moral autonomy. It appeared to attend to public matters yet was concerned primarily with individual morality. The social consciousness that Rauschenbusch intended to vitalize with Christian "spirit" never materialized because the content of his social philosophy was so similar to the already established ideals of the middle-class. In adjusting the Christian message to the regeneration of the social order, Rauschenbusch came out of the struggle with "a crippled formulation" of truth.

Notes

Chapter 1:
The Social Gospel Movement
in Victorian Context

1. Winthrop S. Hudson, *The Great Tradition of the American Churches* (New York: Harper & Bros., 1953), pp. 226–43.

2. C. Howard Hopkins, *The Rise of the Social Gospel in American Protestantism, 1865–1915* (New Haven: Yale University Press, 1940), pt. 2.

3. Walter Rauschenbusch, *A Theology for the Social Gospel* (1917; reprint ed., Nashville: Abingdon Press, 1945), p. 131.

4. Ibid., p. 23.

5. In *Ordeal of Faith: The Crisis of Church-Going America, 1865–1900* (New York: Philadelphia Library, 1959), Francis P. Weisenberger cataloged the crisis of dozens of Victorians.

6. In *The Rise of the Social Gospel,* Hopkins claims that the effect of the movement was a reorientation of both theology and ecclesiastical interests. In *Protestant Churches and Industrial America* (New York: Harper & Bros., 1949), Henry May characterizes the Social Gospel as a form of progressive social Christianity in which the primary concern was a better society. He credits the Social Gospel with influencing American social thought by shattering older economic theories.

7. Washington Gladden, *Recollections* (Boston: Houghton Mifflin, 1909), p. 251.

8. Josiah Strong, *The Twentieth Century City* (1898; reprint ed., New York: Arno Press, 1970), pp. 121–22.

9. My sources for the biographical summary are Lyman Abbott, *Reminiscences* (Boston: Houghton Mifflin, 1915); Ira V. Brown, *Lyman Abbott* (Westport. Conn.: Greenwood Press, 1953); *William Newton Clarke: A Biography with Additional Sketches by His Friends and Colleagues* (New York: Charles Scribner's Sons, 1916); Jacob Henry Dorn, *Washington Gladden: Prophet of*

the Social Gospel (Columbus: Ohio State Press, 1966); Washington Gladden, *Recollections* (Boston: Houghton Mifflin, 1909); William McLoughlin, *The Meaning of Henry Ward Beecher* (New York: Knopf, 1970); Francis G. Peabody, *Reminiscences of Present-Day Saints* (Boston: Houghton Mifflin, 1927); Dores R. Sharpe, *Walter Rauschenbusch* (New York: Macmillan, 1942); Graham Taylor, *Pioneering on Social Frontiers* (Chicago: University of Chicago Press, 1930); and Louise C. Wade, *Graham Taylor: Pioneer for Social Justice, 1851-1938* (Chicago: University of Chicago Press, 1964).

10. Sharpe, *Walter Rauschenbusch*, pp. 42–58. My interpretation of material supplied by Sharpe would not be alien to Rauschenbusch, who assumed that conversion and sexual sublimation in work were related.

11. In *Protestant Churches and Industrial America,* May gives the general impression that the objective of social salvation was a rejection of individual conversion by Social Gospel figures. This impression is given by the writing of Rauschenbusch and is not accurate with reference to other Social Gospel figures or himself. It was an exclusive emphasis on individual conversion and individual piety to which Rauschenbusch objected.

12. To my knowledge, one experience with the Hocking Valley strike in 1884 was Gladden's only experience with a strike. In this case, he was not directly involved in arbitration, but advised the manager of a coal mine to try outside arbitration. Gladden is usually portrayed as having had experience in strike arbitration. Abbott's obituary of Gladden in *The Outlook* of July 17, 1918, reports that Gladden was involved in "more than one important labor dispute." Graham Taylor, by comparison, had served as a mediator on many occasions and doubted the value of the long, wearing process of arbitration.

13. The book is still used as a college and seminary text. Rauschenbusch influenced Reinhold Niebuhr and H. Richard Niebuhr in ways that merit closer critical examination.

14. Rauschenbusch, *A Theology for the Social Gospel,* p. 226.

15. Ibid., p. 178.

Chapter 2:
The Victorian Social
Revolution

1. See the provocative essays by Sidney E. Mead in *The Lively Experiment: The Shaping of Christianity in America* (New York: Harper & Row, 1963) concerning democracy, religion, and culture.

2. Henry Adams, *The Education of Henry Adams* (1918; reprint ed., Boston: Houghton Mifflin, 1961), p. 472.

3. The development of Protestant cultural hegemony is a theme in Robert T. Handy, *A Christian America: Protestant Hopes and Historical Realities* (New York: Oxford University Press, 1971), and in Martin Marty, *Righteous Empire: The Protestant Experience in America* (New York: Dial Press, 1970).

Notes

4. Nancy F. Cott, *The Bonds of Womanhood* (New Haven: Yale University Press, 1977), pp. 23–26.

5. Washington Gladden, *Recollections* (Boston: Houghton Mifflin, 1909), p. 67. The quotation is part of a poem by Oliver Wendell Holmes.

6. Ibid., p. 254.

7. For a good summary of the effect of economics on family organization in the nineteenth century see Kenneth Keniston and the Carnegie Council on Children, *All Our Children* (New York: Harcourt Brace Jovanovich, 1977), chap. 1.

8. Christopher Lasch, *Haven in a Heartless World* (New York: Basic Books, 1977), p. 8.

9. Sondra R. Herman, "Loving Courtship or the Marriage Market:The Ideal and Its Critics, 1871-1911," *American Quarterly* 25 (May 1973): 235-55.

10. Francis G. Peabody, *Reminiscences of Present-Day Saints* (Boston: Houghton Mifflin, 1927), preface.

11. Washington Gladden, *Ruling Ideas* (Boston: Houghton Mifflin, 1895), p. 251.

12. Ibid., p. 246.

13. Gladden, *Recollections,* p. 14.

14. Ann Douglas, *The Feminization of American Culture* (New York: Knopf, 1978), p. 24.

15. Gladden, *Recollections,* pp. 35-36.

16. Walter Rauschenbusch, *Christianizing the Social Order* (New York: Macmillan, 1913), pp. 14-15.

17. Cott, *The Bonds of Womanhood,* p. 132. Whereas Cott testifies to the presence of women in the church, Douglas argues, in *The Feminization of American Culture,* that the culture was feminized through the influence of clergy and women writers.

18. William James, *The Varieties of Religious Experience: A Study in Human Nature* (1902; reprint ed., New York: Modern Library, 1936), p. 357.

19. In "Sexuality, Class and Role in 19th Century America," *American Quarterly,* Summer 1973, pp. 131-54, Charles I. Rosenberg concludes that the outstanding feature of Victorian sexuality was not repression but the conflict for the male between the Christian-gentleman and the masculine-achiever ethos.

20. James, *The Varieties of Religious Experience,* p. 365.

Chapter 3:
The Victorian Intellectual Revolution

1. William Graham Sumner, *What Social Classes Owe Each Other* (1883; reprint ed., New York: Arno Press, 1972), p. 41.

2. In *Social Darwinism in American Thought, 1860–1915* (New York: Braziller, 1955), Richard Hofstadter points out the many forms of Social Darwinism present in American thought.

3. Conrad Cherry, *Nature and Religious Imagination* (Philadelphia: Fortress Press, 1980), p. 122.

4. In chapter 4 of *The Child and the Republic* (Philadelphia: University of Pennsylvania Press, 1968), Bernard Wishy discusses the influence of phrenology on child-care literature in the 1830s.

5. Donald B. Meyer, *The Positive Thinkers: A Study of the Quest for Health, Wealth and Personal Power from Mary Baker Eddy to Norman Vincent Peale* (Garden City: Doubleday, 1965), pt. 1.

6. A. D. Kaplan, *The Baby's Biography* (New York: Brentano's, 1891), p. 67.

7. See Cherry, *Nature and Religious Imagination,* pp. 106–7, concerning Scottish commonsense philosophy on reason, natural law, and moral law.

8. George Combe, *The Constitution of Man* (New York: Fowless and Wells, 1850), chap. 2, sec. 4, on "The Supremacy of the Moral Sentiments and Intellect."

9. Ibid., pp. 371–87.

10. Ibid., p. 50.

11. Ibid., pp. 10–11.

12. Ibid., pp. 10–14.

13. Alcott is not the only source of the rationale behind the family ethos. He is a good example of important elements in the thought of both Combe and the Social Gospel men.

14. William Alcott, *Physiology of Marriage* (1866; reprint ed., New York: Arno Press, 1972), p. 9.

15. Ibid., pp. 11–13.

16. Ibid., pp. 12–19.

17. Ibid., p. 67.

18. Victorians, like the Social Gospel men, were highly critical of the Puritan practice of spiritual self-examination and of Puritan use of civil law to enforce individual morality.

19. Charles Fourier, *The Passions of the Human Soul* (1851; reprint ed., New York: Kelley, 1968), 1:358.

20. Fourier envisioned the free-love stage of Socialism as only an intermediate step between Civilization and Harmonium. Eventually he expected Socialism to give way to Harmonium, a society in which love would be purely spiritual without any taint of materialism.

21. For an extended discussion of natural theology and Scottish commonsense theology in America in the nineteenth century see Cherry, *Nature and Religious Imagination,* pt. 2.

22. Sydney E. Ahlstrom, ed., *Theology in America: The Major Protestant Voices from Puritanism to Neo-Orthodoxy* (Indianapolis: Bobbs-Merrill, 1967), p. 222.

23. This is a standard apologetic device used by a variety of religious liberals cataloged by Henry F. May in *Protestant Churches and Industrial America* (New York: Harper & Bros., 1949).

24. Nathaniel Taylor, *Lectures on the Moral Government of God, Vol. I* (New York: Clark, Austin, and Smith, 1859), p. iii.

25. Bushnell's essay "Our Obligation to the Dead" is reprinted in *God's New Israel,* ed. Conrad Cherry (Englewood Cliffs, N.J.: Prentice-Hall, 1971), pp. 197–209.

26. William Newton Clarke, *Sixty Years with the Bible: A Record of Experience* (New York: Charles Scribner's Sons, 1910), p. 115.

27. Ibid., p. 145.

28. William Newton Clarke, *An Outline of Christian Theology* (New York: Charles Scribner's Sons, 1904), pp. 318, 321.

29. Clarke, *Sixty Years with the Bible,* pp. 199–203.

30. Ibid., p. 208.

31. Combe, *The Constitution of Man,* chap. 9, "The Relation Between Science and Scripture."

32. *Herbert Spencer: An Autobiography* (New York: D. Appleton & Co., 1904), 1:225–31. See also *Herbert Spencer: An Autobiography* (New York: D. Appleton & Co., 1904), 2:523, 522–40, for an account of the development of his faculties.

33. Charles Darwin, *On the Origin of Species by Means of Natural Selection* (1859; reprint ed., Chicago: Encyclopedia Britannica, 1952), p. 4.

34. Ibid., p. 242.

35. Herbert Spencer, *Social Statics* (1850; reprint ed., New York: Robert Schalkenbach Foundation, 1970), p. 391.

36. Hofstadter makes this claim in chap. 2 of *Social Darwinism and American Thought.*

37. Spencer, *Social Statics,* p. 374.

38. Ibid., p. 60.

39. Ibid., p. 370.

40. Ibid., p. 69.

41. Ibid., chap. 2, "The Evanescence of Evil."

42. Ibid., chap. 30.

43. Ibid., chap. 31.

44. Herbert Spencer, *Education: Intellectual, Moral and Physical* (Akron: Werner Co., 1860), pp. 181–82.

45. Spencer, *Social Statics,* pp. 332–40.

46. Moncure Conway, *Autobiography* (Boston: Houghton Mifflin Co., 1904), 2:436–37.

47. Spencer, *Social Statics,* pp. 424–25.

48. Henry Ward Beecher discusses the relationship of God's use of natural law to poverty and prosperity in chap. 4 of *Evolution and Christianity* (Boston: Pilgrim Press, ca. 1885), vol. 1.

49. Charles Darwin, *The Descent of Man and Selection in Relation to Sex* (1871; reprint ed., Chicago: Encyclopedia Britannica, 1952), p. 318.

50. Ibid.

51. Ibid., p. 325.

52. Darwin, *Origin of Species,* chap. 3.

53. Darwin, *The Descent of Man,* p. 323.

54. Henry George, *Progress and Poverty* (1879; reprint ed., New York: Robert Schalkenbach Foundation, 1970), p. 195.

55. Ibid., p. 197.

56. Spencer, *An Autobiography,* 2:536, tells this story about Henry George.

Chapter 4:
Social Change
and Applied Christianity (1865–1900)

1. In *Protestant Churches and Industrial America* (New York: Harper & Bros., 1949), Henry May interprets the Social Gospel as progressive social Christianity in which the primary concern was a search for a better society, as compared to the more conservative evangelical churchmen who were defenders of the status quo in society. He credits the influence of the movement on social thought and its appeal to the middle class to its effectiveness in shattering old economic theory. In *The Modernist Impulse in American Protestantism* (Cambridge: Harvard University Press, 1976), p. 165, William Hutchison follows that interpretation in defining the movement as arguing "as the Social Gospelers did, that social salvation procedes individual salvation both temporally and in importance. Even to give social reform an equal, non-derivative status was a move quite distinct in theory from what evangelicals generally could support. It was this theoretical elevation of social salvation, therefore, that made the Social Gospel a distinctive movement." I am arguing that the Social Gospel placed an equal emphasis, theoretically, on individual and social salvation, and that the Social Gospelers are "new light" evangelicals.

2. Not all Victorians believed that virtue was inherited, but Darwin's theory of sexual selection reinforced the idea for those who did.

3. Although Bushnell never accepted evolutionary theory concerning the origin of the human race, he did endorse the "out-populating power of the Christian stock" in chap. 8 of *Christian Nurture* (1861; reprint ed., New Haven: Yale University Press, 1967). The seeds of Social Gospel doctrines of the coming kingdom, coercive law giving way to spontaneous law-keeping behavior, and the perfection of the race can all be found in *Christian Nurture,* as well as in other books authored by Bushnell between 1858 and 1872.

4. Conrad Cherry, ed., *God's New Israel* (Englewood Cliffs, N.J.: Prentice-Hall, 1971), p. 202.

Notes

5. Henry Adams, *The Education of Henry Adams* (1918; reprint ed., Boston: Houghton Mifflin, 1961), p. 57.

6. Washington Gladden, *Working People and Their Employers* (Boston: Lockwood Brooks & Co., 1876), pp. 11, 12.

7. Ibid., p. 142.

8. Lyman Abbott, *Reminiscences* (Boston: Houghton Mifflin, 1915), p. 270.

9. Washington Gladden, *Recollections* (Boston: Houghton Mifflin, 1909), pp. 371–72.

10. Lyman Abbott, *The Rights of Man* (Boston: Houghton Mifflin, 1902), p. 219.

11. Ira V. Brown, *Lyman Abbott* (Westport, Conn.: Greenwood Press, 1953), p. 95. Brown speculates that "white land sharks" were responsible for the passage of the Dawes Act.

12. Wages-fund theory was an assumption that the wages-fund represented the aggregate wealth of the world. Early in his career Gladden believed, on the basis of this theory, that more men working produced a greater aggregate wealth and that employers could increase the aggregate wealth by subtracting less from the wages-fund for private use.

13. Washington Gladden, *Applied Christianity* (Boston: Houghton Mifflin, 1886), p. 136. The term "applied Christianity" was used by George Combe in *The Constitution of Man* (New York: Fowless & Wells, 1850).

14. Ibid., p. 145. Gladden's advice to employer and employee to empathize with each other presumed face-to-face relations. In "Wealth," *The North American Review,* June 1889, p. 660, Andrew Carnegie pointed out that the idea of personal relationships between employer and employee was impossible because "we assemble thousands of operatives in the factory."

15. Gladden, *Applied Christianity,* p. 50.

16. Brown, *Lyman Abbott,* pp. 107–8.

17. Indians, "negroes," and Mormons were not yet civilized enough to vote. Abbott opposed "woman suffrage" because woman did not need the vote to protect her rights. The "chivalry" of man was better protection for woman than the right to vote. Abbott's discussion of woman suffrage appears in *The Rights of Man,* p. 234.

18. Gladden, *Working People and Their Employers,* pp. 33–44.

19. Henry Ward Beecher, *Evolution and Christianity* (Boston: Pilgrim Press, ca. 1885), vol. 1, chap. 6.

20. Josiah Strong, *Our Country,* rev. ed. (New York: Baker & Taylor, 1885, 1891), chap. 9.

21. To the Victorians, effeminacy meant male lack of moral fiber caused by failure to work productively. Women, who had no need to develop moral fiber by working off the "sex passion," were permitted to enjoy luxury and leisure.

22. Strong, *Our Country,* pp. 122–26.

23. Ibid., chaps. 3 and 4.

24. In chap. 14 of *Our Country* Strong cites the questions addressed as coming from Darwin's *Descent of Man,* and the answers from Bushnell's *Christian Nurture.*

25. Josiah Strong, *The New Era* (New York: Baker & Taylor, 1893), chap. 2.

26. Ibid., p. 193.

27. Gladden and Abbott would have agreed with the analysis of the problem, but not with the solution offered. Strong differs most from them on the issue of legislating morality. This is due in part to his more literal acceptance of the physical aspects of phrenology regarding the relationship of brain size to moral power. He follows Darwin's biological model, while Gladden and Abbott were more influenced by Spencer's social model concerning public opinion as the mode of social change.

28. On the finer nervous system of the Anglo-Saxon race see Strong, *Our Country,* chap. 14.

29. Lyman Abbott, *Christianity and Social Problems* (Boston: Riverside Press, 1896), p. 112.

30. Ibid., p. 138.

31. Gladden, *Recollections,* p. 158.

32. Many of the sermons collected by Robert Cross in *The Church and the City, 1865–1900* (New York: Bobbs-Merrill, 1967) include the use of this dichotomy.

33. Strong, *The New Era,* pp. 191–93.

34. Harold Frederic, *The Damnation of Theron Ware* (1896; reprint ed., Cambridge: Belknap Press, 1960), p. 51.

35. W. D. P. Bliss, *The New Encyclopedia of Social Reform* (1908; reprint ed., New York: Arno Press, 1970), p. 981.

36. Abbott, *The Rights of Man,* p. 250.

37. In *The New Heavens and the New Earth* (New York: Harper & Row, 1974), Cushing Strout interprets prohibition as the greatest success of the Social Gospel, and industrial reform its greatest failure. Gladden and Abbott had no intention of legislating "an austerity of manners" through prohibition.

38. See chap. 7, "Strong Drink," in *Working People and Their Employers,* in which Gladden outlines the connection between alcohol and "beastly" behavior. His position against the "liquor law" appears on pp. 199–203 of *Christianity and Socialism* (New York: Eaton & Mains, 1905). Gladden believed that existing laws should be enforced because they were an embodiment of public opinion. He was cautious about the writing of the new laws unless they did express existing public opinion.

39. Graham Taylor, *Pioneering on Social Frontiers* (Chicago: University of Chicago Press, 1930), p. 24.

40. Gladden, *Recollections,* p. 359.

41. Ibid., p. 365.

42. Josiah Strong, *The Twentieth Century City* (1898; reprint ed., New York: Arno Press, 1970), p. 145.

Notes

Chapter 5:
The Social Problem and the
Kingdom of God (1890–1924)

1. Walter Rauschenbusch, *Christianizing the Social Order* (New York: Macmillan, 1913), p. 6.

2. Ibid., pt. 3, sec. 2.

3. Francis Greenwood Peabody, *The Approach to the Social Question* (New York: Macmillan, 1909), p. 6.

4. Graham Taylor documented his painstaking effort at Chicago Commons to calm the near hysteria that ensued after the Haymarket riot in Chicago in 1886 in *Pioneering on Social Frontiers* (Chicago: University of Chicago Press, 1930), pp. 131–37. From personal experience with so-called anarchists, he was convinced that fears of a revolution were unwarranted.

5. Newspaper circulation increased from 600 to 2,500 daily newspapers between 1870 and 1900. High schools increased from 500 to 2,500 between 1870 and 1900.

6. William Newton Clarke, *The Ideal of Jesus* (New York: Charles Scribner's Sons, 1911), p. 64.

7. In *The Rise of the Social Gospel in American Protestantism, 1865–1915* (New Haven: Yale University Press, 1940), C. Howard Hopkins uses the term *social Christianity* as a general reference to social science, social work, and social reform in the maturity of the Social Gospel between 1900 and 1915. He interprets the Social Gospel development between 1890 and 1900 to be the flowering of Christian socialism out of "socialized" Christianity. He follows the Rauschenbusch criticism of the earlier men in the movement as prone to an individualism that was dropped in the mature form of the movement. In fact, the entire movement relied on the power of personal relationships and individual personality as a medium of social change.

8. Paul F. Bourke, "The Social Critics and the End of American Innocence, 1907–1921," *Journal of American Studies* 3, no. 1 (1969): 67.

9. Francis G. Peabody, *Reminiscences of Present-Day Saints* (Boston: Houghton Mifflin, 1927), p. 213. Peabody devoted a chapter of the book to Henry Drummond.

10. Francis G. Peabody, *Jesus Christ and the Christian Character* (New York: Macmillan, 1906), p. 282.

11. Walter Rauschenbusch, *The Social Principles of Jesus* (New York: Association Press, 1916), p. 76.

12. Theodore Roosevelt, *The Strenuous Life* (1902; reprint ed., St. Clair Shores, Mich.: Scholarly Press, 1970), p. 8.

13. Ibid., p. 25.

14. Peter Gabriel Filene, *Him/Her/Self* (New York: Harcourt Brace Jovanovich, 1974), pp. 79–86. Filene documents the increasing inability to find satisfying work for the middle-class male in the period from 1890 on.

15. Washington Gladden, *Recollections* (Boston: Houghton Mifflin, 1909), p. 385.

16. Henry James in *Living Ideas in America,* ed. Henry Steele Commager (New York: Harper & Row, 1964), p. 645.

17. Ibid., p. 644.

18. Ibid., p. 646.

19. Rockefeller had been entertained in the homes of both Josiah Strong and Walter Rauschenbusch. Washington Gladden was the only Social Gospel figure who publicly condemned the "ill-gotten gains" of men like Rockefeller.

20. Ira V. Brown, *Lyman Abbott* (Westport, Conn.: Greenwood Press, 1953), p. 178.

21. Roosevelt, *The Strenuous Life,* pp. 1–38.

22. Ibid., pp. 3–4.

23. See Filene, *Him/Her/Self,* p. 81: "By 1900, the middle-class economy was becoming corporatized and bureaucratized." Roosevelt helped in the transformation of the older concept of gentlemen as statesmen into national service as an acceptable middle-class career.

24. Gladden, *Recollections,* pp. 386–88.

25. Lyman Abbott, "Gladden Obituary," *The Outlook,* July 17, 1918, p. 442.

26. Brown, *Lyman Abbott,* pp. 165–68.

27. Dores R. Sharpe, *Walter Rauschenbusch* (New York: Macmillan, 1942), chap. 16. Sharpe reveals the enthusiasm of Rauschenbusch for the Spanish-American War. The interpretation of why Rauschenbusch favored that war and objected to the First World War is my own.

28. Peabody, *Jesus Christ and the Christian Character,* p. 292.

29. This is the context of the Peabody criticism of the "effeminate Christ figure" of Washington Gladden. Peabody viewed the thought of the older men as effeminate and too individualistic, both characteristics of pietism.

30. Rauschenbusch, *Christianizing the Social Order,* pt. 2, chap. 5 "A Religion for Social Redemption."

31. Roosevelt, *The Strenuous Life,* p. 330.

32. Ibid., p. 324.

33. Ibid., p. 327.

34. Ibid., pp. 41–62.

35. Francis G. Peabody, *Jesus Christ and the Social Question* (New York: Grosset & Dunlap, 1900), p. 7.

36. Francis G. Peabody, *The Social Teachings of Jesus Christ* (Philadelphia: University of Pennsylvania Press, 1924), pp. 53–61.

37. Peabody, *Jesus Christ and the Social Question,* pp. 149–60.

38. Peabody, *The Approach to the Social Question,* pp. 83–93.

39. Peabody, *The Social Teachings of Jesus Christ,* p. 53.

40. Peabody, *Jesus Christ and the Social Question,* p. 19.

41. Ibid., p. 144.

Notes

42. Ibid., p. 149.
43. See Sharpe, *Walter Rauschenbusch,* chap. 6.
44. Many of the Bellamy imitators hoped to establish organizations like the Nationalism Clubs that sprung up to work toward Bellamy's socialist ideals following the publication of *Looking Backward.* I suspect that Rauschenbusch entertained similar hopes for the spread of groups organized on the principles of the Brotherhood of the Kingdom.
45. Edward Bellamy, *Looking Backward: 2000–1887* (1887; reprint ed., Belknap Press, 1967), p. 264.
46. Rauschenbusch, *Christianizing the Social Order,* pt. 6, chap. 3, "The Socializing of Property."
47. Ibid., chap. 4, "Institutions of Love and Their Dangers."
48. Walter Rauschenbusch, *Christianity and the Social Crisis* (1907; reprint ed., New York: Harper & Row, 1964), pp. 67–68.
49. Rauschenbusch, *Christianizing the Social Order,* pp. 352–53.
50. William Newton Clarke, *A Study of Christian Missions* (New York: Charles Scribner's Sons, 1900), p. 70.
51. Rauschenbusch, *The Social Principles of Jesus,* pp. 72–73.
52. Peabody, *The Social Teachings of Jesus Christ,* p. 52.
53. Benson Y. Landis, ed., *A Rauschenbusch Reader* (New York: Harper & Bros., 1957), p. 79.
54. Rauschenbusch, *Christianity and the Social Crisis,* p. 279.
55. Ibid., p. 135.
56. Samuel Eliot Morison, *The Oxford History of the American People* (New York: Mentor, 1972), 3:131.
57. Clarke, *A Study of Christian Missions,* p. 48.

Chapter 6:
Theology for the
Social Gospel (1900–1924)

1. Because Josiah Strong wrote no theology, my survey of religious thought in the early stages of the Social Gospel refers only to Gladden and Abbott, who were quite similar. With reference to the five men surveyed and cited in this chapter, my emphasis is on concepts that remained central to their thought throughout their careers. Since none of them was systematic in any way, I have attempted to isolate central themes and images in their religious thought. Changes in social context described in earlier chapters are integral to shifts in concepts noted here.

2. In the preface to *A Theology for the Social Gospel* (1917; reprint ed., Nashville: Abingdon Press, 1945), Walter Rauschenbusch wrote: "This book had to be written sometime, and as far as I know, nobody has yet written it."

3. This assumption, shared by most liberal theologians of the period, is stated most clearly in James Freeman Clarke, *Ten Great Religions* (Boston: Houghton Mifflin, 1871, 1883), vols. 1 and 2. The material in the books, especially chap. 4 of vol. 2, is quite similar to material common to Clarke, Peabody, and Rauschenbusch. Clarke was included among Peabody's "saints" (Francis G. Peabody, *Reminiscences of Present-Day Saints* [Boston: Houghton Mifflin, 1927]).

4. Washington Gladden, *How Much Is Left of the Old Doctrines? A Book for the People* (Boston: Houghton Mifflin, 1899), p. 42.

5. Washington Gladden, *Present Day Theology* (Columbus: McClelland & Co., 1913), p. 58.

6. William Dean Howells, *April Hopes*, introduction and notes by Kermit Vanderbilt (Bloomington: Indiana University Press, 1974), introduction and notes.

7. *How Much Is Left of the Old Doctrines?* p. 146.

8. Washington Gladden, *Live and Learn* (New York: Macmillan, 1914), p. 124.

9. Washington Gladden, *Christianity and Socialism* (New York: Eaton & Mains, 1905), pp. 30-32.

10. H. Shelton Smith, ed., *Horace Bushnell* (New York: Oxford University Press, 1965), pp. 148-51. In "Nature and Supernatural," Bushnell defined the supernatural in part as the power of man to act upon the natural world and to obtain knowledge of natural law. He considered the penetration of the laws of nature by the power of reason to be God's way of unveiling the mysteries of the universe. He fully expected that this would bring God closer to man and would make men more aware of the moral laws of life. Gladden applied Bushnell's reasoning by analogy from natural law to moral law.

11. Washington Gladden, *Recollections* (Boston: Houghton Mifflin, 1909), pp. 322-23.

12. Rauschenbusch, *A Theology for the Social Gospel,* p. 178.

13. William Newton Clarke, *The Christian Doctrine of God* (New York: Charles Scribner's Sons, 1923), p. 251.

14. Ibid., p. 377.

15. Rauschenbusch, *A Theology for the Social Gospel,* p. 17.

16. Ibid.

17. Ibid., p. 131.

18. Ibid., p. 177.

19. Ibid., p. 26.

20. Gladden, *How Much Is Left of the Old Doctrines?* p. 23.

21. Unusual natural events were not seen as being contrary to the laws of nature. Events that seemed miraculous or disorderly only appeared to be outside the laws of nature because they were contrary to what was then known of natural law. Eventually events perceived as miracles would be fully understood, not as supernatural events breaking the laws of nature but as the perfection and completion of the natural process.

22. Gladden, *Present Day Theology,* p. 190.

23. Washington Gladden, *Witnesses of the Light* (1903; reprint ed., Freeport, N.Y.: Books for Libraries Press, 1969), pp. 25-26.

24. It is tempting to interpret the God who creates and sustains as an image of unrestrained female fecundity, which would appeal to sexually repressed Victorian men. I suspect that this is true of the image of a ripe and productive Mother Nature commonly used by Victorians. But I have no evidence to suggest that the Social Gospel men were unconsciously using natural imagery to suggest feminine sexual generosity or abandon. It is more consistent with their thought as a whole to interpret their God as containing both male and female elements.

25. Rauschenbusch, *A Theology for the Social Gospel,* p. 167.

26. Benson Y. Landis, ed., *A Rauschenbusch Reader* (New York: Harper & Bros., 1957), p. 134.

27. Rauschenbusch, *A Theology for the Social Gospel,* pp. 47-50.

28. Ibid., pp. 264-67.

29. Ibid., p. 191.

30. *William Newton Clarke: A Biography with Additional Sketches by His Friends and Colleagues* (New York: Charles Scribner's Sons, 1916), p. 205.

31. Francis G. Peabody, *Jesus Christ and the Social Question* (New York: Grosset & Dunlap, 1900), p. 74.

32. John Henry Newman (1801-90), later Cardinal Newman, an Anglican who converted to Catholicism, was a contemporary of Coleridge. Both men gave high priority to the power of the spirit in human personality.

33. Alcott's idealism in the theory of education was radical in 1830, but his educational method was more common in the revolt against rote educational methods in 1880. Lyman Abbott's father and uncles ran a "progressive school" in New York City that was founded in 1845.

34. James Freeman Clarke, in the introduction to *Self-Culture* (Boston: Houghton Mifflin, 1890), advised parents to use nature's way of educating children by discovery and invention rather than by imposing restraint and self-discipline. A happy childhood and youth would be the best preparation for life, which was "hard work, trial and difficulty," because it would provide happy memories when adult life was experienced as difficult and discouraging.

35. Gladden, *Present Day Theology,* p. 80.

36. Walter Rauschenbusch, *Christianity and the Social Crisis* (1907; reprint ed., New York: Harper & Row, 1964), pp. 264-65.

37. Francis G. Peabody, *The Religious Education of an American Citizen* (New York: Macmillan, 1917), chap. 2.

38. Walter Rauschenbusch, *The Social Principles of Jesus* (New York: Association Press, 1916), p. 158.

39. This is an intricate facet of the nineteenth-century attempt to explain sin and its functions in human life. Hegel and Schleiermacher both theorized that a woman developed morally through the experience of childbirth because that event stirred her consciousness of spiritual need through facing possible death in

childbirth. This is also the reason marriage was imperative for a woman from the perspective of sin as a fortunate fall.

40. Clarke, *The Christian Doctrine of God,* p. 251.
41. Lyman Abbott, *The Evolution of Christianity* (New York: Outlook Co., 1892), p. 244.
42. Washington Gladden, *Being a Christian* (1876; reprint ed., Freeport, N.Y.: Books for Libraries Press, 1972), p. 10.
43. Abbott, *The Evolution of Christianity,* p. 1.
44. Ibid., p. 133.
45. Rauschenbusch, *A Theology for the Social Gospel,* p. 271.
46. Ibid., pp. 273–79.
47. Ibid., p. 263.
48. Rauschenbusch used only biblical texts that were empirically possible. The symbolic power of the "spirit of Jesus" is attributed only to suffering and crucifixion. The resurrection is not mentioned by Rauschenbusch.
49. Rauschenbusch, *A Theology for the Social Gospel,* pp. 264–67.
50. Ibid., pp. 108–9.
51. Rauschenbusch, *The Social Principles of Jesus,* pp. 8–13.
52. Rauschenbusch, *A Theology for the Social Gospel,* p. 279.
53. Walter Rauschenbusch, *Christianizing the Social Order* (New York: Macmillan, 1913), pp. 45–47.
54. Rauschenbusch, *The Social Principles of Jesus,* chap. 2.
55. Landis, ed., *A Rauschenbusch Reader,* p. 78.
56. Rauschenbusch, *Christianity and the Social Crisis,* pp. 67–68.
57. Francis G. Peabody, *Jesus Christ and the Christian Character* (New York: Macmillan, 1906), p. 124.
58. Gladden, *How Much Is Left of the Old Doctrines?* p. 239.
59. Rauschenbusch, *Christianity and the Social Crisis,* chap. 7.
60. Peabody, *Jesus Christ and the Christian Character,* p. 69.
61. Rauschenbusch, *A Theology for the Social Gospel,* p. 238.
62. Dores R. Sharpe, *Walter Rauschenbusch* (New York: Macmillan, 1942), pp. 343–49.
63. *William Newton Clarke,* p. 100.

Chapter 7:
The Paradoxes of
the Social Gospel Movement

1. Lyman Beecher, *Autobiography of Lyman Beecher* (Cambridge: Harvard University Press, 1961), 2:380–81.
2. Theodore K. Rabb and Robert I. Rotberg, *The Family in History: Interdisciplinary Essays* (New York: Harper & Row, 1971), pp. 202–3. In Andover, Massachusetts, for instance, only 43 percent of the fourth-generation males

Notes

remained in Andover by the time of the Revolution. The land could no longer sustain the population.

3. In *The Positive Thinkers* (Garden City: Doubleday, 1965), Donald B. Meyer interprets the self-made man to mean a motherless or self-generative man, while the literature for girls concerning fatherless families suggests a fatherless girl. While his interpretation suggests ambivalence toward the parent of the opposite sex, I am suggesting that the economic and social situation in America was one source of antipathy between fathers and sons.

4. The connection between economic language and sexuality is developed in Peter T. Cominos, "Late Victorian Sexual Respectability and the Social System," *International Review of Social History* 8 (1963): 216–50.

5. In *Home Life in America* (New York: Macmillan, 1910), Katherine G. Busbey documented the dimensions of dissatisfaction for both men and women in the Victorian family arrangement.

6. Herbert G. Gutman, "Protestantism and the American Labor Movement: The Christian Spirit in the Gilded Age," *American Historical Review,* October 1966, pp. 74–101.

7. The father of Lyman Abbott remarried after the death of Lyman's mother and did not live with the children of his first marriage.

8. Francis Peabody was seven when his clergyman father died. He later remembered only the unsmiling face of his austere father.

9. Lyman Abbott, *Reminiscences* (Boston: Houghton Mifflin, 1915), p. 355.

10. Washington Gladden, *Recollections* (Boston: Houghton Mifflin, 1909), chap. 25.

11. Walter Rauschenbusch, *Christianizing the Social Order* (New York: Macmillan, 1913), p. 94.

12. Gladden, *Recollections,* p. 205.

13. From the conservative point of view, woman suffrage and prohibition could be seen as complementary. Conservative evangelicals wanted a moral social order without legislation that would limit economic competition. Some Victorians believed that women voting would purify public opinion and indirectly "clean up" political processes. While granting women this limited place in the public sphere, prohibition would protect women and children in the private sphere. Both amendments can be interpreted as indirect attempts to improve the moral tenor of life, both public and private.

14. Josiah Strong, *The New Era* (New York: Baker & Taylor, 1893), chap. 6, "The Two Fundamental Laws."

15. Theologians from Augustine to the present have pointed out the distinction between the nature of God and the limits of thought and language to express the nature of God. In the twentieth century Paul Tillich distinguished between a religious symbol and an "exchangeable metaphor." The thought of the Social Gospel is an "exchangeable metaphor" in that it drains religious language and thought of the power to transcend the concrete. *The Protestant Era* (Chicago: University of Chicago Press, 1957), pp. 61–65.

16. Immanuel Kant, *Critique of Pure Reason* (New York: St. Martin's Press, 1929), pp. 267–68.

17. Ibid., pp. 54–62.

18. Walter Rauschenbusch, *A Theology for the Social Gospel* (1917; reprint ed., Nashville: Abingdon Press, 1945), pp. 92–93.

19. Friedrich Schleiermacher, *The Christian Faith,* ed. H. R. Mackintosh and J. S. Stewart (New York: Harper & Row, 1963), 2:388–89.

20. Albrecht Ritschl, *The Christian Doctrine of Justification and Reconciliation* (Clifton: Reference Book Publishers, 1966), pp. 495–507.

21. Rauschenbusch, *A Theology for the Social Gospel,* pp. 238–39.

22. Dean Hoge, *Division in the Protestant House* (Philadelphia: Westminster Press, 1976), p. 24.

23. Ibid., p. 88.

24. Ibid., p. 110.

Bibliography

Primary Sources

Abbott, Lyman. *Christianity and Social Problems*. Boston: Riverside Press, 1896.

————. *The Evolution of Christianity*. New York: Outlook Co., 1892.

————. "Gladden Obituary." *The Outlook*, July 17, 1918, p. 442.

————. *The Homebuilder*. Boston: Houghton Mifflin, 1908.

————. *Problems of Life*. New York: Dodd, Mead & Co., 1903.

————. *Reminiscences*. Boston: Houghton Mifflin, 1915.

————. *The Rights of Man*. Boston: Houghton Mifflin, 1902.

————. *The Theology of an Evolutionist*. Boston: Houghton Mifflin, 1897.

Adams, Henry. *The Education of Henry Adams*. 1918. Reprint. Boston: Houghton Mifflin, 1961.

Alcott, William. *Physiology of Marriage*. 1866. Reprint. New York: Arno Press, 1972.

Beecher, Henry Ward. *Evolution and Christianity*. Vol. 1. Boston: Pilgrim Press, ca. 1885.

Beecher, Lyman. *Autobiography of Lyman Beecher*. 2 vols. Cambridge: Harvard University Press, 1961.

Bellamy, Edward. *Looking Backward: 2000–1887*. 1887. Reprint. Cambridge: Belknap Press, 1967.

Bushnell, Horace. *Christian Nurture*. 1861. Reprint. New Haven: Yale University Press, 1967.

————. *Moral Uses of Dark Things*. 1869. Reprint. New York: Charles Scribner's Sons, 1903.

Carnegie, Andrew. "Wealth." *North American Review*, June 1889, pp. 653–64.

Clarke, James Freeman. *Self-Culture*. Boston: Houghton Mifflin, 1890.

————. *Ten Great Religions*. Vols. 1 and 2. Boston: Houghton Mifflin, 1871, 1883.

Clarke, William Newton. *The Christian Doctrine of God.* New York: Charles Scribner's Sons, 1923.

_____. *The Ideal of Jesus.* New York: Charles Scribner's Sons, 1911.

_____. *An Outline of Christian Theology.* New York: Charles Scribner's Sons, 1904.

_____. *Sixty Years with the Bible: A Record of Experience.* New York: Charles Scribner's Sons, 1910.

_____. *A Study of Christian Missions.* New York: Charles Scribner's Sons, 1900.

_____. *The Use of the Scriptures in Theology.* Edinburgh: T. & T. Clarke, 1907.

Combe, George. *The Constitution of Man.* New York: Fowless and Wells, 1850.

Conway, Moncure. *Autobiography.* 2 vols. Boston: Houghton Mifflin, 1904.

Crane, Stephen. *The Red Badge of Courage.* 1895. Reprint. New York: Bantam Books, 1972.

Darwin, Charles. *The Descent of Man and Selection in Relation to Sex.* 1871. Reprint. Chicago: Encyclopedia Britannica, 1952.

_____. *On the Origin of Species by Means of Natural Selection.* 1859. Reprint. Chicago: Encyclopedia Britannica, 1952.

Dewey, John. *American Education.* 1904. Reprint. New York: Arno Press, 1969.

Drummond, Henry. *The Ascent of Man.* New York: James Pott & Co., 1894.

Fiske, John. *The Destiny of Man Viewed in the Light of His Origin.* Boston: Houghton Mifflin, 1884.

_____. *Life Everlasting.* Boston: Houghton Mifflin, 1901.

Fourier, Charles. *The Passions of the Human Soul.* Vol. 1. 1851. Reprint. New York: Kelley, 1968.

Frederic, Harold. *The Damnation of Theron Ware.* 1896. Reprint. Cambridge: Belknap Press, 1960.

George, Henry. *Progress and Poverty.* 1879. Reprint. New York: Robert Schalkenbach Foundation, 1970.

Gibbons, James Cardinal. *A Retrospect of Fifty Years.* 2 vols. New York: Arno Press, 1972.

Gladden, Washington. *Applied Christianity.* Boston: Houghton Mifflin, 1886.

_____. *Being a Christian: What It Means and How to Begin.* 1876. Reprint. Freeport, N.Y.: Books for Libraries Press, 1972.

_____. *Christianity and Socialism.* New York: Eaton & Mains, 1905.

_____. *How Much Is Left of the Old Doctrines? A Book for the People.* Boston: Houghton Mifflin, 1899.

_____. *Live and Learn.* New York: Macmillan, 1914.

_____. *Present Day Theology.* Columbus: McClelland & Co., 1913.

_____. *Recollections.* Boston: Houghton Mifflin, 1909.

_____. *Ruling Ideas.* Boston: Houghton Mifflin, 1895.

Bibliography

————. *Who Wrote the Bible? A Book for the People.* 1891. Reprint. Freeport, N.Y.: Books for Libraries Press, 1972.

————. *Witnesses of the Light.* 1903. Reprint. Freeport, N.Y.: Books for Libraries Press, 1969.

————. *Working People and Their Employers.* Boston: Lockwood Brooks & Co., 1876.

Gregg, David. *Ideal Young Men and Women.* New York: E. B. Treat, 1897.

Hegel, G. W. F. *The Phenomenology of Mind.* Trans. J. B. Baillie. New York: Harper Torchbooks, 1967.

Hodge, Charles. *What Is Darwinism?* New York: Charles Scribner's Sons, 1874.

Howells, William Dean. *April Hopes.* Introduction and notes by Kermit Vanderbilt. Bloomington: Indiana University Press, 1974.

James, William. *The Varieties of Religious Experience: A Study in Human Nature.* 1902. Reprint. New York: Modern Library, 1936.

Kant, Immanuel. *Critique of Pure Reason.* New York: St Martin's Press, 1929.

————. *Religion Within the Limits of Reason Alone.* Trans. with an introduction and notes by Theodore M. Greene and Hoyt H. Hudson. New York: Harper Torchbooks, 1960.

Kaplan, A. D. *The Baby's Biography.* New York: Brentano's, 1891.

Landis, Benson Y., ed. *A Rauschenbusch Reader.* New York: Harper & Bros., 1957.

Lloyd, Henry G. *Wealth Against Commonwealth.* New York: Harper & Bros., 1894.

McCosh, James. *Christianity and Positivism.* New York: Carter & Bros., 1871.

————. *The Intuitions of the Mind Inductively Investigated.* New York: B. Carter, 1867.

Norris, Frank. *The Pit.* 1903. Facsimile reprint. Columbus: Merrill, 1970.

Peabody, Francis Greenwood. *Afternoons in the College Chapel.* Boston: Houghton Mifflin, 1898.

————. *The Approach to the Social Question.* New York: Macmillan, 1909.

————. *Jesus Christ and the Christian Character.* New York: Macmillan, 1906.

————. *Jesus Christ and the Social Question.* New York: Grosset & Dunlap, 1900.

————. *The Liquor Problem: A Summary of Investigations Published by a Committee of Fifty, 1893–1903.* Boston: Houghton Mifflin, 1905.

————. *The Religious Education of an American Citizen.* New York: Macmillan, 1917.

————. *Reminiscences of Present-Day Saints.* Boston: Houghton Mifflin, 1927.

————. *The Social Teachings of Jesus Christ.* Philadelphia: University of Pennsylvania Press, 1924.

Rauschenbusch, Walter. *Christianity and the Social Crisis.* 1907. Reprint. New York: Harper & Row, 1964.

————. *Christianizing the Social Order.* New York: Macmillan, 1913.

_____. *The Social Principles of Jesus*. New York: Association Press, 1916.
_____. *A Theology for the Social Gospel*. 1917. Reprint. Nashville: Abingdon Press, 1945.
Ritschl, Albrecht. *The Christian Doctrine of Justification and Reconciliation*. English translation ed. by H. R. McIntosh and A. B. Macaulay. Clifton: Reference Book Publishers, 1966.
Roosevelt, Theodore. *The Strenuous Life*. 1902. Reprint. St. Clair Shores, Mich.: Scholarly Press, 1970.
Schleiermacher, Friedrich. *The Christian Faith*. 2 vols. Ed. H. R. Mackintosh and J. S. Stewart. New York: Harper & Row, 1963.
_____. *On Religion: Speeches to Its Cultured Despisers*. Trans. John Oman with introduction by Rudolph Otto. New York: Harper & Row, 1958.
Sheldon, Charles M. *In His Steps: What Would Jesus Do?* Chicago: Advance Publishing Co., 1897. .
Smith, H. Shelton, ed. *Horace Bushnell*. New York: Oxford University Press, 1965.
Spencer, Herbert. *An Autobiography*. 2 vols. New York: D. Appleton & Co., 1904.
_____. *Education: Intellectual, Moral and Physical*. Akron: Werner Co., 1860.
_____. *Social Statics*. 1850. Reprint. New York: Robert Schalkenbach Foundation, 1970.
Stead, William T. *If Christ Came to Chicago*. Chicago: Laird & Lee, 1894.
Strong, Josiah. *The New Era*. New York: Baker & Taylor, 1893.
_____. *Our Country*. Rev. ed. New York: Baker & Taylor, 1885, 1891.
_____. *The Twentieth Century City*. 1898. Reprint. New York: Arno Press, 1970.
Sumner, William Graham. *What Social Classes Owe Each Other*. 1883. Reprint. New York: Arno Press, 1972.
Taylor, Graham. *Pioneering on Social Frontiers*. Chicago: University of Chicago Press, 1930.
_____. *Religion in Social Action*. New York: Dodd, Mead & Co., 1913.
Taylor, Nathaniel. *Lectures on the Moral Government of God*. 2 vols. New York: Clark, Austin and Smith, 1859.
Twain, Mark. *A Connecticut Yankee in King Arthur's Court*. 1889. Reprint. San Francisco: Chandler, 1963.
Van Dyke, Henry. *The Gospel in an Age of Doubt*. New York: Macmillan, 1906.
Veblen, Thorstein. *The Theory of the Leisure Class*. 1899. Reprint. Boston: Houghton Mifflin, 1973.

Secondary Sources

Abell, Aaron. *The Urban Impact on American Protestantism, 1865–1900*. New York: Hanover, 1960.

Bibliography

Ahlstrom, Sydney E. *A Religious History of the American People*. New Haven: Yale University Press, 1972.

———. *Theology in America: The Major Protestant Voices from Puritanism to Neo-Orthodoxy*. Indianapolis: Bobbs-Merrill, 1967.

Bliss, W. D. P. *The New Encyclopedia of Social Reform*. 1908. Reprint. New York: Arno Press, 1970.

Boller, Paul F. *American Thought in Transition: The Impact of Evolutionary Naturalism, 1865–1900*. Chicago: Rand McNally, 1969.

Bourke, Paul F. "The Social Critics and the End of American Innocence, 1907–1921." *Journal of American Studies* 3, no. 1 (1969): 57–72.

Brown, Ira V. *Lyman Abbott*. Westport, Conn.: Greenwood Press, 1953.

Burgess, John. *Reconstruction and the Constitution*. New York: Charles Scribner's Sons, 1902.

Busbey, Katherine. *Home Life in America*. New York: Macmillan, 1910.

Calhoun, Arthur W. *A Social History of the American Family*, Vol. 3. Cleveland: Arthur H. Clark Co., 1919.

Champney, Elizabeth W. *The Romance of the Feudal Chateaux*. New York: G. P. Putman's Sons, 1905.

Cheney, Mary Bushnell. *Life and Letters of Horace Bushnell*. New York: Harper & Bros., 1880.

Cherry, Conrad. *Nature and Religious Imagination*. Philadelphia: Fortress Press, 1980.

———, ed. *God's New Israel*. Englewood Cliffs, N.J.: Prentice-Hall, 1971.

Cominos, Peter T. "Late Victorian Sexual Respectability and the Social System." *International Review of Social History* 8 (1963): 216–50.

Commager, Henry Steele. *The American Mind: An Interpretation of American Thought and Character Since the 1880's*. New Haven: Yale University Press, 1950.

———, ed. *Living Ideas in America*. New York: Harper & Row, 1964.

Cott, Nancy F. *The Bonds of Womanhood*. New Haven: Yale University Press, 1977.

Cross, Robert. *The Church and the City, 1865–1900*. New York: Bobbs-Merrill, 1967.

Dorn, Jacob Henry. *Washington Gladden: Prophet of the Social Gospel*. Columbus: Ohio State Press, 1966.

Douglas, Ann. *The Feminization of American Culture*. New York: Knopf, 1978.

Ellis, John Tracy. *American Catholicism*. Chicago: University of Chicago Press, 1972.

Filene, Peter Gabriel. *Him/Her/Self*. New York: Harcourt Brace Jovanovich, 1974.

Frederickson, George M. *The Inner Civil War: Northern Intellectuals and the Crisis of the Union*. New York: Harper & Row, 1965.

Gaustad, Edwin S., ed. *The Rise of Adventism*. New York: Harper & Row, 1974.

Gutman, Herbert G. "Protestantism and the American Labor Movement: The Christian Spirit in the Gilded Age." *American Historical Review,* October 1966, pp. 74-101.

Hale, Nathan, Jr. *Freud in America, 1876-1917.* New York: Oxford University Press, 1971.

Handy, Robert T. *A Christian America: Protestant Hopes and Historical Realities.* New York: Oxford University Press, 1971.

————. *The Social Gospel in America.* New York: Oxford University Press, 1966.

Herman, Sondra R. "Loving Courtship or the Marriage Market: The Ideal and Its Critics, 1871-1911." *American Quarterly* 25 (May 1973): 235-55.

Hofstadter, Richard. *Social Darwinism in American Thought, 1860-1915.* Rev. ed. New York: Braziller, 1955.

Hoge, Dean. *Division in the Protestant House.* Philadelphia: Westminster Press, 1976.

Hopkins, C. Howard. *The Rise of the Social Gospel in American Protestantism, 1865-1915.* New Haven: Yale University Press, 1940.

Hudson, Winthrop S. *The Great Tradition of the American Churches.* New York: Harper & Bros., 1953.

————. *Religion in America.* New York: Charles Scribner's Sons, 1973.

Hutchison, William. *The Modernist Impulse in American Protestantism.* Cambridge: Harvard University Press, 1976.

Keniston, Kenneth. *All Our Children.* New York: Harcourt Brace Jovanovich, 1977.

Lasch, Christopher. *Haven in a Heartless World.* New York: Basic Books, 1977.

————. *The World of Nations.* New York: Knopf, 1973.

McLoughlin, William. *The Meaning of Henry Ward Beecher.* New York: Knopf, 1970.

Marty, Martin. *Righteous Empire: The Protestant Experience in America.* New York: Dial Press, 1970.

May, Henry. *The Enlightenment in America.* New York: Oxford University Press, 1976.

————. *Protestant Churches and Industrial America.* New York: Harper & Bros., 1949.

Mead, Sidney E. *The Lively Experiment: The Shaping of Christianity in America.* New York: Harper & Row, 1963.

Meyer, Donald B. *The Positive Thinkers: A Study of the Quest for Health, Wealth and Personal Power from Mary Baker Eddy to Norman Vincent Peale.* Garden City: Doubleday, 1965.

Morgan, H. Wayne. *The Gilded Age: A Reappraisal.* New York: Syracuse University Press, 1970.

Morison, Samuel Eliot. *The Oxford History of the American People.* Vol. 3. New York: Mentor, 1972.

Bibliography

Muller, Dorothea R. "The Social Philosophy of Josiah Strong: Social Christianity and American Progressivism." *Church History* 28 (1959): 183–201.

Niebuhr, H. Richard. *The Kingdom of God in America.* New York: Harper & Bros., 1937.

Parsons, Stow. *The Decline of American Gentility.* New York: Columbia, 1973.

Pivar, David Jay. *Purity Crusade: Sexual Morality and Social Control, 1868–1900.* Westport, Conn.: Greenwood Press, 1973.

Rabb, Theodore K., and Rotberg, Robert I. *The Family in History: Interdisciplinary Essays.* New York: Harper & Row, 1971.

Roemer, Kenneth M. *The Obsolete Necessity: America in Utopian Writings, 1888–1900.* Kent: Kent State University Press, 1976.

Rosenberg, Charles I. "Sexuality, Class and Role in 19th Century America." *American Quarterly,* Summer 1973, pp. 131–54.

Schlesinger, A. M. "A Critical Period in American Religion, 1865–1900." *Proceedings of the Massachusetts Historical Society* 64 (1932): 523–48.

──────. *Rise of Modern America, 1865–1951.* New York: Macmillan, 1951.

Sharpe, Dores R. *Walter Rauschenbusch.* New York: Macmillan, 1942.

Smith, H. Shelton, ed. *Horace Bushnell.* New York: Oxford University Press, 1965.

Smith. H. Shelton; Handy, Robert T.; and Loetscher, Lefferts A. *American Christianity: An Historical Interpretation with Representative Documents, Vol. II: 1820–1960.* New York: Charles Scribner's Sons, 1963.

Strout, Cushing. *The New Heavens and the New Earth: Political Religion in America.* New York: Harper & Row, 1974.

Thomas, John Wesley. *James Freeman Clarke.* Boston: Luce & Co., 1949.

Tillich, Paul. *The Protestant Era.* Chicago: University of Chicago Press, 1957.

Wade, Louise C. *Graham Taylor: Pioneer for Social Justice, 1851–1938.* Chicago: University of Chicago Press, 1964.

Weisenberger, Francis P. *Ordeal of Faith: The Crisis of Church-Going America, 1865–1900.* New York: Philadelphia Library, 1959.

Wiebe, Robert. *The Search for Order.* New York: Hill & Wang, 1967.

William Newton Clarke: A Biography with Additional Sketches by His Friends and Colleagues. New York: Charles Scribner's Sons, 1916.

Williams, Daniel Day. *The Andover Liberals: A Study in American Theology.* New York: King's Crown Press, 1941.

Wishy, Bernard. *The Child and the Republic.* Philadelphia: University of Pennsylvania Press, 1968.

Wright, Conrad. *Three Prophets of Religious Liberalism.* Boston: Beacon Press, 1961.

Ziff, Larzer. *The American 1890's: Life and Times of a Lost Generation.* New York: Viking Press, 1966.

Index

Abbott, Lyman: on the city, 84–85; Dawes Act, 74–75; epistemology in, 134–35, 172; on Indian barbarism, 74–75; on "the Negro," 73; on prohibition, 88; on public opinion, 75; on the Spanish-American War, 109

Acquisitiveness, 79

Adams, Henry, 18, 71–72

Afterlife: as continuing development, 157–58; and evolutionary hypothesis, 48; and morality, 47; Rauschenbusch on, 158, 174

Alcott, Bronson, 38, 144

Alcott, William, 38, 42–45

Altruism: definition of, 40; in industrial conflict, 76; of middle-class family, 93, 145; and the socialist state, 68, 116

Amativeness, 39, 43, 123, 154

Animalism: in "the Negro," the anarchist, the priest, 87; as sin, 145–46, 154

Barbarian, definition of, 42

Barbarism: in the Captain of Industry, 106; William Newton Clarke on, 120–21; of the Indian,

74; and savage man, 42; and social disorder, 42

Beecher, Henry Ward, 31, 37, 59, 79

Beecher, Lyman, 6, 90, 160

Bellamy, Edward, 116–18

Bible: analogical method, 47; authority of, 130; biblical-historical method, 4; intuitionist theory of inspiration, 51, 130, 135; moral inspiration of, 64, 130; theory of biblical dictation, 50

Bliss, W. D. P., 87–88

Brotherhood of the Kingdom, 4, 9, 169

Brotherhood of Man: common use of, 92, 170; in the Social Gospel, 15, 92, 119, 150, 170; like the Victorian family, 23; verification in moral progress, 136

Bushnell, Horace, 49–50, 70–71

Calvinist, "Old Light": autocratic God of, 136; doctrine of human nature, 52, 134, 144; doctrine of predestination, 135; and egotism, 145; as orthodoxy, 129; revolt against, 129

Capitalism: as cause of sexual inequality, 116; effects of, 20, 118;

and the "self-made man," 160
Captain of Industry: Henry G.
Lloyd on, 105; and the male
achiever ethos, 102–103; Francis
G. Peabody on, 110
Catholic: immigrants, 17, 82;
priesthood, 9, 87
Catholicism: and civilization, 110;
Rauschenbusch on, 110. *See also*
"Romanism"
Character, development of, 145, 146,
152–53
Cherry, Conrad, xi
Chivalry: and the Christian
gentleman, 111, 170; and
democracy, 77, 110; and male
self-sacrifice, 27; in marriage, 27;
in the Social Gospel, 32, 166; in
the South, 71; and the Victorian
gentleman, 111
Christ: the cross as duty, 148, 152;
as historical fact, 148; as the ideal
type of humanity, 148
Christian Gentleman. *See*
Gentleman, Christian
Christian Manhood. *See* Manhood,
Christian
Christianized America: and social
institutions, 100; the moral
influence of the Christian citizen
in, 88–89; Rauschenbusch on, 96;
role of family in, 23–24, 85, 108
Church: affluence of, 167;
disestablishment of, 30;
evangelism in, 91–92; feminized,
31, 44, 169; historical destiny of,
96, 102; middle-class values in,
175; role of clergy in, 29–30;
social functions of, 5–7, 16, 17,
29–31, 102; stewardship in, 91–92,
168
City: as immoral environment, 84–
86; Strong on, 84–86
Civilization: in American

democracy, 56; definition of, 41,
42; Henry George on, 62; and
progress in history, 62; in the
Social Gospel, 69, 99. *See also*
Morality, Civilized; and Cultures,
civilized and barbarian
Civilized Morality. *See* Morality,
Civilized
Civil War: as freedom from
paternalism, 159–60; as vicarious
sacrifice of the North, 50, 71
Clarke, William Newton: on afterlife, 158; on barbarism, 120–21;
on change in the church, 31; faith
of, 143–44; on progress in reason,
52; *Sixty Years With the Bible,*
46; on the "social spirit," 126; *A
Study of Christian Missions,* 126
Coleridge, Samuel Taylor, 54
Combe, George: *The Constitution
of Man,* 38–42, 171–72;
epistemology in, 52, 171–72; and
moral law, 40–41, 52, 171–72; and
natural law, 41; and phrenology,
38–42
Competition: and character
development, 78; and
commercialism, 45; and progress,
79
Conversion: in adolescence, 146–47;
as "change of heart," 10; in
conversionist psychology, 37; "old
light" expectations of, 29; and
sexuality, 101–102, 146–47
Crane, Stephen, 104
Cultures, civilized and barbarian,
44, 60, 71–72, 174

Darwin, Charles: on civilized
morality, 61; *The Descent of
Man,* 59, 60; on moral sense, 59;
Origin of the Species, 46, 53, 54;
Social Darwinism, 35; on theory
of natural selection, 54, 60; on

theory of sexual selection, 60
Democracy: and the family ideal, 23, 124; and private property, 74–75, 113–14
Dilthey, Wilhelm, x
Douglas, Ann, xi
Drummond, Henry, 99

Economics, laissez-faire. *See* Laissez-Faire Economics
Egotism: in children, 145; and competiton, 79; definition of, 40
Ellis, Havelock, 22
Emerson, Ralph Waldo, 26
Epistemology: Abbott on, 134–35; Combe on, 52; Gladden on, 134–35; Kant on, 172; in the Social Gospel, 134–35, 172–73
Ethical Idealism: on acts and ideals, 137; complementarity of the sexes in, 101; faculty psychology in, 101; family in, 101; Social Darwinism in, 101–102, 132; and the social status quo, 120; and theology, 131; and vocation, 154
Evangelical, "New Light": 5, 29, 129; and manifest destiny, 64; the Social Gospel as a masculine form of, 162
Evolution, biological, 54–55
Evolutionary Hypothesis: and afterlife, 48; and doctrine of God, 138; and Paley's analogy, 47; and theology, 129–30

Faculty Psychology. *See* Psychology, Faculty
Family: as building block of society, 23, 42–43, 53, 120, 122; changes in, 22, 24–26, 112, 159–61; and a Christianized America, 23–24, 85, 108; as a means of natural selection, 63, 69, 101, 117; as a microcosm of the Kingdom of

God, 114–15, 156
Family Ethos: Peabody on, 114–15, 121–22; in Social Darwinism, 64; in the Social Gospel, 64, 163–64; unrewarding to men, 161
Father, Victorian: autocratic, 161; remote, 159–61
Fatherhood of God: common use of, 92, 162, 170; in Social Gospel thought, 15, 92, 119, 170; use by labor leaders, 162; verification in moral progress, 139–40
Feminists, 22, 95, 112
Finney, Charles Grandison, 6, 29, 37, 101
Fourier, Charles: on civilized morality, 45; on "familistic" socialism, 45, 111–12; *Passions of the Human Soul*, 45
Fourierites: and "familistic" socialism, 45, 111–12; and "free love" communes, 111–12
Frederic, Harold, 22, 87
Freedom: in democracy, 121, and moral development, 119–20, 123

Gentleman, Christian, 32, 102, 109, 111, 165, 170
Gentleman, Victorian, 32, 111
George, Henry: influence on Social Gospel, 61–63; and the land tax, 62; on progress in history, 62; *Progress and Poverty*, 36, 61
Gladden, Washington: on arbitration, 76; biography of, 12, 19; on the Civil War, 72; on conversion, 19, 155; epistemology in, 134–35, 172; on industrial conflict, 76; "Is It Peace or War?", 76–78; on legislation, 184; on nativism, 90–91; nature romanticism in, 85; *Present-Day Theology*, 14; on prohibition, 88; *Recollections*, 18; on

reconstruction, 72–73; on "tainted money," 169; on wages-fund theory, 78; on war, 104, 109; on "the worker class," 19

God: as the Creator, 42; and the evolutionary hypothesis, 138; as First Cause, 47, 132, 135; as "light," 143; as Vital Energy, 132

God the Father: forgiving, 139–40; as the God of democracy, 142; like a Victorian father, 141, 144; like a Victorian mother, 140–41; and the middle-class, 141; a mother-father figure, 141; as procreator, 139; unchangeable, 140; verifiable, 136

God concept, the, 141

Hegel, G. W. F., 158, 173, 189
Hoge, Dean, xi, 174
Hodge, Charles, 50

Idealism, Ethical. See Ethical Idealism
Ingersoll, Robert, 4
In His Steps, 166
Indian, American, 74
Industrialization: and division of labor, 20; and effect on the family, 21, 24; and industrial development, 18–20; and industrial warfare, 20
Ireland, Bishop John, 81–82

James, William: on the church, 31–32; on manhood, 32; "The Moral Equivalent of War," 104–105
Jesus Christ: as the friend, 148; as the God within, 148–49

Kant, Immanuel, 172–73
Kingdom of God: and the family ideal, 15, 124, 151; as inspiration of faith, 152; and manifest destiny, 15, 81, 170; as the national hope, 98, 163; as norm of Rauschenbusch's theology, 137; as a social ideal, 98, 150–51

Laissez-Faire Economics: effect on youth, 102–105; and international expansion, 109; and manhood, 102–103, 160; Peabody on, 114; and the "self-made man," 160; in Social Gospel thought, 79; and survival of the fittest, 77

Legislation, Progressive: Rauschenbusch on, 113, 118–19; and Roosevelt, 20, 113; in the Social Gospel, 35, 70, 80, 88; Strong on, 83–84, 86, 92

Lloyd, Henry G.: on Captain of Industry, 106–107; on trusts and monopolies, 106–107; Wealth Against Commonwealth, 92, 106

Maguires, Molly, 19, 87

Manhood: and male achiever ethos, 21, 102; and manly virtues, 28; and moral self-sacrifice, 27, 165; and the public sphere, 21, 27–28, 44, 170; and work, 20, 27–28. See also Gentleman, Christian; Gentleman, Victorian; and Manhood, Christian

Manhood, Christian: leadership potential of, 111, 156–57, 169; and manifest destiny, 90; as perpetual incarnation, 148–49, 166; and purity of woman, 123; as salvation, 146; and Theodore Roosevelt, 103–104

Manifest Destiny: and American expansionism, 107–108; as a Christianized America, 89, 164, 170; as Kingdom of God on earth, 81; and social conflict, 82; and Social Darwinism, 63; and

survival of the fittest, 35
Marriage: complementarity of the
sexes, 26, 43–44; crisis of, 22;
nature of, 23; purity in, 43;
Rauschenbusch on, 122; Victorian
ideal of, 26–28
Marty, Martin, 175
Masturbation, 40, 44
Men and Religion Forward
Movement, 30, 32
Middle Class: and alcohol, 83–84;
economic insecurity of, 11, 13, 20;
independence of, 25; moral
anxiety of, 86, 164, 168; as
physically superior, 83–84; and
the status quo, 58, 175
Moody, Dwight L., 10, 99
Moral Evolution: as interpretation
of Civil War, 72–73; and manifest
destiny, 82; and "spirit of Jesus,"
119; and survival of the fittest, 61,
72
Moral Sense: and character
development, 145; Darwin on,
59–61; in faculty psychology, 55;
and public opinion, 58, 133–34;
Spencer on, 53, 55–58, 133–34
Morality, Civilized: in Darwin, 61;
in Fourier, 45–46; in
Rauschenbusch social ethic, 119,
as standard of character, 75
Mother, Victorian, moral influence
of, 88, 122

Natural Selection: theory of,
Darwin on, 48, 53–54; family as
means of, 63; in Social Gospel,
68; Social Gospel response to, 49,
59, 61; Strong on, 82; theory of
sexual selection, 60, 80
Natural Theology, 47–50, 172
Nature Romanticism: and the city,
85; and theology, 139–40
"Negro," 55, 73–74

"New" Liberal Theology. See
Theology, "New" Liberal
"New Light" Evangelical. See
Evangelical, "New Light"
Newman, Cardinal John H., 143
Norris, Frank, 80

"Old Light" Calvinist. See
Calvinist, "Old Light"

Paley, William, 47
Paradox: in the Christian theological
tradition, 174; definition of, 16; in
Social Gospel movement, 166,
170; in Social Gospel thought, 15,
159, 174
Peabody, Francis Greenwood: on
Captain of Industry, 110–11; on
Dwight L. Moody, 10, 99; and
the family, 114–15, 121–22; Jesus
Christ and the Social Question,
113; and laissez-faire economics,
114; and Social Darwinism, 99,
113–14; and socialism, 113–14
Phrenology: William Alcott on, 38;
in Baby's Biography, 38; Combe
on, 38–42; as epistemology, 135;
and faculty psychology, 37–41;
influence on child care, 38–39; a
"science," 37, 41, 135; Spencer on,
53
Philoprogenitiveness, 39, 154
Progress, Social, 61, 78, 79, 82,
124–25, 164. See also Reason,
Progress in
Progressive Legislation, See
Legislation, Progressive
Prostitution, 22, 44, 87–88, 118
Psychology, Conversionist, 37
Psychology, Faculty: amative
faculty, 43, 154; Combe on,
39–40; as epistemology, 172; in
ethical idealism, 100–101; as
moral philosophy, 39; moral sense

in, 55; moral sense and public opinion in, 58, 133–34; Rauschenbusch on, 36, 154; in Social Gospel, 68, 69, 75, 145, 154, 163–64, 172; Spencer on, 55–57

Public Opinion: a force for social change, 6, 58; and moral sense in Spencer, 58, 133–34; and personal persuasion in the Social Gospel, 167

Rauschenbusch, Walter: on atonement, 150, 166; biography of, 8–10; on Catholicism, 110; and Christian socialism, 115–16, 126; *Christianizing the Social Order,* 96, 102, 152; and civilized morality, 119, 121–22; on faculty psychology, 36; on the family, 122–23; on feminism, 124; and Henry George, 36, 116; on the God concept, 141–42, 171; on income tax, 118; and Kingdom ideal, 4, 16, 151, 153, 175; on legislation, 113, 118–19; on love, 153–54; on Moody, 99; on mysticism, 167; on parenthood, 122; on pietism, 29, 101–102, 166, 169; on purity of woman, 117, 122; on private property, 116–17; on Social Darwinism, 99; on social nature of sin, 146, 150, 173; on Spanish-American War, 96; *A Theology for the Social Gospel,* x, 1, 3–4, 13–16, 137, 158, 175; on virile manhood, 111, 169; on the "worker class," 115–16; on World War I, 9–10, 110, 174

Reason, Progress in, 49, 52, 54, 136–37, 171–72

Ritschl, Albrecht, 158, 173, 174

"Ritschlians," 132, 158, 173

"Romanism," "perils of," 17, 82

Roosevelt, Theodore: as Christian gentleman, 107; as evangelist of manifest destiny, 107; on family and nation, 108; and "progressive" legislation, 20, 113; on Spanish-American War, 103–104, 107

Salvation: as character development, 146; as Christian manhood, 146; different for male and female, 147

Schleiermacher, Friedrich, 158, 173, 189

Second Great Awakening, and conversion, 10; and later Social Gospel, 101; and personal persuasion, 6–7

"Self-Made Man": definition of, 160; as fatherless, 160–61; and laissez-faire economy, 160

"Sex-Passion": amativeness, 39; Rauschenbusch on, 122, 154; and the sexual ethos, 26–28; and work, 9, 72, 154

Sin: as animalism, 145–47, 154; social nature of, 146, 149

Social Darwinism: Darwin on, 35, 53–62; and faculty psychology, 36, 53; and "new" liberal theology, 5; Peabody on, 44; "progressive," 67; Roosevelt on, 107–108; and sexuality, 36; in the Social Gospel 68–69, 75, 80, 92, 125–26, 145, 154, 163–64, 172, 175; Spencer on, 53–54; and the Victorian world-view, 5–6, 18, 36, 46

Social Evolution: and social order, 96, 115: and the "spirit of Jesus," 119

Social Gospel: definition of, 4; and the social movement, 14; and socialism, 137

Social Gospel Movement: biography of figures, 11–12; evangelism in,

6, 20, 67, 91–92, 167; as fatherless
sons, 10, 163, 164; masculine
nature of, 169; origins of, 3–5, 18;
"pioneers" of, 4–5, 7–8, 13, 17, 33;
and progressive legislation, 35, 70,
80, 88; prophetic consciousness
of, 9, 50; and sexual selection, 80;
and socialism, 95, 113–19; work
patterns of, 12
Social Gospel Thought: and ethical
idealism, 99–100; and family
ideal, 15, 121–22, 124–25;
Fatherhood of God in, 15, 92,
170; Social Darwinism in, 80, 92,
125–26, 175; and the "social
question," 97–98; a theology for
men, 32; three pillars of, 15, 92
"Social Problem": as class inequality,
126; as an opportunity for faith,
137, 155
Social Reformers, 95, 112
Socialism: and anarchism, 97,
111–12; and Christianity, 115;
"familistic," 45, 111–12; and social
reform, 95; as a threat to the
family, 115, 120, 122–23
Society, definitions of, 100, 126
Spanish-American War: Abbott
on, 109; as "blood sacrifice," 107;
Gladden on, 109; Rauschenbusch
on, 96, 110; Roosevelt on,
103–104, 107
Spencer, Herbert: *Education:
Intellectual, Moral and Physical,*
57; and laissez-faire government,
56–57; and moral sense, 53,
55–58, 133–34; and phrenology,
53; on public opinion and social
change, 58; and Social
Darwinism, 35–36, 53–58; *Social
Statics,* 53, 55–57; on
transcendental physiology, 55
Spirit, democratized, 108, 155, 156;
in later Social Gospel, 151–52; as

social-psychology, 142; and the
"social spirit," 126
"Spirit of Jesus": as moral
inspiration, 145; as self-sacrificing
love, 167; and social regeneration,
100; and unchanging truth, 131
Strong, Josiah: on the city, 84–86;
on manifest destiny, 81–82, 89,
170; on natural selection, 82; and
"new" theology, 89; *The New Era,*
81; *Our Country,* 30, 81, 89; on
progress and natural selection, 82;
"progressive" legislation in 83, 86,
92; secretary of Evangelical
Alliance, 30
Sumner, William Graham: and
laissez-faire economics, 59, 78;
and survival of the fittest, 35;
*What Social Classes Owe Each
Other,* 35
Survival of the Fittest: as laissez-
faire economics, 77; as manifest
destiny, 35; as moral evolution,
61, 72; William Graham Sumner
on, 35

Taylor, Graham, 6, 91, 139, 185
Taylor, Nathaniel, 48, 49
Temperance, 40, 164
Temperance Movement, 87–88
Theological Method: analogical, 49;
analogy as identity, 171; historical
evidences, 50; natural analogy,
133–34; spiritual intuition, 130–31
Theology, "New" Liberal, as
evolutionary theology, 49; and
Social Darwinism, 5–6, 48–49,
136; and the Victorian world-
view, 89
Transcendentalism, 85, 144

Unitarian, 47, 144

Veblen, Thorstein, 80

Victorian: definition of, 18; middle-class ethos, 64

Victorian world-view; and faculty psychology, 39; and family ethos, 23, 26–28, 123; and idealism, 133; and sexual ethos, 25–28; and Social Darwinism, 5, 18, 36, 46; and temperance, 40; and work, 20

Violence. *See* Warfare

Wages-Fund Theory, 76, 78, 183

Warfare (Violence): in civilization, 62, 78, 103; conflict as temporary evil, 16, 56, 58; industrial, 19; as source of manhood, 104

Womanhood: and childbirth, 104, 147, 189; and domestic sphere, 21, 27–28, 44, 170; moral purity of, 45, 118; and salvation, 147; and sexual purity, 22, 27

Woman Suffrage, 124

Work: and "the sex-passion," 9, 72, 154; and the sexual ethos, 27

"Worker Class," 20, 83–84, 91–92, 115–16

WESTMAR COLLEGE LIBRARY